Eventscapes

Eventscapes: Transforming Place, Space and Experiences directly examines the interrelation between events' simultaneous dependence on and
transformation of the places in which they are held.

This event–environment nexus is analysed through a variety of international case studies including different kinds of well-known sporting and
cultural events such as Vivid Sydney, the Vancouver 2010 Winter Olympics and the Tour Down Under international cycle race, among others.
Chapters focusing on visual design explore the opportunities, at different
spatial scales, to develop an event 'look' and the ways in which an event
experience can be enhanced through connecting and engaging with the
local culture and community. As well as the planning and management of
events, the book draws on event experience, dramaturgically examining
the roles played by authors, actors and the audience, and emphasises the
participation of multiple groups in the co-creation of event experiences.

This will be invaluable reading for those studying events and the
environment. Adopting a multidisciplinary approach, it also draws on geography, urban and cultural studies, image studies, architecture and design,
environmental psychology, and event management, and will be of use to a
broad academic audience.

Graham Brown is Professor of Tourism Management, University of
South Australia.

This book provides a long overdue and much-needed account of eventscapes. Graham Brown has produced a thoroughly researched review of the ideas and principles underpinning this complex concept. Brown uses a range of fascinating examples and his book will be appreciated by anyone wanting to learn more about event design, but also those with wider interests in place management and the experience economy.

Dr Andrew Smith, *School of Architecture and Cities,*
University of Westminster, UK

The concept of eventscapes directs attention to the effects of the physical environment on the way events are experienced while revealing their impact on the places they occupy and the spaces they move through. The book assists understanding of event planning, design, experience and impacts by analysing eventscapes from diverse perspectives. It is a thought-provoking book which brings a much-needed critical edge to event studies. A major contribution!

Dr I. Sunny Lee, *Senior Lecturer in Event and Tourism Management,*
University of South Australia

Eventscapes

Transforming Place, Space and Experiences

Graham Brown

Routledge
Taylor & Francis Group

LONDON AND NEW YORK

First published 2020
by Routledge
2 Park Square, Milton Park, Abingdon, Oxon OX14 4RN

and by Routledge
52 Vanderbilt Avenue, New York, NY 10017

Routledge is an imprint of the Taylor & Francis Group, an informa business

British Library Cataloguing-in-Publication Data
A catalogue record for this book is available from the British Library

Library of Congress Cataloging-in-Publication Data
A catalog record has been requested for this book

ISBN: 978-1-138-09724-7 (hbk)
ISBN: 978-1-138-09726-1 (pbk)
ISBN: 978-1-315-10500-0 (ebk)

Typeset in Times New Roman
by Wearset Ltd, Boldon, Tyne and Wear

MIX
Paper from
responsible sources
FSC   FSC® C013056
www.fsc.org

Printed and bound in Great Britain by
TJ International Ltd, Padstow, Cornwall

Contents

List of plates   viii
List of figures   ix
List of tables   x
List of contributors   xi
Preface   xiii
Acknowledgements   xvii

1 Introduction   1

Background 1
Orientation 3

2 Events   7

Urban rhythms 7
Eventful cities 11
Mega-events 14
Event planning 17
Event design 21
Event impacts 27
Event experiences 35
Summary 41

3 The study of scapes   48

Visions of the world 48
Landscapes 50
Landscapes of leisure 60
Sportscapes 67

Servicescapes 71
Eventscapes 80
  Eventscapes: a conceptual model 82
Summary 83

4   Eventscapes   93

Introduction 93
The resource base 93
Spatial patterns 99
  Single sites 99
  Precincts 104
  Multiple settings 119
  Routes 123
Mapping eventscapes 132
Summary 138

5   Transformations by design   145

Introduction 145
Design culture 145
Place branding 147
Olympic design 150
The Olympic look 153
  The Winter Olympic Games 156
    Lillehammer 1994 156
    Salt Lake City 2002 157
    Vancouver 2010 157
  The Summer Olympic Games 163
    Barcelona 1992 163
    Sydney 2000 163
    Beijing 2008 166
    London 2012 168
    Rio de Janeiro 2016 175
Summary 176

6   Transformations by light   182

Introduction 182
Day and night 183
Then there was light 186
Responses to light 189
Heat and light 194

Illuminations 199
Festivals of light 206
    Vivid Sydney 209
Summary 217

7   **Conclusion**   224

Reflections 224
Research directions 229

Index   234

Plates

1 Rio 2016: visual identity
2 Byron Bay Bluesfest
3 Mysteryland, Holland
4 The stage at Mysteryland
5 Mapping the 2016 Games
6 Interacting with the eventscape
7 Salt Lake City skyline
8 Vancouver 2010: constructing the core graphic
9 Sydney 2000: colour, movement and the fluid graphic
10 Sydney 2000: iconic setting
11 London 2012: venue design
12 London 2012 Festival
13 *Starry Night over the Rhône*
14 Vivid Sydney
15 Supertrees in Singapore
16 Strengthening communities through culture

Figures

2.1	Pedestrian stroll and celebration sites in the Village of Whistler	20
2.2	Millennium Marquee logo	23
2.3	Tourism impact map	29
3.1	View from the Glacier Express	58
3.2	Poster: Midland Railway, 1896	64
3.3	Poster: Midland Railway, 1904	65
3.4	Emotion in eventscapes	75
3.5	View from the Olympic Museum	77
3.6	Eventscapes: a conceptual model	83
4.1	Beach volleyball, Rio 2016 Olympic Games: Copacabana Beach	95
4.2	Beach volleyball, London 2012 Olympic Games: Horse Guards Parade	96
4.3	Riverbank precinct, Adelaide	109
4.4	The Olympic Green, Beijing	113
4.5	Olympic Park, Munich	115
4.6	Sultan's Elephant in the Mall, London	125
4.7	Tour Down Under, Stage Five, 2019	129
4.8	Artistic cartography at London 2012	135
4.9	Disruptive cartography at London 2012	137
5.1	Vancouver 2010: posing with Canadian symbols	158
5.2	Barcelona 1992: street art	164
5.3	Beijing 2008: visual brand – scope and timeline	167
5.4	London 2012: the dynamic grid	172
5.5	London 2012: countdown clock	174
6.1	Expo 2010: UK Pavilion	189
6.2	London's Burning: sculpture on the Thames	198
6.3	Light festivals: development process	207

Tables

2.1	Event participation	10
2.2	Impacts on arts and culture	30
3.1	Ten views of the eventscape	69
3.2	Environmental variables in service contexts	73
5.1	Contribution to design by host cities	155

Contributors

Anthony Bastic, CEO and Creative Director, AGB Events, Sydney, Australia.

Martin Berthod, Director of Sport and Events at Tourism St Moritz, Switzerland.

Sandra Chipchase, CEO, Destination New South Wales. Executive Producer, Vivid Sydney, Australia.

Philip Cox, AO, Founding Director, Cox Architects and Partners, Sydney, Australia.

Heather Croall, Director and Chief Executive, Adelaide Fringe, Australia.

Hailian Gao, PhD, Lecturer in Nanjing Agricultural University in China with research interests in tourism in China, cultural values and tourist behaviour.

Alison Gardiner, Former Vice-President, Brand and Creative Services, Vancouver Organizing Committee for the 2010 Olympic and Paralympic Winter Games (VANOC).

Grant Hall, Lecturer at the University of South Australia with research interests in the transformative power of culture and the arts.

Rosanne Janmaat, Director International, ID&T, Amsterdam, Holland.

Nicola John, Postgraduate student in Management at the Technical University Munich, Germany, specialising in sports management.

Chris Krolikowski, PhD, Lecturer at the University of South Australia with research interests in tourism, event-led urban regeneration and placemaking.

David Musch, Founder and Director, Mapped Design, Adelaide, Australia.

Nick Sykes, CEO, FutureBrand, London, England.

Preface

The seeds for many of the ideas included in this book were sown while I was studying my undergraduate degree in geography at Plymouth, in the south west of England. The following pages have afforded me an absorbing return to this discipline. Discussions of space, place and people–environment interactions are important, integrative themes throughout the book. The material about events which gives form to the discussions is the product of insight gained around the world over the last 30 years. During this time, exposure to diverse ontological realms, alternative epistemologies and different approaches to event management have been instructive.

My time as a graduate student at Texas A&M University (TAMU) was very influential and it is no coincidence that there is a similarity between the title of this book and Clare Gunn's *Vacationscape: Developing Tourist Areas*. It was published in 1972 and was recognised by Kozak and Kozak (2016) as, both, one of the earliest books on tourism and hospitality and one of the first to be widely distributed outside North America. Dr Gunn, who was a Professor at TAMU, trained as a landscape architect and, in 1984, Mark Havitz and I worked as his Research Assistants to prepare a tourism development strategy for Mineral Wells, a small town north of Dallas. I was impressed by Mark's command of the canoe and by Dr Gunn's artistic skills. He produced drawings with ease of streetscape designs that were included in the final report to make statements about the development proposals.

My PhD thesis was about *Tourism and Place Identity* and examined psychological bonds between people and the places visited as tourists. I owe much to the members of my committee particularly Carlton Van Doren, a geographer, who was the Chair of my committee and to John Crompton. John is recognised with justification as one of the leading contributors to the study and management of Recreation, Tourism and Events. My graduate programme in leisure and tourism was supplemented with courses in Social Psychology, Management and Services Marketing. This mix of courses demonstrated the value of interdisciplinary analysis. It shaped much of my subsequent research and teaching and is reflected in the structure of this book. While in Texas, I was exposed to the role of festivals and events in community development. This was an important part of the work conducted by the Extension Service, based in the Department of Recreation, Park and Tourism Science at the university.

Events held in Texas were included as examples in courses I developed for the new tourism degree at the Dorset Institute in 1985. The tourism programme prospered and gained an international reputation for what is now Bournemouth University. There were strong links with the local tourism industry and I learned much from Ken Male who was the Director of Tourism in Bournemouth at the time. Events were used strategically to attract new tourist markets and Ken provided valuable information that I used in my teaching. He also opened doors to industry organisations and his colleagues who supported the development of the programme at Bournemouth. By the time I arrived in Australia in 1990, the relationship between events and destination marketing had become one of my main research interests.

Once again, at Sothern Cross University, I was very involved in the design and development of undergraduate and postgraduate tourism courses as well as what became a successful Executive Development Programme. It was organised in collaboration with the Pacific Asia Travel Association. My work on the Byron Shire Tourism Committee and, particularly, as a Trustee at Cape Byron provided opportunities to be involved in the promotion of tourism and the protection of the region's unique environment. Meetings held in the Lighthouse cottages at the Cape with views across the Pacific were a bonus.

The announcement, in 1993, that Sydney would host the 2000 Olympic Games proved to be very significant for me. From my base in northern New South Wales (NSW), I regularly visited Sydney for meetings and to conduct research about the Olympics. This was made possible by free flights provided by Ansett Airlines, which became the official airline for the 2000 Games. I was fortunate that Maggie White was appointed as the Olympic Manager at the Australian Tourist Commission (ATC). I knew Maggie when she was responsible for the ATC's 'Theme Years' promotional campaign in which events featured prominently in the Years of Sport (1993) and Art & Culture (1995). Maggie introduced me to members of the Olympic 'family' such as Olympic sponsors and key people at the Sydney Organising Committee for the Olympic Games (SOCOG). Workshops I attended at SOCOG exposed me to a new 'insider' language with words like *wrapping* taking on a completely new meaning. Significantly, the workshops explained the rules and requirements imposed by the International Olympic Committee (IOC) and the immense scale and complexity of planning for this mega-event. I became a member of the state government's Tourism Olympic Forum (TOF) that was chaired by the Chief Executive of Tourism NSW and included representatives of the major tourism industry bodies. In 1996, I participated in one of the TOF 'missions' to Atlanta to learn from people who had been involved in the Olympic Games that preceded Sydney 2000. More than any of the other Olympic sponsors, Visa recognised the benefits of co-branding activities with the host city and its tourism agencies. I am grateful to Scot Smythe who was Visa's Vice-President, Sponsorship and Event Marketing and supported my research. He provided valuable contacts and facilitated the distribution of questionnaires to guests of Visa's hospitality programme at the Games in Sydney and, two years later, at the Salt Lake Winter Olympics.

It is common for the Olympic Games to attract the interest of academics in the host country and that was certainly the case in Australia. A research grant from the federal government's Collaborative Research Council (CRC) for Sustainable Tourism provided the catalyst for collaboration with researchers at a number of Australian Universities. My work with Leo Jago, Laurence Chalip and others during the Sydney Olympics marked the start of enduring research partnerships. Laurence and I participated in pre-Games evaluations for the 2002 and 2010 Winter Olympics in Salt Lake City and Vancouver, respectively. I returned to both cities during the Games where I could not fail to notice the Olympic 'looks' that had been created in the host cities. The visual transformations offered examples of *eventscapes*. They made me reconsider the rationale for the 'look' that had been created during the Sydney Games and I was able to refer to the very large design manual that I had been given by SOCOG. It explained the objectives of the visual presentation of all Olympic communications with detailed guidelines for the use of graphic material.

I became aware of different types of *eventscapes* on visits to other Olympic host cities. In Beijing, the prominence of the Birds Nest and the Water Cube underlined the multifaceted impact of iconic structures and the location and layout of the Olympic Green demonstrated the importance of site planning. In London, the survey that was conducted with Andrew Smith took advantage of Andrew's knowledge about the use of public spaces for events and my interest in measuring spectator attachment to sport venues. A related study in Plymouth, with a sample who watched the Games on television, drew on the local knowledge and Olympic expertise of Stephen Essex. I was fortunate to work with Arianne Reis on two research projects in Brazil. The first was focused on Fortaleza during the 2014 FIFA World Cup and the second on Rio during the 2016 Olympic Games.

The information above clearly demonstrates a bias towards evidence gathered at the Olympic Games and I do not claim that the Olympics are a typical event. Their size, the amount of resources that are required to stage the Games and the global attention they command make them quite distinctive. They also attract critical scrutiny in the media and from academics with much of the scholarly interest from people in disciplines such as sociology and urban studies who would not normally be interested in sport events. In addition, many of the operational requirements, whilst on a larger scale, are typical of activities that form part of planning and management at all events. The Olympics offer examples of practices that can be adapted to the benefit of many types of events, big and small.

I have been in Adelaide, South Australia for nearly 20 years and, although we are yet to host the Olympic Games, the 'Festival State' offers a wealth of art, cultural and sport events. They include the famous Arts Festival and a Fringe that is just behind Edinburgh as the second largest in the world. In addition, research conducted at the Tour Down Under has revealed a very different, spatially dispersed form of eventscape. The research at this cycling event was conducted with my colleague Sunny Lee and with Richard Shipway and Katherine King from Bournemouth University.

I have been able to convert an affection for Canada into periods of sabbatical leave at the universities of Waterloo, Victoria and Calgary. The experience at each of the universities was valuable partly due to the different settings – Leisure at Waterloo, Business in Victoria and Calgary. In the context of this book, the ongoing success of Canada Olympic Park in Calgary can be regarded as an *eventscape* legacy from the 1988 Winter Olympics. I was invited to Calgary by Don Getz who has been a pioneer in the generation of knowledge about festivals and events. In *Event Studies*, he provides a detailed review of the disciplines that contribute to this knowledge and advocates the type of interdisciplinary approach that has been adopted in this book.

REFERENCE

Kozak, M. and Kozak, N. (2016). Institutionalisation of Tourism Research and Education: From the 1900s to 2000s. *Journal of Tourism History*, 8(3): 275–299.

Acknowledgements

Over an extended period, many people have provided access, support and ideas that have made this book possible and I express my thanks to you all. In addition to your knowledge, some of you offered friendship and I would like to note that conducting research with Laurence Chalip, Andrew Smith and Arianne Reis in different parts of the world was always fun. I am particularly grateful to people who made distinctive contributions in the form of the boxes that give life to the text. I learned a lot from your work, enjoyed our discussions and was so pleased that you were all enthusiastic about being involved. Thank you to Roseanne Janmaat of ID&T and Helen Marriage of Artichoke who were among the first to provide material for the book and to Anthony Bastic, Sandra Chipchase, Heather Croall, Alison Gardiner, Nick Sykes and Martin Berthod. I hope I have adequately reflected the impressive contributions you have all made to the creation of eventscapes in Australia, Canada, England and Europe. Tracking down and gaining authorisation to use some of the images that are included was not easy but it introduced me to interesting, creative people in England, France, Brazil and the USA. Conversations by phone and email at all hours of the day and night with Katherine Baxter, James Harper and others proved to be insightful and enjoyable. Thank you to Jeremy Brown who produced some of the figures and images and clicked the right buttons to rescue my manuscript from time to time and to Stella for supporting the project and enduring my commitment to the computer and to periods of absence overseas.

A number of my colleagues at the University of South Australia have provided encouragement at key times and, Sunny Lee and Chis Krolikowski, in particular, have been invaluable sources of support and ideas. I presented material included in the book to students studying postgraduate courses in Sport Tourism and Events and Venues Management who provided valuable feedback. Finally, thank you to the editors at Taylor & Francis – to Emma Travis who provided words of wisdom at our initial meeting at the IBG conference in London in 2016, to Calotta Fanton, who gave advice during the project and to Lydia Kessell, who always responded quickly, guiding me through the critical final stages.

1 Introduction

In *Mega Events and Social Change: Spectacle, Legacy and Public Culture*, Roche (2017) suggests that a book's Introduction should answer three questions: why the book has been written; what it is about; and how it is structured. So, here we go. In some ways, my answer to the first question is 938 which, some of you will note is larger than 42 – the answer to everything in the *Hitchhiker's Guide to Galaxy* by Douglas Adams. Prior to the Sydney Olympics, on one of many visits to the offices of the organising committee (SOCOG), I was given a package, weighing over 3 kg, that stated on the cover, 'Your copy of the Sydney 2000 Olympic Games Image Guidelines'. On the thick plastic cover, it was clearly marked as number 938 of a limited number produced by SOCOG. Typical of the style of the content, 938 was in white on the cover, beneath a thick blue resin in an ergonomic shape of the fluid graphic that became a central feature of the look of the Games. The content of the Guidelines provided information about the rationale for design decisions, explained how a distinctive visual identity for the Games would be created and gave instructions about how to use the design features. It was, and remains, a shock to see the level of detail that was given and the controls that dictated the format for any Olympic-related communication. I return to this in Chapter 5. While the Games were being planned, when information was distributed and during the Games, I saw endless examples of the application of the information in the Guidelines – from business cards, letterheads and folder covers to street signs, flags and volunteer uniforms. The look was everywhere and the city was transformed. I may have noticed some of this more than people who were happy to just enjoy the new festive appearance of the city. I enjoyed it too but, through a new critical lens that has influenced the way I have looked at events and their surroundings for over 20 years. I have tried to reflect these perceptions in this book.

The book uses eventscapes as an analytical framework to examine the relationship between events and the environments where they are held. This is complex due to the need to understand the way different settings are selected, designed and managed to achieve a wide range of event-related outcomes. The aim is to analyse the visual and spatial characteristics of eventscapes to better understand events and the impacts they create. But, hopefully, the book will do more than this. I would like the way the information is presented to create an interest in event settings and a desire to learn more about the places and cities that are featured – to understand the processes that shape them and the role that events play in the production and consumption of cities and urban experiences. I hope this book will demonstrate the value of geographical analysis in event management studies. However, informed scholarship requires a breadth of understanding that draws on a wide range of disciplines. It is noteworthy that Getz (2007) focused on this theme in *Event Studies* after making contributions, over many years, to teaching and research in event management and event tourism. It is challenging to break away from the comfort of a familiar discipline but it is rewarding and readers may find value in considering issues addressed in this book based on writings and research in Art, Drama, Literature, History, Leisure, Environmental Psychology, Sociology, Design, Marketing, Management and Urban Studies. With more time and a larger word limit, many issues could have been examined in greater depth.

Events are shaped by the places where they are held but places are also transformed by events. This is demonstrated by two observations. First, 'thousands of young kids travelling in for the festival transformed the small old steel town, and Borlange became a festival city. A Music City' (Wynn, 2015: 3). Second, events 'are shaped by the cities they take place in, with their form, duration, content and effects being determined to a large extent by urban space, place and process' (Richards and Colombo, 2017: 527). It is important to emphasise the reflexive nature of this relationship between events and place as it represents a defining characteristic for the analysis of eventscapes throughout the book. Both of the quotes refer to events and festivals held in cities and many of the examples in the book are about events in urban environments. The rich resource base of cities enhances their ability to host different types of events including large and mega-events. The scale and resource requirements of the latter are beyond the capacity of small communities. However, examples of events that are held in small communities and in rural areas are discussed, as are the factors that affect their relationship with the local environment. In addition, the fluid nature of events that cross urban and rural landscapes gives rise to particular forms of eventscapes that forge connections between places and communities that are spatially dispersed.

Some of the discussion refers to research about festivals when it helps inform understanding of eventscapes. For example, in Jonathan Wynn's ethnographic study of Austin, Nashville and Newport as *Music Cities*, he describes festivals as 'carefully scripted products of maneuverings and agreements between powerful stakeholders and cultural institutions' (2015: 4). Using Erving Goffman's (1963; 1967) sociology of occasions, the festivals are regarded as moments of intense sociability characterised by 'concentrated investment and participation in urban cultural activities' (Wynn, 2015: 19). In this book, the moments are not restricted to urban environments and a broad definition of cultural activities and institutions enables consideration of sport and art events and the wide range of individuals and organisations that engage with eventscapes. By drawing attention to the significance for festivals of a city's spatial resources, both public and private, Wynn's (2015) study is of direct relevance to an analysis of eventscapes. He also describes three approximations to ideal types of spatial patterns associated with urban festivals. These ideal types are used to help characterise different eventscapes in Chapter 4. Consistent with the approach adopted in this book, Wynn considers festivalisation to be 'a process where cultural activity meets place making' (Wynn, 2015: 12) and his language is rich in geographical references. He identifies the role of festivals in *territorial* trade marking, the way festivals present corporations with an opportunity to impose an imprint in the visual *landscape* and suggests, with reference to the work of Suttles (1984) that festival symbols shape *the texture of a city*. Visual transformations associated with events are a key theme that are discussed throughout this book as they are considered to be one of the main ways to identify and define eventscapes.

ORIENTATION

An attempt is made throughout the book to give life to the subjects under discussion by making frequent reference to examples. It will be encouraging if readers feel more suitable examples should have been included as this will demonstrate thoughtful consideration of the applicability of concepts in different situations. In fact, if this were a task-oriented textbook, it would ask readers to identify local examples of different types of eventscapes and to consider opportunities to apply design practices. The inclusion of case studies has given license for me to describe some of my experiences and discuss the lessons they offer for event management. The other case studies have been written by people with specialist knowledge; people who have managed organisations that created eventscapes that have offered experiences for large numbers of people and captured the attention of domestic and international audiences. These voices reveal humanistic dimensions of event management.

In addition to the Introduction and Conclusion, the book has five chapters. The first two chapters discuss the elements of eventscapes – events and scapes. Chapter 2 considers the place of events in contemporary society, examining the relationship between events and urban rhythms; the patterns of movements and activities that give structure to life in modern cities. It reviews the literature that supports the proposition that cities are increasingly eventful (Richards, 2017; Richards and Palmer, 2010; Richards and Columbo, 2017). Event planning and event design feature prominently as decision-making in these areas influence the creation and form of eventscapes. The nature of event experiences is discussed primarily in the context of mega-events as most of the case studies relate to the Olympic Games or events that are transformative due the scale of their impacts. Chapter 3 reviews an extensive literature to identify the way scapes have been defined and analysed in different disciplines. The wide range of uses of the term is, in some ways, problematic but the issues addressed in the book are assisted by the breadth of philosophical and analytical perspectives. Key scapes such as landscapes, sportscapes and servicescapes are examined drawing, in particular, on the influential work of Bale and Bitner. Bale (1993, 1994, 2000, 2003) demonstrated the value of a wide range of perspectives associated with sportscapes and Bitner's (1992) servicescapes concept has been discussed extensively in a variety of disciplines and has been applied on a wide range of spatial scales. Other studies that are reviewed promote alternative ways of seeing in art and design and help explain the ideologies that accompany these creative practices. The practical utility of scapes is revealed by examining the way environmental settings are managed to achieve specific outcomes. The chapter concludes with the development of a conceptual model of eventscapes. Chapter 4 is more descriptive and the text is supported by a large number of photographs. After reviewing the relationship between events and resources, the variability in the form of eventscapes is analysed. Consideration is given to the role of spatial anchors and the patterns that emerge in both urban and rural landscapes and the impacts that are created. The management implications of the different patterns and of network relationships are identified.

Chapters 5 and 6 discuss transformations associated with eventscapes. Chapter 5 provides an opportunity to include material from 938. Many illustrations are included as the chapter is about the effect of graphic design and its role in creating a distinctive look at the Olympic Games. The discussion is placed in the context of design culture (Julier, 2006) and place branding and draws on the wealth of design manuals and reports about the development of visual identities that have become available in recent years. Please forgive the indulgence but I think Chapter 6 is particularly interesting. Consistent with Bill Bryson's comments about the Blackpool Illuminations, this is partly a product of expectations. My interest in Vivid Sydney required the inclusion of a chapter about light festivals but my reading took me in unexpected directions. The discussions refer to authors who provide a social history of attitudes towards light and dark and I draw on some of the work of Tim Edensor (Edensor, 2014; 2015; Edensor and Lorimer, 2015; Edensor and Millington, 2013), who has published extensively on various forms of illumination. A series of insightful case studies are included and it is demonstrated that light has been used throughout human existence and remains a powerful expression of cultural traditions in festivals that continue to be held around world. Light changes the atmosphere of a place and the visual appearance of the environment, so it is not surprising that it is an integral part of events. Chapter 6 provides examples of these visual transformations and describes the dramatic impact created by Vivid Sydney, an event that relies on a combination of artistic creativity and technological innovation and has become a major tourist attraction.

In the Conclusion, the utility of eventscapes as an analytical framework is revisited and future research directions are mapped. Some of the dots that emerge in different parts of the book are connected but I hope readers will be stimulated to identify additional relationships in eventscapes that have both conceptual and practical value.

REFERENCES

Bale, J. (1993). *Sport, Space and the City*. London: Routledge.

Bale, J. (1994). *Landscapes of Modern Sport*. London: Leicester University Press.

Bale, J. (2000). *Sportscapes*. Sheffield: The Geographical Association.

Bale, J. (2003). *Sports Geography*, 2nd edn. London: Routledge.

Bitner, M. J. (1992). Servicescapes: The Impact of Physical Surroundings on Customers and Employees. *Journal of Marketing*, 55(April): 57–71.

Edensor, T. (2014). The Rich Potentialities of Light Festivals. In: J. Meier, U. Hasenöhrl, K. Krause and M. Pottharst, eds, *Urban Lighting, Light Pollution and Society*. London: Routledge, 85–98.

Edensor, T. (2015). Light Design and Atmosphere. *Visual Communication*, 14(3): 331–350.

Edensor, T. and Lorimer, H. (2015). 'Landscapism' at the *Speed of Light*: Darkness and Illumination in Motion. *Geografiska Annaler: Series B Human Geography*, 97(1): 1–16.

Edensor, T. and Millington, S. (2013). Blackpool Illuminations: Revealing Local Cultural Production, Situated Creativity and Working-Class Values. *International Journal of Cultural Policy*, 19(2): 145–161.

Getz, D. (2007). *Event Studies: Theory, Research and Policy for Planned Events.* Oxford: Butterworth-Heinemann.

Goffman, E. (1963). *Behavior in Public Places: Notes on the Social Organisation of Gatherings.* New York: Free Press.

Goffman, E. (1967). *Interaction Ritual: Essays on Face-to-Face Interaction.* Garden City, NY: Doubleday.

Julier, G. (2006). From Visual Culture to Design Culture. *Design Issues*, 22(1): 64–76.

Richards, G. (2017). Emerging Models of the Eventful City. *Event Management*, 21: 533–543.

Richards, G. and Columbo, A. (2017). Rethinking the Eventful City: Introduction. *Event Management*, 21: 527–531.

Richards, G. and Palmer, R. (2010). *Eventful Cities: Cultural Management and Urban Revitalisation.* Oxford: Elsevier.

Roche, M. (2017). *Mega-Events and Social Change: Spectacle, Legacy and Public Culture.* Manchester: Manchester University Press.

Suttles, G. (1984). The Cumulative Texture of Local Urban Culture. *American Journal of Sociology*, 90: 283–304.

Wynn, J. (2015). *Music City: American Festivals and Placemaking in Austin, Nashville, and Newport.* Chicago, IL: University of Chicago Press.

2 Events

Congratulations Vienna! In 2018, Vienna was recognised as the most liveable city in the world in the rankings prepared by the Economist Intelligence Unit. For the previous seven years, Melbourne had been in first place. The rankings are determined by scores for 30 factors across five categories: stability, health care, culture and environment, education and infrastructure (Economist Intelligence Unit, 2018). It could be argued that these measures represent an operationalisation of the good city – 'the kind of urban order that might enhance the human experience' (Amin, 2006: 1009). Amin (2006) suggests that utopian ideas from Plato to Le Corbusier about harmony and order have shifted to meanings of a good life derived from temporary, hedonistic projects. Vienna and Melbourne are famous for the quality of the events they host each year. Melbourne's sporting events include the Australian Tennis Open, the Australian Formula One Grand Prix and the Melbourne Cup horse race that 'stops the nation'. The Melbourne Cricket Ground staged the Olympic Games in 1956 and the Commonwealth Games in 2006 and is the nation's spiritual home for cricket and Australia Rules Football. Vienna is one of the world's great cultural cities with a unique musical heritage that is expressed at famous events such as the annual concert series held at the Schönbrunn Palace. The Austrian capital and the capital of Victoria in Australia may be exceptional in the scale of their events but they are not alone in the importance placed on events as part of a strategy to make cities attractive places for residents, visitors and investors. Events also influence the structuring of time in cities, creating rhythms that enhance the lifestyle they offer.

Building on principles associated with time-geography (Hagerstrand, 1970) and rhythmanalysis (Lefebvre, 2004), Edensor (2016) has discussed the multiscalar temporalities that shape urban life; the rhythms associated with daily, weekly and annual patterns of behaviour. The routines of daily life that produce the domestication of time (Amin, 2008) include children walking to school along the same streets, commuters parking in the same spots or passing through the same turnstiles and the performance of rituals of homework, housework and shopping. Transport schedules impose order and habitual practices become unreflexive. However, regular exposure to features in the urban landscape can produce a sense of spatial belonging and mobile homeliness (Edensor, 2016), which is enhanced when family and friends share the habitual routines (Herzfield, 1997). Operating at a different beat, weekly activities provide another layer of structured orderliness. Places such as shops and cafés act as meeting points and become part of the geographies of communality as space is mapped by repetitive choreographies. Mobility allows choice and place attachment may result from the selection of meaningful spatial anchors at leisure settings, tourist destinations and event venues (Smith, Brown and Assaker, 2017). Places are constituted by the flows that pass through them with rhythms imposing a consistency on the landscape. Places in cities are part of broader spatial networks that operate when national and global rhythms pulse through them. They are dynamic and, although permanently in a process of becoming, can be stabilised by the regularity of interventions (Edensor, 2016).

Edensor provides examples when rhythms are suspended including when intoxication, music and crowds at festivals combine to create 'new physical and emotional rhythms that underpin an alternative experience of self-in-world' (Jackson, 2004: 30). In a more sober vein, adherence to practices that form part of the slow movement resist normative temporalities when a commitment is made 'to occupy time more attentively' (Parkins, 2004: 364). When events force the closure of roads, normal patterns of circulation are disrupted as streets are used differently; people slow down and interact more (Stevens and Shin, 2014). The temporary and, in many cases, repetitive nature of events means they can disrupt normal urban rhythms while imposing their own rhythm. Allen, O'Toole, Harris and McDonnell (2011) note that events have always served as temporal markers citing examples of rituals linked to seasonal changes in agrarian societies when space and time is used 'to define occasions worthy of celebration' (Rojek, 2013: 2). According to Richards and Palmer, life in medieval cities 'revolved around a festive calendar with a rich spectrum of feasts and Saint's days, as well as major celebrations such as carnivals' (2010: 5). In the UK, fairs that were held in city streets and on common land to coincide with Saint's days were the most significant events in urban public spaces during the seventeenth, eighteenth and nineteenth centuries (Smith, 2016).

In recent times, the Bicentenary and the Sydney Olympics defined milestones in the life of Australians (Allen *et al.*, 2011) and Roche (2003) has described mega-events as international timekeepers. When discussing the power of events such as the Olympics, the FIFA World Cup and the Rio Carnival, Rojek suggests that 'periodically, they burst into social consciousness as part of an established cycle of global festivity. – They issue license for us to break out of our daily bubble of existence' (2013: vi–vii). For residents of a host city during the Olympics, the 'usual notions of time and space seemed to be turned upside down' (Dyck and Gauvin, 2010: 198). Interestingly, Dyck and Gauvin suggested that the visible evidence that the Games had arrived was the presence in restricted traffic lanes of sport utility vehicles bedecked with Olympic insignia. Barker has suggested that television coverage of sporting events and royal ceremonies 'situate me in the rhythms of a national calendar' (1990: 6). Local events also register cycles of time and provide structure to contemporary life. In so doing, cities, as the setting for events are made more meaningful (Smith, 2016) and for those who attend events the implications may be profound, as illustrated in Table 2.1, which gives hypothetical examples of event participation based on the cycle of events in Adelaide, South Australia

According to Collins (2004) physical co-presence and participation in rituals produce emotional energy, what Durkheim (1915) called collective effervescence, in ways that facilitate the development of social ties (Richards, 2015). Richards suggests that iterative events, held at regular intervals at the same location, have the potential to enhance bonding and social cohesion among local individuals and groups in contrast with, one-off, pulsar events that are more likely to transform local social structures while providing access to global networks, fostering innovation and creating new relationships. It is suggested that there are interesting differences in terms of the environmental requirements of iterative and pulsar events. The former needs a sustainable resource that can be used repetitively, and the example is provided of the Piazza in the centre of Siena that has been conserved in its original form since the Middle Ages to stage the famous Il Palio horse race. Pulsar events are likely to require new facilities or to have temporary access to places that are not normally used as event venues.

Making arrangements to attend an event, especially with friends, requires making a commitment and involves cost and disruption to normal routines. For iterative events, the processes of planning, anticipation and attendance is attuned to key dates. The event venue is the setting for performative enactments and social interactions that reconnect friends and confirm

Table 2.1 Event participation

Participant	Event (duration, frequency)	Activities
Male, 6 years old	Christmas Pageant (one day, every November)	Counting the days to see Santa in the procession again.
Female, 17 years old	Royal Adelaide Show (10 days, every September)	Previously attended each year for one day with parents. This year will be attending on three nights with friends.
	Tour Down Under, UCI World Tour cycle race (7 days, every January)	Watched two stages of the race for the last three years. This year, after training every Sunday, will participate with brother in the, mass participation Challenge Tour.
Male, 35 years old	Adelaide 5000 Car Race (5 days, every March)	As in last two years, will buy 4-day Grandstand Pass to attend with three local friends.
	Adelaide Fringe Festival (Mid-February–mid-March, every year)	Will attend a mix of comedy and cabaret shows with friends who come every year from Melbourne to enjoy the excitement of 'Mad March'.
Female, 56 years old	Adelaide Festival (17 days, every March)	Booked seats to four World Premieres during the priority booking period for 'Friends of the Festival'.
	Colours of Impressionism Masterpieces from the Musée D'Orsay (March–July 2018)	As a Member of the Art Gallery of South Australia, receive invitations to opening night presentations of touring exhibitions.

Participant	Event (duration, frequency)	Activities
Male, 60 years old	Cricket: Australia v. England (Ashes series) (Adelaide Oval – every four years)	Attend every day of the match with brother who visits from England as part of the 'barmy army'.

identities at a particular time and place each year. The venue becomes an eventscape as it is temporarily transformed; stabilised by the distinctive pulse of people and the flow of resources. Drawing on ideas associated with Castells' (1996) 'network society', the eventscape is a physical location: a place of local actors but also a space of flows which make connections with external networks. The eventscape may be rhythmically expressive with a distinctive tempo that is perceived as slow or fast, static or dynamic, continuous or intermittent (Wunderlich, 2010). A designed aesthetic of colours, sounds and smells stimulates cognitive, affective and conative responses. Active engagement in events, combined with place transformations, may stimulate a heightened sense of environmental awareness, contrasting with the unreflexive behaviour associated with the daily rhythms of urban life. The presence of national and international flows, including media coverage, can enhance network connections, raise the profile of the event and put the host city on the map. This combination of benefits explains why cities strive to be eventful.

EVENTFUL CITIES

It has been claimed that 'the "eventful city" concept, developed out of the basic observation that cities are using events to achieve a growing range of policy objectives, including economic growth, image change, social cohesion, and physical development' (Richards and Columbo, 2017: 527). These objectives have influenced the places where events are held and the type of spatial and sectoral relationships that are produced. In the 1980s, cultural quarters and cultural events assisted in the revitalisation of decaying areas in post-industrial cities (Richards and Palmer, 2010). Neoliberal urban policies stressed the aesthetics of place and the resuscitation of the symbolic and economic value of specific landscapes to create spectacular consumptive environments (Silk, 2011). With spectacle acting as one of the seductive forces that sustain a consumption economy (Debord,

1994), events offered flexible support for themes expressed in architecture and landscape design. Consumption and entertainment became increasingly indistinguishable while creating relationships between shopping, dining and recreation (Amin and Thrift, 2002).

The 'experience economy' was defined by a move from the provision of services to the co-creation of experiences with value added by a 'heightened ambience or sense of theatre' (Pine and Gilmore, 1999: 1). A consumer was willing to spend time and money to enjoy events that were staged 'to engage him in a personal way' (Pine and Gilmore, 1999: 2). Although Pine and Gilmore directed their theatrical recommendations to the business practices of firms, urban planning responded with the development of mixed-use hubs: lively, productive environments where residents, artists, business people and festival goers coexist. Richards and Palmer (2010) explain that Montreal's Quartier des Spectacles has 25 event venues and is managed as a coordinated space by a partnership that includes representatives of the culture, real estate, education and business sectors, local residents, the City of Montreal and the Government of Quebec. By adding spectacle and symbolic capital (Richards and Palmer, 2010), events make cities more attractive places to live in and appeal to the 'creative class' (Florida, 2002). As media spectacles, 'entire skylines and multiple public arenas are built and re-imagined for the sake of worldwide mass media coverage' (Kolamo and Vuolteenaho, 2013: 503). Florida claimed that the talented are attracted by 'visual and audio cues such as outdoor dining, active outdoor recreation, a thriving music scene, active nightlife and bustling street scene' (2005: 99). The creative city model places culture and creativity at the forefront of inter-urban competition (Richards and Palmer, 2010) and encourages the capitalisation of city landscapes (Silk, 2011). Capitalisation includes the development of event-related, place images that are designed to inspire pride among local residents and to capture the attention of the mobile global community. This represents 'a particular expression of self within the logics of the global market' (Silk, 2011: 736) but by selecting only images that are conducive to the market and the tourist gaze (Silk, 2011), the city may be reduced to a stylised exotic (Hall, 1991). If packaged as a surface aesthetic of symbolic novelty (Banjeree and Linstead, 2001), the city may represent an elitist depiction devoid of a local sense of place (Yeoh and Chang, 2001).

In the belief that cities are a natural location for events, Richards and Palmer (2010) refer to the resources they offer: the availability of transport, accommodation and linkages to communication systems, as well as spaces where people can gather. They caution that while event places need to be managed to attract, animate and entertain people, they also need 'to ensure safety, not disrupt mobility, promote accessibility and avoid con-flict' (Richards and Palmer, 2010: 75). Events are faced with practical issues in attempts to encourage access to venues while preventing security threats and keeping cities operational but this is part of broader socio-political practices concerning 'the surveillance-relevant role of space and, in turn, the space-producing role of surveillance' (Klauser, 2013: 289). Klauser refers to the 'splintering' (Graham and Marvin, 2001) of urban environments into a patchwork of 'purified insides separated from more or less dangerous outsides' (Franzen, 2001: 207) with 'capsular civilisation' (de Cauter, 2004) a logical response to fear. Regulation may impose restriction on the flows of people while freeing flows of information that make it possible to identify and verify who and which objects are moving across space and entering event venues.

The management of space is particularly complex when large parts of cities become event stages, as occurs when Fringe activities at the Edin-burgh and Adelaide Festivals are held in a multitude of venues and spaces that are widely dispersed throughout the cities. Regular users of public spaces want to ensure that any transformation and loss of amenity is tem-porary with the environment returned to 'normal' as soon as possible after an event. In the context of what he calls the 'urbanization of events', Smith (2016, 2017) has discussed how the intensity of event programming in London's parks is challenging their functions and meanings. This is regarded as the product of a neoliberal, entrepreneurial approach to the management of the city's resources (Peck and Tickell, 2002) producing benefits that include the identification of the 'potentialities' of the, often underutilised, spaces – releasing them from traditional uses and restrictive constraints. The idea of reclaiming city spaces is central to the rationale espoused by organisers of mass events such as the Sultan's Parade that is discussed in Chapter 4. By opening up the spaces and attracting new users, they can become safer due to the presence of visitors and security staff. But, Smith also describes the pressures placed on the parks, practical issues related to waste management and the impact of noise and safety in local neighbourhoods. There is particular concern about ticketed events which signal the privatisation of public spaces that become platforms for commercialisation and are accompanied by barriers, both physical and symbolic, controls and restricted access to 'our parks' (Smith, 2017).

A need to find suitable places to stage events is compounded by innovative inclinations to offer new experiences in new places. While technical and operational requirements dictate certain spatial configurations, event organisers recognise that space shapes experience and that the animation of place needs to be managed. They also have the capacity to produce a unique atmosphere and imbue places with meanings. The term 'festivalisation' (Häußermann and Siebel, 1993) describes situations when events are used as a unifying forces for public policy. Ploger (2010) draws on Foucault's (1980) concept of 'eventilisation' to distinguish between spontaneous 'presence events' and planned 'serial events' (Richards, 2017). Due to the use of events to achieve strategic objectives, many cities have established specialist departments to develop, attract or oversee events (Getz, 2012). Decisions about whether to specialise in particular types of events or to develop a diversified portfolio (Ziakas, 2014) are influenced by market objectives and the implications for other sectors. Getz (2017) has suggested that eventful cities need to have a healthy population of events that contribute to sustainability policy fields and three policy models, as ideal types, have been proposed by Richards (2017). The event-centric model focuses on the identification of new event-related products and markets with an event unit responsible for the city's overall event programming strategy. A sector-centric model requires recognition of all stakeholders that can benefit from events, using events as platforms to achieve a wide range of economic, social and cultural outcomes in different sectors. A network-centric model uses events to generate 'network value' (Stokes, 2006) by creating links beyond the city to global ideas and organisations. Inevitably, the most extensive networking opportunities are offered by mega-events.

MEGA-EVENTS

In the pursuit of definitional clarity and to enhance comparative analysis, it has been suggested that mega-events should be assessed based on the number of ticketed visitors, the value of broadcast rights, event costs and the proportion of the budget devoted to urban capital and infrastructure spending (Muller, 2015). Muller (2015) also proposes that urban transformation should be measured by capital investment in transport infrastructure and the construction of event venues and other buildings. But, this emphasis on quantifiable indicators fails to recognise the significance of other transformations, particularly those associated with the festival atmosphere that invades the host city as it becomes a stage for new experiences (Hillier and Wanner, 2015). As the public crave affective experiences, spectacular events such as the Olympic Games construct drama and emphasise the qualities of the theatrical (Jirásek and Kohe, 2015). While the drama has universal appeal, it includes situated content with local meaning (Tzanelli, 2018).

Rojek (2013) believes mega-events serve as a distraction from serious problems in the world but that they also generate psychological energy with participation being like giving a gift to yourself. While making people feel good, the gift sends a message to others about values and, in this context, events are 'components of lifestyle architecture through which we now build competent, relevant, credible images of ourselves' (Rojek, 2013: 2). For Roche (2000), mega-events should be interpreted as projects by host communities that mark and symbolise collective identities. They are the products of particular times and places, of when and where they are held, and are 'material and performative spectacles which are physically embedded in cities' (Roche, 2000: 10). Roche nominated the Olympic Games and International Expos as the most spectacular mega-events within a dense social eco-system of public events (Roche, 2000) and as the most significant markers and catalysts of social change in host cities (Roche, 2017). The reference to an eco-system draws attention to the importance of systematic interactions and the relationship between events and their environment.

In another analysis related to gift giving, Tzanelli (2018) describes a system of global reciprocity as mega-events circulate among the community of nations. An investment by a host city to develop an event equates to giving a gift to the world with reciprocity taking the form of recognition of a city's achievements (Tzanelli, 2018). Unconditional giving is synonymous with sacrifice; a form of symbolic power that cannot be contested (Tzanelli, 2004). This is similar to the idea of 'propaganda of a good deed' (Häußermann and Siebel, 1993: 14), when developing events signal a political capacity to unify heterogeneous local interests and achieve public consensus (Jacob, 2013). Tzanelli regards hospitality at the Olympics as peaceful place-making and hopeful future-making. The host city welcomes the world during the Games and seeks to impress with the level of hospitality that is provided. A distinctive form of hospitality at events, particularly mega-events, is corporate hospitality. For Olympic sponsors, it is a key activation of their contract with the International Olympic Committee and is used to reward staff achievements, secure contracts, enhance partnerships and build relationships with influential business and political decision makers. The hospitality offers exclusivity which is made possible by the manipulation of event power (Rojek, 2013). Rojek (2013) suggests that hierarchical authority is imposed at mega-events to keep citizens at arm's length and to create highly controlled event environments. Citing Graham (2010), Rojek (2013) states that, at the 2012 Olympics, more troops were deployed in London than to the war in Afghanistan and a wide range of security measures divided the Olympic zone from the rest of the city. The imposition of an 'Olympic state of exception', characterised by the suspension of normal juridical order and the deployment of extreme security has become a feature of the Olympic Games (Marrero-Guillamón, 2012). Other controls can be more subtle such as the visual policy of the London Olympic Delivery Authority (ODA), which prohibited photography at the Olympic Park during construction while producing carefully designed official images (Marrero-Guillamón, 2012). In an analysis that resembles the ideology of map making (see Chapter 4), Marrero-Guillamón (2012) describes the ODA's preferred view of the Olympic stadium prior to the Games. It was a computer-generated image that created a visual connection between the stadium and Canary Wharf, London's symbol of financial capitalism. The grandeur of an aerial perspective was combined with 'a lighting trick: while the stadium is powerfully lit, the city is kept in the dark, silent, under control' (Marrero-Guillamón, 2012: 134).

Tzanelli challenges the view that the Olympics are only about politics, power and money, claiming it to be 'an enterprise engaged in knowledge production about human environments and the aesthetic landscapes humans inhabit' (2018: 9). The term 'imagineering' is used to describe the aesthetic frames that are produced by artists, architects, ceremonial directors and choreographers at Olympic Games with the forces of globalisation reworked locally to produce artistic symbolisations of urban ecologies. After Sassen (2006), she suggests that the work of imagineers is contextualised by flows of capital, corporate power and global media systems to create geopolitical belongings that prioritise the city over the nation state. Understanding requires the mapping of spaces, or 'moorings', where the flows, movements and performances are concentrated while understanding the non-spaces, across the world, that give shape to the patterns (Tzanelli, 2018). As space-bound transnational enterprises, mega-events implicate host cultures to the politics of place-making (Cresswell, 2010) with the mobility of ideas, humans and materialities acting as the governing principle (Baernholdt, 2013).

The spatial patterns associated with imagineering and their related production and consumption processes are examined in the context of event-scapes in this book. There is a particular focus on the visual dimensions of eventscapes and Tzanelli contributes to this theme by describing developments in Rio de Janeiro for the Olympic Games 'as a successful marriage between architectural craft as technology and decorative design as art' (2018: 14). Referring to Heidegger (1993) and Lazzarato (2004) respectively, Tzanelli describes the 'pictorial intentionality' (2018: 14) of Rio's, recently constructed, Museum of Tomorrow and the way the city's life-worlds are refashioned as bits of a picture postcard. Under scrutiny by the machine of surveillance that accompanies mega-events, she suggests that an impeccable picture of the urban ecology must be presented with a city-scape tamed for the visitor's gaze (Urry, 2004) and local territories made legible for outsiders (Tzanelli, 2018). A demand-driven approach to the arrangement of consumable signs, images and promised experiences (Urry and Larsen, 2011) supports the development of the urban experience economy (Pine and Gilmore, 1999) and allows elite coalitions to showcase the city as an attractive place for investment (Hillier, 2006). The images, which are inserted into world markets as part of the digital commons (Becker, 1982), amplify mobility, encouraging performances by globetrotting collectors of places. The rhetoric of honouring commitments made to the IOC confers legitimacy on relocating residents, disciplining urban space and 'blitzkrieg planning' (Silvestre and de Oliveira, 2012: 209).

EVENT PLANNING

The spatial pattern of some events demands planning at a national scale. As the name implies, the Tour de France visits places throughout France and widely dispersed communities become part of the event. At the FIFA World Cup, the need for large stadiums requires big cities with necessary facilities to host games during the tournament. A map that accompanied an article by Fox Sports in Australia showed the location of the ten cities in Russia that would host games at the 2018 World Cup. It provided detailed information about the three cities and the stadiums where the Australian team, the Socceroos, would be playing games (Fox Sports, 2017). At the previous tournament in Brazil, not all cities that wished to host games were successful in their bids and the selection process was influenced by a desire to spread economic benefits to specific regions (Brown, Assaker and Reis 2018). In addition to the submission of formal bids to organising bodies, a pro-active approach makes it possible for many types of communities to attract event-related activities. Prior to the 2000 Olympic Games, local and state government agencies in Australia prepared information about places with high quality sport facilities and accommodation that were suitable for different-sized groups. It was sent to national sport federations encouraging them to send teams for pre-Games training. While helping to achieve training and acclimatisation objectives, the relative seclusion of remote locations can be ideal for athletes who need to relax and avoid media attention. The Gold Coast City Council delegated responsibility for pre-Games training initiatives to its Community and Recreation Facilities department. It attracted visits of varying duration by teams from 15 countries including the entire British team, who made several visits prior to the event and was based on the Gold Coast throughout the Games. The Olympic Task Force established in the Hunter Valley

Region in NSW was located in the Economic Development agency as pre-Games training was seen as an opportunity to create long-term business relationships for the region. The networks that were created resulted in reciprocal trade missions with a number of countries and sales of a wide range of, mainly agricultural, products (O'Brien and Gardiner, 2006). Despite these examples, most major events are held in cities and urban planning has to identify the resource needs of events and to prepare for the impacts they create.

Transport planning is essential at mega-events with demand projections used to assess event-related needs and their impact on existing services. At the Sydney Olympics, this was the responsibility of the Olympic Roads and Transport Authority (ORTA) and it was predicted that the Games would create the highest continuous demand for passenger transport ever experienced in Australia (ORTA, 1999a). An additional 400,000 people were expected to visit central Sydney on a typical day during the Games with activity peaking around 4 pm and with crowds regularly extending beyond midnight (ORTA, 1999b). The *Olympic City* transport strategy was the product of a taskforce, led by ORTA that included the organising Committee for the Games (SOCOG), the Olympic Coordination Authority (OCA), state agencies for Police, Roads and Rail, and the Bus and Coach Association (ORTA, 1999b). Olympic spectator services included regional bus routes to the Sydney Olympic Park at Homebush and shuttle routes, running from railway stations to the other Olympic venues. The Sydney Harbour zone and the Horsley Park Equestrian venue were approximately 15 kilometres from the Olympic Park. Penrith Lakes, where canoeing and rowing were held, was nearly 40 kilometres to the west of Homebush. Bus and car fleets, carrying Olympic officials, athletes, accredited media and sponsors and their guests were able to use designated road routes that operated during the Games (ORTA, 1999a).

The OCA was responsible for the development and delivery of sporting facilities and venues for the 2000 Olympics. This involved managing agreements with existing venues and for planning new venues. It established an Urban Domain Planning Team due to the belief that 'areas of impact surrounding venues and the common domains in which the normal day to day management arrangements of State and Local Government agencies will not be sufficient to deal with the anticipated Games impacts and issues' (Churches, 1999). Central Sydney was the host for Olympic 'assets' such as the Torch Relay, the Triathlon, the Marathon and the Olympic Arts Festival. Ships, providing accommodation for Games visitors were moored in the harbour and many hotels, shops, bars and restaurants used by visitors were in the centre of the city. The OCA worked with the management agencies of Darling Harbour, Sydney Cove, the Royal Botanic Gardens and the Sydney Airport Authority as one of its key 'interventions' was to plan 'Live Sites'. Live sites have become an integral part of major events in recent years and they normally include large screens to watch events, stages for performances and interviews, shops selling event merchandise and opportunities for sponsors to showcase products. They attract event visitors and are particularly popular with local residents who can connect with the event without having tickets to the competition venues. The location of Live Sites affects the spatial pattern of an eventscape by influencing where people congregate. Programming influences the timing of visitor flows and their related impacts and each of the Live Sites in Sydney played a role in pedestrian management (OCA, 1999). Martin Place was a focal point where city workers gathered at lunchtime and after work. Belmore Park provided a place where crowds on very busy days were entertained to ease pressure on the area around the central railway station.

Live Sites are part of the event 'overlay' – a term used to describe the provision of temporary infrastructure. It includes the construction of paths, bridges, fencing and wayfinding, the creation of a distinctive look for the event and the addition of seating to increase the capacity of venues. At the London Aquatic Centre, two temporary wings were constructed to provide 14,000 extra seats for the duration of the 2012 Olympics. The term 're-use legacy' has been used to describe infrastructure that can be adapted for a new purpose after an event (Preuss, 2015) such as athlete villages. In 1997, the Sydney Park Authority signed a contract with a consortium of building companies and banks to design, finance and construct an Olympic Village to accommodate 15,300 competitors and team officials. After the Games, the consortium was required to carry out reinstatement work and to sell the properties. Nearly 900 townhouses and 700 apartments now form part of the suburb of Newington, bordering the Olympic Park. Environmental sustainability was at the forefront of the Olympic committee's objectives and every home had solar panels and water recycling facilities. At the time, it was the largest solar-powered suburb in the world (Walsh, 2012). The village constructed for the 2018 Commonwealth Games on the Gold Coast was built to accommodate 6,600 athletes and provided residential, retail, recreation, dining and medical facilities. Once again, it met environmental standards achieving the highest standard of accreditation with the Urban Development Institute of Australia for its commitment to ecosystems, waste, energy, water, materials and community (Kerslake, 2018). After the Games, the village became part of a mixed-use residential, health and knowledge precinct at Parklands in the north of the Gold Coast.

The media needs to be located close to event venues and at Sydney 2000, the main Media Centre, for accredited media was located at the Homebush Olympic Park. A second Media Centre, for non-accredited media, was developed at a harbourside location in the city. This was the first time a second media centre had been provided in a host city and was a response to lessons learned from the 1996 Atlanta Games. The provision of a home, for the duration of the event, with the resources needed by journalists made it possible to provide press briefings and supply information that was consistent with the objectives of the organising committee and the positioning of the host country and the tourism agencies. It proved to be an excellent example of the benefits that result from supportive media management (Brown, 2001).

While transportation is critical for movement across cities, the facilitation of pedestrian flows is a key part of site planning. This is illustrated by plans prepared by the community of Whistler, which was the Alpine Village for the 2010 Winter Olympics. The plans acknowledged that ancillary activities add to the emotional impact of the Games and an interactive network of spaces dedicated to sport, culture and the arts was designed. The Celebration Sites programme featured a series of plazas connected by a 'meandering pedestrian stroll' (Figure 2.1). The route was illuminated for

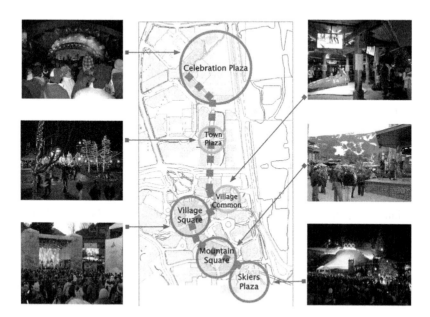

Figure 2.1 *Pedestrian stroll and celebration sites in the Village of Whistler.*
Source: Resort Municipality of Whistler, 2007.

atmospherics and animated by street performers. Screens in the plazas showed coverage of competition highlights and provided an extensive range of entertainment and cultural programming. Live music was focused in Village Square where Games-time infrastructure included a covered stage, an LED screen and a front of house tent controlling lighting, audio, video and live feeds to the other plazas. A back of house compound included dressing rooms, a crew room with catering and private washrooms.

A Snow & Glow event, held nightly at the Skiers Plaza, included music, lighting and snowboarders flying through flaming Olympic rings erected on the slopes at the edge of the village. With a capital budget of $14,200,000, Celebration Plaza was planned to be the focus of Games-time activities and to serve as a legacy of the Games. In the first phase of development, it was able to accommodate up to 8,000 spectators attending Olympic medal ceremonies, concerts and live entertainment. In phase 2, after the Games, it was designed to become a public space staging outdoor performances and exhibitions. Phase 3 was designed to include galleries, and studio spaces for artists, educational facilities, a new museum and a Centre for Sustainability. It intended to construct a pavilion: an iconic landmark to cover outdoor skating in winter and performances and exhibitions in the summer (Resort Municipality of Whistler, 2007). Eight years after the Games, the Whistler home page promoted the Celebration Plaza as a state-of-the-art outdoor performance facility and community space where free performances are offered on winter afternoons and summer evenings. In winter, the pavilion is transformed into a skating rink (Resort Community of Whistler, 2019).

EVENT DESIGN

The development of the Celebration Sites at Whistler, described above, is a good example of design responding to needs identified in the planning process and some authors, such as Berridge, consider design to be integral to 'any intentional or deliberate effort to solve a problem' (2012: 276). Berridge acknowledges that this is an 'expansive' perspective but it helps explain the diversity of approaches that have been taken in event design (Richards, Marques and Mein, 2015). The approach adopted in this book is more focused and is oriented towards the application of design 'tools' to the settings from which experiences emerge (Goldblatt, 2004). Examples of this approach are discussed in detail in Chapter 5. The tools are associated with artistic skills and creativity in theming, programming and service delivery. Getz (2007) mentions the of role theatrical techniques in event design and Nelson (2009) advocates the application of Goffman's (1959) dramaturgical perspective with stagecraft used to facilitate performances and create specific types of experiences. Scenery, lighting, sound and props are used to create dramatic effect and to capture audience attention. It is useful to distinguish between the tangible settings where environmental design is applied and experience design which involves the use of techniques associated with programming and atmospherics.

There is an important role for what Berridge (2012) calls 'process design' when describing space planning, seating arrangements and queuing systems and Getz (2007) discusses the way design is used to manage access and visitor flows. He refers to the enduring value of Lynch's (1960) insight about cognitive mapping and wayfinding where environments are made legible by nodes that act as focal points for activities, paths that direct movements and edges that provide orientation in relation to surrounding areas. Getz's (2007) model of the planned event experience has, at its core, a liminal zone where extraordinary experiences are gained. People are made aware that they are entering a special space by banners, logos, themes and ceremonies (Getz, 2007). In this way, places, be they indoor arenas or open public spaces, are replete with symbols and are transformed by the meanings they convey. However, design and programming are more complex in expansive, dispersed environments. A stylistic template can be applied to produce consistency across event settings with design having the power 'to mobilize people and networks by combining aesthetics, processes, ideas' (Bevolo, 2015: 65). This integrative function is valuable due to the range of stakeholders involved in event design (Richards *et al.*, 2015). An example of the design process is provided in **Designing the Millennium Marquee**.

DESIGNING THE MILLENNIUM MARQUEE

One of the benefits of Olympic sponsorship is the right to entertain guests in an exclusive manner (Schier, 1998). It is one of the main ways sponsors leverage benefits from their investment as, unlike other major sporting events, non-sponsors cannot purchase tickets and hospitality packages at the Olympic Games (Brown, 2007). Sponsor hospitality centres were first introduced in 1984 at the Los Angeles Games to offer an exclusive facility close to competition venues. The 24 Team Millennium Olympic Partners, the top tier of sponsorship at the Sydney 2000 Olympics, were expected to bring 60,000 guests to the Games, in 3–5 waves, over the period of the Games (Schier, 1998).

The Sydney organising committee (SOCOG) aimed to create the best ever hospitality suites at a high quality venue called the Millennium Marquee at Sydney Olympic Park. The venue exhibited a distinctly Australian style and a flexible design system was developed to brand and identify the numerous areas of applications such as wayfinding and services (Leavy, 2000). The design team at SOCOG included a Programme Manager, Image Programme Manager; a Design and Production Manager, Image Design and Programme Manager; a Creative Director; a Senior Designer and a Digital Artist. The Millennium Marquee comprised a series of catered suites where a staff of 1,500 looked after the needs of an average of 15,000 guests per day. Open from 08.00–23.30 each day, it was expected that there would two peaks with approximately 4,000 people between 11.00 and 14.00 and 4,500 between 16.00 and 19.00. With most guests attending an event in the afternoon, fewer than 1,000 were expected to be in the Millennium Marquee between 14.00 and 16.00 (Tracey, 1999).

The name, Millennium Marquee, focused on the dawn of a new age. The Roman numeral, MM for 2000 appeared above the Fluid Energy Graphic that was an integral element of the visual identity of the Sydney Games. With a human ergonomics shape, the graphic points to the future. The name, using a futuristic style of typeface, appeared in configurations as a single line or over two lines to provide flexibility in applications (Figure 2.2).

The Millennium Marquee was developed on two sites at the eastern side of the Park near a special drop-off facility for the use of sponsors and a short walk, using a dedicated footbridge,

Figure 2.2 *Millennium Marquee logo.*
Source: SOCOG, 1998

to competition venues. The Grand Parade precinct included nine suites averaging 450 square metres and the Australia Avenue precinct included 14 marquees. The environment of the precincts was designed to have a distinctive look and feel and an architect prepared a plan for the venue, buildings and landscaping. It included the design of markers, lighting, canopies and screens. A rainforest setting was created in the café area at each precinct. A nursery at Alstonville in northern New South Wales spent two years, growing 19,000 plants and the striking colours of the native plants were used to line the terraces. Macadamia nut husks provided moisture and nutrients for the plants. Many design decisions reflected environmental considerations such as the use of decorative Armacel screens and finials for the lighting features. They were made from cardboard and paper in PET plastic, allowing for recycling after their Games-time use. Crushed terracotta roof tiles, damaged in a hail storm in Sydney in 1999 were used in landscaping and the International Olympic Committee Pavilion was constructed from recycled Australian hardwood (SOCOG, 1999).

A separate department was established within SOCOG to manage sponsor hospitality and, throughout the planning, there was intensive coordination between SOCOG and the Olympic Partners (Schier, 1998). Sponsors were able to purchase exclusive hospitality facilities at the Millennium Marquee at a cost of AUS$2,500 per square metre. Most purchased between 300 and 600 square metres (Brown, 2007) and this marked the start of an extended period of design decisions, programme and service planning. Sponsors were able to create 'sub environments' within their suites with choices about furnishing and décor reflecting a desire to create a corporate look in the context of an Australian, Olympic experience. Programme decisions were based on the role of hospitality at the Millennium Marquee in relation to the overall package offered to guests. The main elements of the package were travel – business or first-class flights to Sydney for most guests, accommodation – in a five-star Sydney hotel and event tickets. Guests had two bases during their four–five-day stay – the hotel and the hospitality suite at the Millennium Marquee and these were the locations where guests could relax and where relationships could be reinforced or developed. Important guests qualified for special treatment: they were given expensive gifts and arrangements were made for meetings or social interaction with sponsor representatives. Sponsors wanted all guests to leave the Millennium Marquee feeling privileged as the beneficiaries of a unique experience.

Sponsors made decisions about catering and entertainment that often included access to people such as famous sport stars contracted to work with the sponsor. These decisions were not made independently as most sponsors employed specialist marketing companies which were responsible for developing the packages and communicating with guests. The invitation sent by one sponsor stated, 'The Millennium Marquee is an exclusive sponsor hospitality venue – and we have designed our own private suite within the facility for the enjoyment of our guests' (Westpac, 2000). There was ongoing communication between SOCOG, the sponsors and the representatives of the marketing companies and three major workshops were held: over three days in 1999, one year before the opening of the Games, and for two days in February and June, 2000. These were critical gatherings where SOGOC provided updates about Games and host city activities. Detailed information about the Millennium Marquee was provided with discussions following separate presentations by the architect and managers responsible for the venue, staffing and catering. The wide range of issues that needed to be understood by participants is evident by the topics of the other presentations. They were about the IOC, Sydney Olympic Park, Spectator Services, Transport and Airport operations, Ticketing, Security, Accreditation, Olympic Arts Festivals and the Paralympic Games.

Sponsors and their representatives used the workshops to explain what they needed in order to fulfil their programme objectives and it was interesting to observe the social dynamics in the room. At the start, it was an exercise in networking as business contracts were negotiated to provide mutual support among members of the sponsor 'club'. People who had been involved in previous Olympic Games reconnected with friends and new sponsors were able to learn from those with relevant experience. Subsequently, discussions were forthright and concerns about costs and quality were frequently raised. These were met with reassurances from SOCOG about an approach oriented towards cost recovery, rather than profit. The workshops were a gathering of people involved in a similar process with similar objectives who were constrained by the same deadlines. It was a very supportive environment and at the start of the last workshop there was sadness that the work and many of the relationships were coming to an end. Participants were reminded by the Sponsor Hospitality Manager that 'it was the last love in', that there would be 'tears at the end of the day' and that it was 'the last time that the room would be used'. This may be attributable to the culture at SOCOG and the skills of Lisa Schier, the sponsor hospitality manager, but it may also be related to the type of experiences that were being designed.

During the Games, the experience started as guests approached the Millennium Marquee. Psychological separation accompanied the physical separation as guests moved away from the crowds. This signalled a transfer into a quiet sanctuary that was set apart – unknown and hidden from those without a pass and a guide. The appearance of the landscape was very Australian as were the entertainers who mingled with guests as they approached the suites. On two occasions, the experience in the outdoor areas had a distinctive atmosphere and form of service. Before the Opening Ceremony and after the Closing Ceremony, Carnivales were held, as events that allowed sponsors and their guests to co-mingle. In the glow of specialty lighting, guests were encouraged to move around following entertainers and the smell of food that was presented in clusters of stalls (Bantock, 2000). Inside, the suites were comfortable and relaxing with an emphasis on the ability to make choices. In addition to a wide range of food, it was possible to sit with others near television screens or find a quiet personal space where a piano could be heard in the background. Attentive staff would make sure questions were answered and needs were addressed and would inform when it was time to leave for next event – or, if you preferred, how long you could stay in the suite before the return journey to the hotel.

Event settings include physical resources that affect spatial planning associated with site layout and the location of facilities while cultural resources can be incorporated in a theme to position the event within a distinctive local context. Theming is an important component of design and although, it is normally used to create and signal a recognisable relationship between activities at a particular event, it can be used strategically over an extended time-frame. The Australian Tourist Commission (ATC) organised 'theme years' from 1993–1997 to focus attention on celebrations of Australian sport, the outdoors, art and culture, the festivals of Oz and good living. This was excellent preparation for the Olympic Arts Festivals: the Festival of the Dreaming in 1997, A Sea Change in 1998, Reaching the World in 1999 and Harbour of Life in 2000. Maggie White who had been the manager of the theme years campaign was then appointed as the ATC's Olympic Manager and was responsible for many of the successful tourism initiatives linked to the Games.

EVENT IMPACTS

The scope of the changes that can be attributed to events is evident in a study by PriceWaterhouseCoopers for the Canadian Government that monitored the impacts of the 2010 Olympic and Paralympic Winter Games in British Columbia and Canada. The extent of spatial coverage is noteworthy as is the duration of the study. It sought to measure impacts before, during and after the Games from 2008 to 2013. After identifying over 200 studies, articles and reports that address various aspects of Olympic Games impacts, it was claimed that the comprehensive nature of the project and the analytical methods used to identify impacts distinguished it from previous work (Price-WaterhouseCoopers, 2009). There were eight areas of analysis in the study:

1 Economic development
2 Sport development
3 Tourism
4 Environmental sustainability
5 Social development
6 Arts and culture
7 Employment
8 Business development

It included not only traditional economic measures of business revenue, value added to the economy, tax revenue and employment but also instrumental impacts such as the creation of business partnerships, participation in sport and the attraction/retention of qualified workers. Most pleasingly for those who advocate the importance of intangible benefits of events, it sought to identify intrinsic impacts including the creation of social bonds and the expression of communal meanings. The total impact was the product of the combined effect of economic, instrumental and intrinsic impacts. For each of the eight areas of analysis, an impact map was developed. The impact map for tourism is shown in Figure 2.3.

A table for each area of analysis identified constituency groups and for each group a list was provided of anticipated impacts, impact measures and the proposed methods of analysis (PriceWaterhouseCoopers, 2009). A report produced in 2009 described the anticipated impacts for each area of analysis, as shown in Table 2.2 for Arts and Culture.

The PriceWaterhouseCoopers study is an example of research which seeks to amalgamate the economic, social and environmental impacts of events into a single framework. The term Triple Bottom Line (TBL) is used to describe this approach and Hede (2007) has suggested that the TBL should be applied in event planning to enhance outcomes for stakeholders. Despite recent interest in holistic approaches, the academic literature has been dominated by research about economic impacts with an evaluation of the 1986 Adelaide Grand Prix by Burns, Hatch and Mules (1986) regarded as a pioneering study. Economic impacts stem from consumption by event organisers, investments in infrastructure and spending by people attending the event with the main categories of spending on accommodation, transport, entertainment and food (Preuss, 2005). Preuss (2005) has provided a theoretical differentiation of the impacts of event-affected persons based on their patterns of movement:

> **Event visitors** travel to the region because the event is being held. This is an important group from an economic impact perspective as their spending is new – money that would not have come to the region without the event.

> **Extentioners** are tourists who would have come to the region anyway but stay longer because of the event. In this case, the event causes an increase in the economic impact of this group.

> **Home stayers** are residents who decide to stay at home and spend their money in the region rather than taking a vacation outside of the region. Thus, money is retained, rather than lost to another region.

> **Runaways** are residents who take a vacation in another region. Money spent in the other region is lost to the home economy.

> **Changers** are residents who take a vacation in another region at the time of the event. The event merely changes the time when the money is lost to the other region.

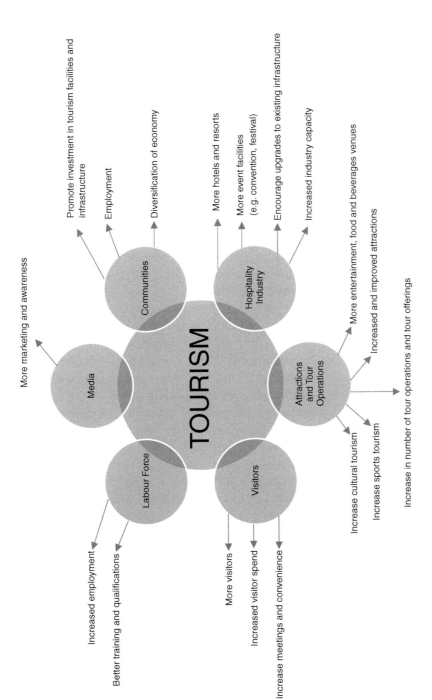

Figure 2.3 *Tourism impact map.*

Source: PriceWaterhouseCoopers, 2009.

Table 2.2 *Impacts on arts and culture*

Constituency	Expected timing of impacts
Communities	As the host city, impacts on Vancouver will be the greatest and are believed to begin in 2008 with the introduction of the Cultural Olympiad series. Impacts on Vancouver are expected to increase in 2009 peaking in 2010 with the Olympic and Paralympic Arts Festivals. As venue cities, Whistler, Richmond, Surrey and West Vancouver may also experience impacts from holding events for the Cultural Olympiads and the Olympic and Paralympic Arts Festivals. Impacts on other communities involved with the torch relay, live sites and other festivals will experience impacts closer to 2010 when the Winter Games are held.
Institutions (education, museums, galleries)	Impacts on non-profit institutions are believed to have begun in 2007 when funding became available for the Arts-Infused Education programme and/EDU launched by VANOC. Impacts resulting from these programmes will increase in 2009 and peak in 2010. Impacts on museums and galleries are expected to occur during the Olympic and Paralympic Games in 2010.
Aboriginal communities	Impacts on aboriginal communities are believed to have begun in 2007 with the introduction of programmes for the development and showcasing of original work including the Arts Partners in Creative Development, and the Cultural Olympiads being held in 2008 and 2009. Impacts on Aboriginal communities will peak in 2010 with the Olympic and Paralympic Arts Festivals. Global exposure during the Olympic and Paralympic Winter Games could result in Aboriginal communities benefiting from increased national and international partnerships resulting in opportunities to provide Aboriginal products and services.

Constituency	Expected timing of impacts
Visitors	Impacts on visitors are believed to begin in 2009 with the introduction of the first Cultural Olympiad. Impacts on visitors are expected to increase in 2009 with the second Cultural Olympiad and then peak in 2010 with the Olympic and Paralympic Arts Festivals. A slight downturn in visitor participation may occur in 2010 caused by audience fatigue. This effect was experienced after Expo '86 and it is anticipated it may occur again. However, previous experience indicates that overall, the arts and culture sector will continue to experience incremental increases after 2010 as more visitors become aware of arts and culture opportunities.
Not-for-Profit Organisations	Impacts on non-profit organisations which deliver arts and culture products and services are believed to have begun in 2007 as funding became available through Arts Partnerships in Creative Development to support the creation and development of original works. Impacts increased with the 2008 Cultural Olympiad. Impacts will continue to build through 2009 and are expected to peak in in 2010 with the presentation of the Olympic and Paralympic Arts Festivals. After 2010, there may be a downturn in the creation of original artistic works if public funding shifts to other societal activities. However, global exposure during the Olympic and Paralympic Winter Games could result in non-profit organisations benefiting from opportunities to tour nationally and internationally.

(Continued)

Table 2.2 *Continued*

Constituency	Expected timing of impacts
For-Profit Industries	Impacts on for-profit creative industries are believed to begin in 2008 as the Cultural Olympiad focuses attention on arts and culture. The development of original artistic work encourages employment opportunities and increased demand for products and services. Impacts on for-profit creative industries are expected to continue after as a result of the development of the sector. More people will be trained in arts and culture, which may facilitate the use of creative processes in the development of other sectors.

Source: PriceWaterhouseCoopers (2009: 15).

Casuals are tourists who would have visited the region even without the event. The event merely changes the timing when the benefit is received.

Time switchers are tourists who visit the region at the time of the event but would have visited at another time. Once again, the event merely changes the timing when the benefit is received.

Avoiders are people who stay away but would have visited without the event. This is known as the displacement effect. It includes people who cancel their trip and tourists who still visit but decide to come before or after the event (Pre/Post Switchers). An economic benefit is lost with the former but not with the latter.

An event may cause changes in the places people normally visit within the host region and attendance figures at tourist attractions fell in Los Angeles during the 1984 Olympics (Preuss, 2005). The same occurred in Atlanta during the 1996 Olympic Games, giving rise to the belief among business operators in the city that you are either part of the Games or you are competing with it (ATC, 1996 cited in Brown, 2008). During the 2000 Olympics, destinations outside Sydney such as the Blue Mountains attracted little business from the day excursion market partly because fewer buses were available due to allocations made as part of Games commitments. At the same time, places in Sydney attracted large increases in visitation and visitor expenditure. Over two million people visited Darling Harbour in September 2000, double the figure for the month in the previous year

(Brown, 2001). In a spatial sense, visitor expenditures are drawn to businesses located within the eventscape and away from traditional attractions during a major event. However, impacts can vary dramatically from place to place, even from one street to the next. The level of sales in shops and cafés along a road which serves as a major pedestrian route to a venue may increase considerably but those located in the next street may miss the passing trade and fail to gain economic benefits. However, they may avoid negative impacts associated with congestion, noise, littering and disruptions to the normal way of life.

In recent years, attitudes towards event evaluation and planning have started to change. 'It is no longer suitable merely to host an event in the hope that desired outcomes will be achieved; it is necessary to form and implement strategies and tactics that capitalise fully on the opportunities each event affords' (Chalip, 2004: 245). Events become a resource that can be leveraged but as every event is unique, a strategy needs to be innovative and responsive to the local context (Ziakas, 2015). Activities include those that are timed to coincide with the event and are designed to maximise visitor spending, retain income and build new markets and those that seek longer-term benefits by enhancing the destination's image and improving its market position (Chalip, 2004). An event can have an impact on a destination's image, if a meaningful match between the two is perceived (Brown, Chalip, Jago and Mules, 2004). A conceptual explanation of this process has been described in the literature about brand alliance effects (Gwinner and Eaton, 1999; Till and Shrimp, 1998). Drawing on cognitive psychology, knowledge consists of a set of nodes that are connected through a network of associations. The transfer of an image from one brand to another occurs when consumers assimilate a node from one brand's association set into the association set of the brand with which it is paired (Till and Shrimp, 1998).

An enhanced image represents an event-related improvement in a destination's location factors; the characteristics that are considered when selecting a destination to visit or as a place to make an investment (Preuss, 2015). However, Preuss explains that changes have only latent value until they become value in use. 'This means the changes only create an impact if the opportunity arises and the location factors attract social or economic activity' (Preuss, 2015: 660). The prospects for change are enhanced when there is an alliance between event organisers, event stakeholders such as event sponsors, government development agencies and local business associations. Prior to the Sydney Olympic Games, the Tourism Olympic Forum (TOF) was established by the NSW state government to coordinate planning for the Games and to communicate information about leveraging opportunities. The Forum was an alliance of organisations that were involved in planning for the Games and its membership and activities are discussed by Brown (2004). The work of the TOF can be divided into three phases. Between 1994 and 1996, the activities responded to uncertainty about the likely impact of the event, the demands that would be placed on resources and the timing of any event-specific regulations that might be imposed. Thus, an emphasis was placed on information gathering which took the form of network extension by forming relationships with informed decision makers. The TOF proved to be an invaluable communication channel between key decision makers at SOCOG and members of TOF who provided information to the businesses and organisations they represented. A specialist library was established and research was commissioned including a study of accommodation provision in the city. Between 1996 and 1999, the emphasis shifted towards planning and a number of sub-committees were established to address issues such as access, capacity, retail/shopping and regional dispersion. During the final year, TOF's emphasis shifted towards implementation with activities associated with hosting/welcome and service quality (Brown, 2004).

The Sydney Olympics saw an extensive campaign that was led by the Australian Tourist Commission (ATC) to leverage the Games for the long-term benefit of the tourism industry. The four-year, AUS$12 million strategy was launched in 1996 and The Director of Marketing of the International Olympic Committee said it represented a model that should be followed at subsequent Games (Brown, 2008). Activities included working closely with overseas ticket agents to assist in packaging tours and with broadcast rights holders to help develop programme ideas and to profile Australian lifestyles and regions throughout the country. A 'Colors of Australia' television advertisement produced by NBC with the support of the ATC was broadcast during prime-time slots in the USA. An expansion of the ATC's Visiting Journalist Programme took advantage of the heightened interest in Australia created by the Games, generating AUS$2.3 billion worth of publicity about the country (Brown, 2001). Collaboration with Olympic sponsors was an important part of the strategy and involved support for an 'Enjoy the Best of Australia' promotion by Kodak that appeared in magazines such as *Gourmet Traveller* and a billboard campaign by Visa in Shanghai's Bund that featured images of Australia. Visa formed a destination marketing consortium with the ATC, the Sydney Convention and Visitor Bureau and Tourism New South Wales that included a three-year global campaign with the title 'Australia Prefers Visa'. It resulted in more than AUS$40 million in marketing value for Australia (Brown, 2001).

The structures that remain as legacies of an event can be both tangible and intangible and they have been categorised by Preuss (2015) as:

Infrastructure Roads, airports, public transport, venues, parks, power supply, sewage plants, recycling factories, harbours, beaches, fairgrounds.

Knowledge Volunteering, bidding processes, employee up-skilling, school education programmes, event organisation, research, service skills.

Policy Education (school curricula), security, sport, environment, social, public policies (city, state and nation), laws.

Networks Politicians, sport officials, environmental activists, security persons.

Emotions Image, celebration, camaraderie, memories, stories 'to talk about', a sense of belonging, activism.

Infrastructure can be further classified as primary structures such as stadiums and theatres, secondary structures such as athlete villages and tertiary structures such hotels, roads and communication services (Solberg and Preuss, 2007). A key concern is the extent to which the development of structures are consistent with a host's long-term needs and, where possible, investment in structures that are only needed for an event should be avoided. It may also be difficult to assess whether a legacy is positive or negative as different stakeholders will be affected in different ways and there have been calls for the inclusion of a social welfare function in event planning (Preuss, 2015; Ziakas, 2015). Consequently, it has been suggested that:

> the government must start with good city planning, to fit the event into long-term city development. Then, it must optimise the way structures are produced or changed by the event, and sometimes, it must make additional investments to produce optimal structures. Finally, its task must be ongoing – it must stimulate a succession of new impacts by exploiting the location factors that have been created by the event.
>
> (Preuss, 2015: 661)

EVENT EXPERIENCES

Experiences are influenced by a wide range of factors including personal needs, past experiences and selective sensory focusing (McIntyre and Roggenbuck, 1998) and vary to the extent they are constructed socially, psychologically, emotionally, cognitively or environmentally (Beard, 2014). Getz (2007) has noted that the key cognitive, affective and conative dimensions proposed by Mannell and Kleiber (1997) capture the way people think, feel and behave at events. Some experiences are fleeting and superficial but deliver the type of enjoyment for people seeking passive forms of entertainment. Other people may seek to be more actively involved, wishing to be part of a creative process that delivers experiences that are personally meaningful. In this context, the categories proposed by Hover and van Mierlo (2006), as reported in Getz (2007), offer a valuable way to distinguish levels of experience:

- Basal experience – an emotional reaction to a stimulus, but with insufficient impact to stay for long in one's memory.
- Memorable experiences – emotion that can be recalled at a later date.
- Transforming experiences – producing durable changes on an attitudinal or behavioural level.

It is to be expected that different people, playing different roles, will gain different types of experiences but the power of events seems inescapable. Herb Elliott, one of Australia's greatest Olympians stated, 'there is nothing in the world like being in the Olympic City during the Games. The brew is one of excitement, anxiety, colour and athletic endeavor' (SOCOG, 1998). An academic, present in Athens during the 2004 Games stated, 'at that time, in that place, the Olympics were just part of life. The Olympics were us, and we were the Olympics, even without thinking about it' (Traganou, 2016: 1). During the Vancouver Olympics,

> SkyTrain and SeaBus commuters reported otherwise routine trips being transformed into uncharacteristically jovial journeys by voluble Olympic volunteers who 'held court' on train cars and face-painted spectators who sociably chatted with others onboard about the merits of seeing the Olympic cauldron.
>
> (Dyck and Gauvin, 2010: 198)

During Vivid Sydney, the driver of a regular bus service asked if the 'grumpy' passengers would like the interior lights turned off when cross-ing the Harbour Bridge so they could see the illuminations. After enjoying the visual experience, passengers applauded and, according to the news-paper report, smiled for the rest of the journey (Sydney Moring Herald, 2018).

This section mainly focuses on the experiences gained by people in the host city of a mega-event with the main consideration being the impact on residents. The event object producing the impact may range from winning a ticket in a consumer competition to attend the event to being evicted from home due to event-related constructions. In the case of the Olympics, the long planning period imposes complexity but key milestones add structure to the timing of experiences. Citizens gather in public places around the world to respond with a single voice when it is announced which city has been selected to host the Games. Media coverage conveys the celebrations in the successful city and the disappointment experienced in the other cities. All of the cities incurred financial costs in the preparation of their bids and sections of their populations invested emotionally in the expectation of winning. Even in the successful city, the announcement marks the end of direct engagement with the event for some organisations. Hotels that hosted international delegations and meetings of the IOC evaluation committee may not receive more Games-related guests until the start of the event. At the Sydney Olympics, Qantas supported the bid but ceased to be directly involved in the Games when Ansett Airlines was selected as the official airline.

The preparation period for the Olympics is usually fraught with controversies (Hillier and Wanner, 2015). It is unrealistic to expect that the excitement created by the announcement will remain for seven years especially when the organising committee has to come to terms with IOC procedures and adapt to local realities as the world changes around it. During the preparations for the Rio Olympics, there was a global economic recession, wars in the Middle East that induced waves of refugee movements, the state government ran out of money and concerns about the Zika virus and pollution in Guanabara Bay received global attention (Tzanelli, 2018). Irrespective of the nature and scale of problems, there would seem to be a law which dictates the nature of domestic and, to a certain extent, international media reporting. This is significant as information in the media influences levels of awareness, attitudes in the host community and can stimulate pre-event excitement and anticipation. The positive coverage that reflects public sentiment at the time of the bid announcement is followed by an extended period of negative stories about costs, ticketing policies, changes to plans and a wide range of impacts. Media organisations turn the dial to positive again just before the Games when the Torch Relay captures attention and a wave of enthusiasm follows it on its journey across the host country. During the planning period, the organising committee has to focus on meeting deadlines, leaving residents on the sidelines (Hillier and Wanner, 2015). However, some sections of the host community, particularly children, are encouraged to feel a sense of engagement by participating in programmes organised in schools and community groups. The programmes often focus on education about the Olympics or encourage participation in sport. During the preparations for Sydney 2000, the programmes were promoted in national newspapers owned by Olympic sponsors.

During the Games, citizens move to a new rhythm. Spontaneity is mixed with reactions primed by messages about how to respond to the new realities. In London, billboards showing images of businessmen pole vaulting over crowds, advised people to 'travel a different way' during the Games. In Sydney, new leisure spaces were connected by colourful crowds flowing through streets. Some of the spaces were brought to life with daily programmes of entertainment and activities that had been the subject of detailed planning. For many people, these peripheral products were their only event-related experiences. At certain places, social worlds collided and the 'fantasy city' (Richards and Palmer, 2010) created a sense of community and Richards and Palmer (2010) discuss the importance of 'being there' to experience communitas. Memorable experiences are recounted by emphasising that 'I was there when –' and this expression that captures the interaction of time and place has been exploited by destination marketers. A television advertisement promoting British Columbia prior to the 2010 Winter Olympics featured beautiful scenery, images of Olympic winter sports and a number of famous Canadian athletes and film stars each of whom asserted 'you gotta be there'.

At the heart of an eventscape is the arena or stadium, which offers the core event experience. At the greatest distance from the arena and beyond the site boundary are car parks and drop off/pick up areas. Their location requires people to walk a considerable distance, forming lines as they move towards the venue. The seating at a venue must offer the opportunity to see and hear a performance in safety and comfort. The venue or adjacent areas include essential services where toilets and first aid facilities are located and include places to purchase food, drinks and merchandise. This zone may offer places for people to congregate before, during or after attending the event. The edge of the site is marked by signs and points of entry and exit. The need for security dictates the inclusion of physical barriers to deny vehicle access and technology to identify people seeking to enter this zone. Simple mag and bag checks are being replaced by techniques that allow personal records and physical features to be recorded and checked against electronic databases. Despite the use of smart technologies, levels of accreditation determine the speed with which people gain entry, the places to which they have access and the levels of service they receive. Category membership determines which venues can be accessed, the zone within the venue, the standard of seating and the type of transport which is available. At the Sydney Olympics, the top level of accreditation qualified for a chauffeur-driven car, access to all Olympic venues with seating in the official stand for all events and ceremonies and butler service at a top hotel. However, it was explained at one of the SOCOG workshops that bodyguards accompanying guests were not allowed to take firearms into Olympic venues!

When VIPs are invited to events and corporate hospitality features prominently, eventscapes are places that offer access for some guests to zones of privilege. Travel patterns and event behaviour vary greatly from one group to the next and, drawing on the information presented above, differences in the typical activity pattern of a local resident with that of the guest of a sponsor at the Olympic Games are described in **Contrasting Event Experiences**.

CONTRASTING EVENT EXPERIENCES

A resident of the host city

The normal pattern of travel for a local resident may be disrupted throughout the period of the Olympic Games as bus and train timetables are changed. This may be extended beyond 16 days subject to pre-Games or post-Games contingencies. Ticketing procedures may make it difficult to obtain a ticket to an Olympic event and, for high-demand events, it may be expensive, relative to local income levels. But local people still represent a large proportion of event attendees with some receiving free tickets, at the last minute, to fill the stands at less popular events. To watch an event at the Games, it will be necessary to travel from home to the venue by public transport and it would not be unusual to spend most of the day travelling to and from a single event. A considerable period of time will be spent in lines for security checks and gaining access to the stadium. It is a good idea to bring food from home to eat during the day but it is not possible to take food and drinks into the stadium. With the exception of visits to Live Sites, most of the excitement of the Games for local residents is shared with friends in or near the home. Expenditure is largely the same as the rest of the year with the exception of any purchases made when visiting the Olympic store.

The guest of an Olympic sponsor

Most guests receive information about the Games before leaving home with all their arrangements managed by a special marketing organisation, contracted to the sponsor. The guest and partner fly in Business Class to the host city, where they are met by a sponsor representative and taken to an assembly area, reserved for sponsor guests in, or immediately outside, the airport terminal. Transfer to the hotel is by a bus contracted to the sponsor or, if a VIP, by a limousine. As one 'wave' of guests arrives at the hotel, which has been reserved for exclusive use by the sponsor, people in the previous 'wave' depart. Guests receive a welcome pack with information about their event programme (updated daily in a newsletter), event tickets, event merchandise and special gifts. The gifts are famous local products that are symbolic of the host country. VIPs receive more luxurious gifts. A welcome party is held on the first night, usually in the hotel. There may be opportunities to meet famous, current or former, athletes who are contracted to the sponsor. The next day, guests travel from the hotel directly to a special drop-off point where an 'operations gate' for group entry makes it possible to avoid lines before moving to premium seats in the stadium. After the event, guests are escorted to the sponsor's hospitality suite where lunch is offered. In the afternoon, guests are able to return to the hotel or attend a second event. Once again, transport is by sponsor bus, which collects guests from a special loading area, near the stadium. It is possible to attend an event and be back at the hotel after only three or four hours. Typically, five nights are spent in the hotel and for most of the time, the itinerary is tightly controlled. It may include visits with fellow guests to a top restaurant one evening and, during a morning or afternoon break from attending events, a visit to a local attraction may be arranged. But most activities, including a farewell party, take place in the hotel. On day six, guests are taken to the airport to take their flight home.

SUMMARY

This chapter has provided an overview of the place of events in contemporary society, revealing approaches to event analysis that will be used in subsequent chapters. The ability of events to disrupt urban rhythms while adding structure to the lives of citizens was discussed as was the role of events in urban development. The focus on mega-events helped demonstrate the significance of global networks and the spatial and temporal dimensions of event impacts. It was explained that planning has to meet event needs while recognising opportunities to create positive legacies. A growing interest in the aesthetic appeal of places of event consumption is drawing scholarly analysis of design into the event literature. The application of design to shape experiences and perceptions of event settings is examined throughout the book.

REFERENCES

Allen, J., O'Toole, W., Harris, R. and McDonnell, I. (2011). *Festival and Special Event Management*, 5th edn. Milton: John Wiley.

Amin, A. (2006). The Good City. *Urban Studies*, 43(5/6): 1009–1023.

Amin, A. (2008). Collective Culture and Urban Public Space. *City*, 12(1): 5–24.

Amin, A. and Thrift, N. (2002). *Cities: Reimagining the Urban*. Cambridge: Polity.

Australian Tourist Commission, (1996). *1996 Olympic Games Atlanta Report for the Tourism Olympic Forum*, September. Australian Tourist Commission.

Baernholdt, J. O. (2013). Governmobility: The Power of Mobility. *Mobilities*, 8(1): 20–34.

Banjeree, B. and Linstead, S. (2001). Globalization, Multiculturalism and Other Fictions: Colonialism for the New Millennium. *Organization*, 8(4): 683–722.

Bantock, P. (2000). Millennium Marquee Carnivale Plan. *Presentation at Team Millennium Olympic Partner Hospitality Workshop*, SOCOG, 1 March.

Barker, C. (1990). *Television, Globalisation and Cultural Identities*. Buckingham: Open University Press.

Beard, C. (2014). Designing and Mapping Event Experiences. In: L. Sharples, P. Crowther, D. May and C, Orefice, eds, *Strategic Event Creation*. Oxford: Goodfellow Publishers, 123–140.

Becker, H. (1982). *Art Worlds*. Berkeley, CA: University of California Press.

Berridge, G. (2012). Designing Event Experiences. In: S. J. Page and J. Connell, eds, *The Routledge Handbook of Events*. London: Routledge, 273–288.

Bevolo, M. (2015). The Discourse of Design as an Asset for the City: From Business Innovation to Vernacular Event. In: G. Richards, L. Marques and K. Mein, eds, *Event Design: Social Perspectives and Practices*. Abingdon: Routledge, 65–77.

Brown, G. (2001). Sydney 2000: An Invitation to the Games. *Olympic Review* 27(February–March): 15–20.

Brown, G. (2004). The Impact of a Mega Event on Destination Networks and Partnerships: A Case Study of the Sydney Olympic Games. In: C. S. Petrillo and J. Swarbrooke, eds, *Networking and Partnerships in Destination Development and Management.* Proceedings of the ATLAS Annual Conference. Naples: Enzo Albano, 347–355.

Brown, G. (2007). Sponsor Hospitality at the Olympic Games: An Analysis of the Implications for Tourism. *International Journal of Tourism Research*, 9: 315–327.

Brown, G. (2008). The Games of the xxvii Olympiad in Sydney (2000). In: M. Weed, *Olympic Tourism*. Oxford: Butterworth-Heinemann, 137–151.

Brown, G., Assaker, G. and Reis, A. (2018). Visiting Fortaleza: Motivation, Satisfaction and Revisit Intentions of Spectators at the Brazil 2014 FIFA World Cup. *Journal of Sport & Tourism*, 22(1): 1–19.

Brown, G., Chalip, L., Jago, L. and Mules, T. (2004). Developing Brand Australia: Examining the Role of Events. In: N. Morgan, A. Pritchard and R. Pride, eds, *Destination Branding: Creating the Unique Destination Proposition*, 2nd edn. Oxford: Butterworth-Heinemann, 279–305.

Burns, J. P. A., Hatch, J. H. and Mules, T. J. (1986). An Economic Evaluation of the Adelaide Grand Prix. In: G. Syme, B. Shaw, P. M. Shaw, P. M. Fenton and W. S. Mueller, eds, *The Planning and Evaluation of Hallmark Events*. Aldershot: Avebury, 172–185.

Castells, M. (1996). *The Rise of the Network Society, the Information Age: Economy, Society and Culture (Vol. 1)*. Oxford: Blackwell.

Chalip, L. (2004). Beyond Impact: A General Model for Sport Event Leverage. In: B. W. Ritchie and D. Adair, eds, *Sport Tourism: Interrelationships, Impacts and Issues*. Clevedon: Channel View Publications, 226–252.

Churches, D. (1999). *Presentation to the Tourism Olympic Forum* by the Director, Games Planning, Olympic Coordination Authority, 18 May.

Collins, R. (2004). *Interaction Ritual Chains*. Princeton, NJ: Princeton University Press.

Cresswell, T. (2010). Towards a Politics of Mobility. *Environment and Planning D*, 28(1): 17–31.

Debord, G. (1994). *The Society of the Spectacle*. New York: Zone Books.

De Cauter, L. (2004). *The Capsular Civilisation: On the City in an Age of Fear*. Rotterdam: Nai Publishers.

Durkheim, E. (1915). *The Elementary Forms of the Religious Life*. London: George Allen and Unwin.

Dyck, N. and Gauvin, R. (2010). Dressing Up to Join the Games: Vancouver 2010. *Visual Studies*, 27(2): 196–203.

Economist Intelligence Unit (2018). *The Global Liveability Index 2018*. A Report by the Economist Intelligence Unit. https://pages.eiu.com/rs/753-RIQ-438/images/The_Global_Liveability_Index_2018.pdf.

Edensor, T. (2016). Introduction: Thinking About Rhythm and Space. In: T. Edensor, ed., *Geographies of Rhythm: Nature, Place, Mobilities and Bodies*. London: Routledge, 1–18.

Florida, R. L. (2002). *The Rise of the Creative Class: And How It's Transforming Work, Leisure, Community and Everyday Life*. New York: Basic Books.

Florida, R. L. (2005). *Cities and the Creative Class*. New York: Routledge.

Foucault, M. (1980). *Power/Knowledge: Selected Interviews and Other Writings 1972–1977*. London: Harvester Press.

Fox Sports. (2017). *Socceroos World Cup Venues for World Cup: Kazan, Samara, Sochi*. www.foxsports.com.au/football/world-cup/socceroos-world-cup-venues-for-world-cup-kazan-samara-sochi/news-story/c723d7d59e24e83efc5e05c37807 b5fc.

Franzen, M. (2001). Urban Order and the Preventive Restructuring of Space: The Operation of Border Controls in Micro Space. *Sociological Review*, 49(2): 202–218.

Getz, D. (2007). *Event Studies: Theory, Research and Policy for Planned Events*. Oxford: Butterworth-Heinemann.

Getz, D. (2012). *Event Studies*. London: Routledge.

Getz, D. (2017). Developing a Framework for Sustainable Even Cities. *Event Management*, 21: 575–591.

Goffman, E. (1959). *The Presentation of Self in Everyday Life*. New York: Anchor Books.

Goldblatt, J. J. (2004). *Special Events: Event Leadership for a New World*. Hoboken, NJ: John Wiley.

Graham. S. (2010). *Cities Under Siege*. London: Verso.

Graham, S. and Marvin, S. (2001). *Splintering Urbanism*. Cheltenham: Routledge.

Gwinner, K. P. and Eaton, J. (1999). Building Brand Image Through Event Sponsorship: The Role of Image Transfer. *Journal of Advertising*, 28(4): 47–57.

Hagerstrand, T. (1970). What About People in Regional Science? *Papers in Regional Science*, 24(1): 7–21.

Hall, S. (1991). The Local and the Global: Globalization and Ethnicity. In: A. D. King, ed., *Culture, Globalization and the World-System*. London: Macmillan, 19–39.

Häußermann, H. and Siebel, W. (1993). Die politik der festivalisierung und die festivalisierung der politik: Große ereignisse in der stradpolitik. In: H. Häußermann and W. Siebel, eds, *Festivalisierung der Stadtpolitik: Stadtentwicklung Durch Große Projekte*. Wiesbaden: Springer VS, 7–31.

Hede, A.-M. (2007). Managing Special Events in the New Era of the Triple Bottom Line. *Event Management*, 11: 13–22.

Heidegger, M. (1993). *Basic Writings*. San Francisco, CA: Harper Collins.

Herzfeld, M. (1997). *Cultural Intimacy: Social Poetics in the Nation State*. London: Routledge.

Hillier, H. (2006). Post-Event Outcomes and the Post-Modern Turn: The Olympics and Urban Transformations. *European Sport Management Quarterly*, 6(4): 317–332.

Hillier, H. H. and Wanner, R. A. (2015). The Psycho-Social Impact of the Olympics as Urban Festival: A Leisure Perspective. *Leisure Studies*, 34(6): 672–688.

Hover, M. and van Mierlo, J. (2006). *Imagine Your Event: Imagineering for the Event Industry*. Unpublished manuscript. Breda University of Applied Sciences and NHTV Expertise, Netherlands: Event Management Centre.

Jackson, P. (2004). *Inside Clubbing: Sensual Experiments in the Art of Being Human*. Oxford: Berg.

Jacob, D. (2013). The Eventification of Place: Urban Development and Experience Consumption in Berlin and New York City. *European Urban and Regional Studies*, 20(4): 447–459.

Jirásek, I. and Kohe, Z. (2015). Readjusting our Sporting Sites/Sight: Sportification and the Theatricality of Social Life. *Sport, Ethics and Philosophy*, 9(3): 257–270.

Kerslake, H. (2018). *Inside the Commonwealth Games Village*. 19 March. Gold Coast. https://gc2018.com/article/inside-commonwealth-games-village.

Klauser, F. (2013). Spatialities of Security and Surveillance: Managing Spaces, Separations and Circulations at Sport Mega Events. *Geoforum*, 49: 289–298.

Kolamo, S. and Vuolteenaho, J. (2013). The Interplay of Mediascapes and City-scapes in a Sport Mega Event. The Power Dynamics of Place Branding in the 2010 FIFA World Cup in South Africa. *International Communication Gazette*, 75(5–6): 502–520.

Lazzarotto, M. (2004). From Capital-Labor to Capital-Life. *Ephemera Theory Multitude*, 4(3): 187–208.

Leavy, P. (2000). Sydney 2000 Olympic Games Sponsor Environments. *Sydney Olympic Games Sponsor Hospitality Programmes. Design Evidence*. Sydney Organising Committee for the Olympic Games.

Lefebvre, H. (2004). *Rhythmanalysis: Space, Time and Everyday Life*. London: Continuum.

Lynch, K. (1960). *The Image of the City*. Cambridge, MA, MIT Press.

Mannell, R. C. and Kleiber, D. A. (1997). *A Social Psychology of Leisure*. Pittsburgh, PA: Venture Publications.

Marrero-Guillamón, I. (2012). Photography Against the Olympic Spectacle. *Visual Studies*, 27(2): 133–139.

McIntyre, N. and Roggenbuck, J. W. (1998). Nature/Person Transactions During an Outdoor Adventure Experience: A Multi-Phase Analysis. *Journal of Leisure Research*, 30: 401–422.

Muller, M. (2015). What Makes an Event a Mega-Event? Definitions and Sizes. *Leisure Studies*, 34(6): 627–642.

Nelson, K. B. (2009). Enhancing the Attendee's Experience Through Creative Design of the Event Environment: Applying Goffman's Dramaturgical Perspective. *Journal of Convention and Event Tourism*, 10: 120–133.

O'Brien, D. and Gardiner, S. (2006). Creating Sustainable Mega Event Impacts: Networking and Relationship Development Through Pre-Event Training. *Sport Management Review*, 9: 25–47.

OCA (Olympic Coordination Authority) (1999). Olympic City. Central Sydney Celebrations for the 2000 Games. OCA, July.

ORTA (Olympic Roads and Transport Authority) (1999a). Olympic Spectator Routes. ORTA, June.

ORTA (Olympic Roads and Transport Authority) (1999b). Olympic City: Central Sydney Roads and Transport for the 2000 Games. ORTA, July.

Parkins, W. (2004). Out of Time: Fast Subjects and Slow Living. *Time and Society*, 13(2/3): 363–382.

Peck, J. and Tickell, A. (2002). Neoliberalizing Space. *Antipode*, 34(3): 380–404.

Pine, J. and Gilmore, J. (1999). *The Experience Economy*. Boston, MA: Harvard Business School Press.

Ploger, J. (2010). Presence Experiences – the Eventilisation of Urban Space. *Environment and Planning D: Society and Space*, 28(5): 848–866.

Preuss, H. (2005). The Economic Impact of Visitors at Major Multi-Sport Events. *European Sport Management Quarterly*, 5(3): 281–301.

Preuss, H. (2015). A Framework for Identifying the Legacies of a Mega Sport Event. *Leisure Studies*, 34(6): 643–664.

PriceWaterhouseCoopers (2009). *Gauging the Games: Research and Benchmarking Services for the 2010 Olympic and Paralympic Winter Games. Framework Report*. PriceWaterhouseCoopers International Limited.

Resort Municipality of Whistler (2007). *Whistler Celebration Sites*. Unpublished document.

Resort Municipality of Whistler (2019). *Whistler Olympic Plaza*. www.whistler.ca/culture-recreation/parks/whistler-olympic-plaza.

Richards, G. (2015). Events in the Network Society: The Role of Pulsar and Iterative Events. *Event Management*, 19: 553–566.

Richards, G. (2017). Emerging Models of the Eventful City. *Event Management*, 21: 533–543.

Richards, G. and Columbo, A. (2017). Rethinking the Eventful City: Introduction. *Event Management*, 21: 527–531.

Richards, G., Marques, L. and Mein, K. (2015). Introduction: Designing Events, Events as Design Strategy. In: G. Richards, L. Marques and K. Mein, eds, *Event Design: Social Perspectives and Practices*. Abingdon: Routledge, 1–13.

Richards, G. and Palmer, R. (2010). *Eventful Cities: Cultural Management and Urban Revitalisation*. Oxford: Elsevier.

Roche, M. (2000). *Mega-Events and Modernity: Olympics and Expos in the Growth of Global Culture*. London: Routledge.

Roche, M. (2003). Mega-Events, Time And Modernity: On Time Structures in Global Society. *Time and Society*, 12(1): 99–126.

Roche, M. (2017). *Mega-Events and Social Change: Spectacle, Legacy and Public Culture*. Manchester: Manchester University Press.

Rojek, C. (2013). *Event Power: How Global Events Manage and Manipulate*. London: Sage.

Sassen, S. (2006). *Territory, Authority, Rights*. Princeton, NJ: Princeton University Press.

Schier, L. (1998). *111 Weeks to Go*. Presentation to the Tourism Industry. Olympic Commerce Centre, 29 July.

Silk, M. (2011). Towards a Sociological Analysis of London 2012. *Sociology*, 45(5): 733–748.

Silvestre, G. and de Oliveira, N. G. (2012). The Revanchist Logic of Mega-Events: Community Displacement in Rio de Janeiro's West End. *Visual Studies*, 27(2): 204–210.

Smith, A. (2016). *Events in the City: Using Public Spaces as Event Venues*. Abingdon: Routledge.

Smith, A. (2017). Animation or Denigration? Using Urban Public Spaces as Event Venues. *Event Management*, 21: 609–619.

Smith, A., Brown, G. and Assaker, G. (2017). Olympic Experiences: The Significance of Place. *Event Management*, 21: 281–299.

SOCOG (1998). *Sydney 2000 Olympic Games Image Guidelines*. Sydney Organising Committee for the Olympic Games.

SOCOG (1999). *The Millennium Marquee, Sydney Olympic Park*. Sponsor Hospitality Fact Sheet, 01. Sydney Organising Committee for the Olympic Games.

Solberg, H. A. and Preuss, H. (2007). Major Sport Events and Long-Term Tourism Impacts. *Journal of Sport Management*, 21: 213–234.

Stevens, Q. and Shin, H. (2014). Urban Festivals and Local Social Space. *Planning Practice and Research*, 29(1): 1–20.

Stokes, R. (2006). Network-Based Strategy Making for Events Tourism. *European Journal of Marketing*, 40(5/6): 682–695.

Sydney Morning Herald (2018). *Compelling Spontaneity in Sydney: How a Sydney Bus Driver Made his Passengers See the Light*. www.smh.com.au/national/how-a-sydney-bus-driver-made-his-passengers-see-the-light-20180615-p4zlsi.html.

Till, B. D. and Shrimp, T. A. (1998). Endorsers in Advertising: The Case of Negative Celebrity Information. *Journal of Advertising*, 27(1): 67–82.

Tracey, T. (1999). *The Millennium Marquee*. Presentation at Team Millennium Olympic Partner Hospitality Workshop, SOCOG, 16 September.

Traganou, J. (2016). *Designing the Olympics: Representation, Participation, Contestation*. New York: Routledge.

Tzanelli, R. (2004). Giving Gifts (And Then Taking Them Back): Identity, Reciprocity and Symbolic Power in the Context of Athens 2004. *Journal for Cultural Research*, 8(4): 425–446.

Tzanelli, R. (2018). *Mega Events as Economies of the Imagination: Creating Atmospheres for Rio 2016 and Tokyo 2020*. London: Routledge.

Urry, J. (2004). Death in Venice. In: M. Sheller and J. Urry, eds, *Tourism Mobilities*. London: Routledge, 205–215.

Urry, J. and Larsen, J. (2011). *The Tourist Gaze*, 3rd edn. London: Sage.

Walsh, A. (2012). Sydney's Newington Olympic Village 12 Years After the Closing Ceremony. *Property Observer*, 8 August. www.propertyobserver.com.au/finding/residential-investment/17667-newington-olympic-story.html.

Westpac (2000). Invitation to the Sydney 2000 Olympic Games. Document sent to guests by Westpac Banking Corporation, Australia.

Wunderlich, P. M. (2010). The Aesthetics of Place-Temporality in Everyday Urban Space: The Case of Fitzroy Square. In: T. Edensor, ed., *Geographies of Rhythm: Nature, Place, Mobilities and Bodies*. London: Routledge, 45–56.

Yeoh, B. and Chang, T. (2001). Globalising Singapore: Debating Transnational Flows in the City. *Urban Studies*, 38(7): 1025–1044.

Ziakas, V. (2014). Planning and Leveraging Event Portfolios: Towards a Holistic Theory. *Journal of Hospitality Marketing & Management*, 23(3): 237–356.

Ziakas, V. (2015). For the Benefit of All? Developing a Critical Perspective in Mega-Event Leverage. *Leisure Studies*, 34(6): 689–702.

3 | The study of scapes

VISIONS OF THE WORLD

> And time it is when raging war is done
> to smile at scapes and perils overblown
>
> (*The Taming of the Shrew*, Act 5, Scene, 2)

In Shakespeare's *The Taming of the Shrew*, Lucentio expresses pleasure at having escaped from the dangers of war. Today, a *smile at scapes* is more likely to be interpreted as the response to a scenic view for, as a suffix, scape commonly refers to a view of the initial part of the word such as a view of the land in landscape. In this context, eventscape directs attention to events and frames the event setting. Scape can operate as an analytical toolbox due to the way it is used in different disciplines. We talk about streetscapes in everyday language but the term also features in scholarly literature about art, architecture, geography and urban planning. It refers to visual characteristics of the urban environment in the context of architecture (Kolodney, 2012) and urban planning (Rosenfield, Fitzpatrick-Lins and Johnson, 1987) with iconic buildings the most visible manifestation of a cityscape (Evans, 2015). At night, a new map of the city emerges (McQuire, 2008) as features are transformed by streetlamps, illuminated signs and floodlit buildings but 'despite contemporary familiarity with illuminated cityscapes, views from on high of the nocturnal city still have the power to thrill' (Edensor, 2015: 333). Edensor notes that tourist destinations such as New York's Times Square and London's Piccadilly Circus as 'environments of congregation, leisure and consumption continue to be atmospherically charged by illumination' (2015: 333).

In a study of the 2010 FIFA World Cup in South Africa, mediascapes were described as concentrations of media publicity that communicated staged representations of urban spaces 'that were constituents of the branded cityscape' (Kolamo and Vuolteenaho, 2013: 504). In a marketing study of outdoor advertising, images were collected from the 'London Olympic cityscape' at public areas around event venues, transportation sites and tourist attractions (Nadeau, O'Reilly and Heslop, 2015).

In other uses, artscapes refers to locations that specialise in artistic production (Chang and Huang, 2005), musicscapes are associated with entertainment zones and, in a particular context, described the patterns on hand-drawn maps of sites that were significant in the lives of musicians (Cohen, 2012). Storyscapes are associated with heritage interpretation (Chronis, 2005) and nostalgiascapes describe places that offer a connection with a cherished former way of life (Gyimothy, 2005). Dreamscapes are mentioned in popular literature to describe romance, fantasies and exotic settings and appear as the title of books which present photographic essays about garden design (Takacs, 2018) and tourist attractions (Drebin, 2016). In Drebin's *Dreamscapes*, it is claimed that:

> we cruise the beaches of the Amalfi Coast; smell and taste downtown San Francisco; gawk at the cityscape of Manhattan; revel in the boulevards of Paris. Reflections of light, dramatic color, and evocative staging invite readers to reflect, relax, and lose themselves in a fascinating and experiential daydream.
>
> (Drebin, 2016)

Drebin's references to light, colour and drama are important themes that are discussed later in the book when their role in shaping the experiences gained at eventscapes is examined.

Appadurai (1996), an anthropologist, has invoked metaphorical scapes including mediascapes, ideoscapes and ethnoscapes to describe global flows of information, ideas and people, as processes that connect dispersed communities. These types of global flows influence the creation of events and the form of eventscapes. They shape points of cultural reference and shared imaginations, which can take tangible form through the transnational symbolic grammar of themed environments (O'Dell, 2005) and ethnic festivals, as translocal eventscapes (Shaw, 2014). The review of scapes in this chapter is designed to assist an understanding of eventscapes and how they can be studied. To this end, a detailed discussion is provided of landscapes, servicescapes, designscapes and sportscapes. Operating at different spatial scales, they help inform the relationship between both leisure and business activities, their environmental settings and processes of production and consumption. A conceptual model of eventscapes is provided at the end of the chapter.

LANDSCAPES

In colloquial use, landscape conveys an all-encompassing perspective such as when talking about the political landscape or the education landscape. Similarly, the media landscape may refer to all organisations involved in the distribution of news but it has a more specific definition when used to 'denote the various ways in which urban outdoor spaces are used as media spaces by those who place text and images on urban surfaces and infrastructure' (Iveson, 2012: 161). Saturation with images sees the emergence of 'screen landscapes' (Gandy, 2017). An expansive meaning of landscape refers to 'anything I see and sense when I am out of doors' (Relph, 1976: 22). An interest in the visual combined with a holistic, experiential approach to relations between humans and the environment have been part of a renaissance in humanistic geography that emerged in the 1980s in opposition to scientific approaches which had dominated geographical studies in the post-war period (Cosgrove, 1985). Cosgrove suggests that the renewed interest in landscape brought 'a refreshing willingness by geographers to employ landscape representations – in painting, imaginative literature and garden design – as sources for answering geographical questions' (1985: 46), although he stressed the need to recognise that visual ideology has always been integral to landscape painting.

The Dutch word landschap referred to paintings of the countryside at the start of the seventeenth century when French artists, based in Italy, such as Poussin and Lorrain were painting idyllic scenes with harmonious compositions. At this time, Dutch artists such as van Ruisdael and Hobbema infused their work with metaphorical meanings that depicted the power of nature. The Rococo period in the eighteenth century saw the development by French and English painters of a lyrical approach to outdoor scenes that depicted stylish men and women engaged in leisure pursuits. With the Romantic movement in the nineteenth century, landscapes became more dramatic and the importance of light and atmosphere in the work of artists such as Turner challenged the dominance of a linear perspective, which had served as the guarantor of pictorial realism since its introduction in Renaissance Italy (Cosgrove, 1985). Renaissance art had involved a shift from symbolism to more realistic renderings that made possible a closer engagement with the subject matter and the expression of ideas (Jirásek and Kohe, 2015).

The invention of the tin tube for paint and the portable easel allowed artists to venture out of their studios and outdoor painting became the dominant practice of the Impressionist painters. The developing train network at this time made it possible for the artists to travel to the countryside around

Paris. The Impressionists favoured subjective forms of expression and applied theories and scientific discoveries about colour, using newly available pigments to capture the fleeting effects of light as it appeared before their eyes. In the twentieth century, the cityscape took a prominent place in the work of modern artists in the United States such as Georgia O'Keeffe, John Marin and Marsden Hartley as traditional ideas about landscape disappeared within abstract images of the built environment, under the glare of artificial light. These artists were contemporaries of photographers such as Alfred Stieglitz and Ansel Adams who were using emerging photographic and printing technologies in ways that challenged the hierarchies of painting (Vickery, 2015). Photography rearranged the circulation of images bringing landscapes to the attention of new audiences. According to Cosgrove (1985), representations of the landscape direct the environment to the external observer, giving mastery to the eye and making space an appropriated object. The way a view is framed affects the way of seeing and 'one of the consistent purposes of landscape painting has been to present an image of order and proportioned control, to suppress evidence of tension and conflict between social groups' (Cosgrove, 1985: 58). Hence, the need to critically examine visual and social values inherent in representations of landscape and to question what they say about the way the world is structured.

A non-representational approach, informed by phenomenology, does not negate the act of viewing but places emphasis on the role of embodied experiences in everyday interactions between people and things (Vickery, 2015). Sight remains important when landscapes are experienced, particularly under the conditions of natural light but, at night, there is a reliance on other senses (Edensor and Lorimer, 2015). This was noted poetically by Shakespeare in *A Midsummer Night's Dream*:

> Dark night, that from the eye his function takes,
> The ear more quick of apprehension makes,
> Wherein it doth impair the seeing sense.
> It pays the hearing double recompense
> (Shakespeare, 1992: Act 3, Scene 2)

As we become more responsive to sounds, smells and the feel of surroundings at night, the landscape can be exciting, mysterious or frightening. The former Director of the Fête des Lumières in Lyon, has suggested that light festivals should be used to question our relationship with the night (Roger Narboni cited in Giordano and Ong, 2017) and although the bright lights of urban areas can create nocturnal 'blandscapes' (Schlor, 1998), the spectacle of calculated illumination stimulates 'fantasy-scapes,

– appreciated and consumed for the ways in which they add to the experience of cities' (Giardano and Ong, 2017: 712). The term 'landscapism' was used to describe a calculated, scripted experience that was enacted en masse, by participants at the *Speed of Light* event that was held at the 2012 Edinburgh International Festival (Edensor and Lorimer, 2015). Active engagement with scapes takes many forms and landscape architects combine scientific knowledge and artistic appreciation to improve the scenic qualities of the physical environment. They create atmospheres by controlling the way sunlight is filtered by vegetation (Böhme, 2016). Design is used to change the appearance of many types of scapes – to affect perception and attitudes towards environmental settings. In services-capes, environments are managed to influence consumer behaviour and to achieve business outcomes. This topic is discussed in more detail later in this chapter as it helps to demonstrate how eventscapes can be managed.

Returning to the study of landscape by geographers, the Chair's theme at the Annual Conference of the Royal Geographical Society in 2018 was *Geographical Landscapes/Changing Landscapes of Geography.* It was a large conference and landscapes appeared in the title of 58 of the 180 special sessions. In addition, scapes were mentioned in the form of food-scapes, seascapes, timescapes, soundscapes and sandscapes. The conference theme and the calls for papers about visualising seascapes and soundscapes are described in **Geographical Landscapes**. This information presents a contemporary perspective of the relationship between geography and land-scape studies. According to the Conference Chair, the relevance of geography has been enhanced by the popularity of books, television shows and radio broadcasts about seeing, moving through and engaging with land-scape. The description of the seascapes session refers to the diversity of stakeholders, to growing environmental risks, which are changing social values and the power of the visual to create new meanings of the seascape. Drawing on the ideas of rhythmanalysis (Lefebvre, 2004) and temporality (Ingold, 1993), a soundscape is shaped by recurrent social activities and cyclical natural events that are distinctive to particular locations (Wunder-lich, 2010) with acoustic colourations caused by echoes and reverberations as sound is absorbed and reflected from surfaces in the environment (Wrightson, 2000). Acoustic spaces range from a room to an entire metro-politan region, if the listener or sound sources are moving through space with music used to promote products and invoke emotional responses (Gandy, 2017). In both of the sessions at the IBG conference, scape is used as a framework to bring to bear critical perspectives to assist understanding of the theme. The sessions were organised by different academics who were part of the Geography of Leisure and Tourism Research Group.

GEOGRAPHICAL LANDSCAPES

International conference of the Royal Geographical Society with the Institute of British Geographers. 28–31 August 2018, Cardiff University.

Chair's Theme: Geographical landscapes/changing landscapes of geography

The theme of geographical landscapes/changing landscapes of geography provides an opportunity to explore ideas of landscape within geographical scholarship, the popularity of landscape beyond the academy, and the shifting landscapes of geography as an academic discipline.

Landscape has long been a central concept within geography. The conference will offer critical reflection on the position of landscape within contemporary geography. It will also seek to develop dialogue between human and physical geographers, and engage with researchers from other cognate disciplines working on landscape. The conference will provide a broad perspective on geographical landscapes in terms of spatial and temporal context, methodological approaches and thematic coverage.

Beyond academic scholarship, landscape has emerged as one of the key public faces of geography through the publication of numerous popular books and broadcasts of television shows and radio programmes on seeing, moving through and engaging with landscape. This has provided geography with a greater sense of recognition and relevance, even though the term 'geography' is often absent from these texts. The conference will explore this popular interest in landscape from the perspectives of those within and beyond the academy.

The landscapes of geography are also changing. The conference will encourage critical discussion of the shifting contours of geography as an academic discipline. It will also engage with the changing external landscapes within which geography is positioned. Brexit and recent rounds of restructuring of the (higher) education sector in the UK are presenting new challenges for the discipline in relation to internationalism, marketisation and understandings of excellence in the context of research, impact and teaching. How are these changes impacting on geography and geographers in the UK, and to what extent are such shifting external landscapes evident in other countries?

Professor Paul Milbourne,
(Royal Geographical Society, 2018a)

Call for papers

Visualising seascapes: encounters with coastal and marine environments

Co-badged session between the Geography of Leisure and Tourism Research Group and the Coastal and Marine Research Group.

There is now considerable effort to frame the importance of the sea to diverse stakeholders and the public. Initiatives ranging from the Blue Planet to Blue Growth build new perspectives around the values and importance of the ocean and create new narratives of meaning for coastal and marine environments. These narratives help shape individual and collective identities alongside particular experiences and encounters with the ocean and liminal environments where land and water meet.

This session will explore how the meanings of coastal and marine environments are created with a particular focus on the mediating power of the 'visual' and its role in shaping particular understandings and relationships with the sea. Encounters with visual stimuli may often be regarded as routine, yet it is the banality of such that can be so influential. This session approaches the 'visual' in terms of a range of visual discourse (e.g. art, sculpture, architecture, film, television, photography etc.) and that of visuality (e.g. sensory seeing, notions of the visible and invisible, spectacle, imaginings etc.).

From the perspective of coastal and marine environments and associated activities (e.g. transport, fisheries, coastal and marine tourism/leisure etc.), this session invites papers and dialogues that embrace the 'visual' in exploring and shaping the meanings of coastal spaces and seascapes. The following offers some, but not exclusively, themes for consideration:

Representations/non-representations of seascapes
Coastal identities: communities, tourists, leisure-seekers
Seascape imaginings: spaces for commerce, tourism, leisure
Visual topographies of the coastline: natural and built
Sense of place and place attachment: residents, workers, visitors
Mapping histories: connecting the past to the present
Maritime heritage: installations and visual interpretations
Convened by Tim Acott (University of Greenwich, UK) and
Jo-Anne Lester (University of Brighton, UK)

Call for papers

Sonic spaces: music landscapes, soundscapes and identity.

Sponsored by the Geographies of Leisure and Tourism Research Group.

Sonic spaces can be an important feature in leisure and tourism consumption, extreme examples might include Abbey Road or Graceland as sites of music pilgrimage. Sonic spaces feature in a broad spectrum of research, and proposals for this session are welcome from any area of geography, cultural/media studies, critical tourism studies and other social sciences that engage with musical spaces and places. This forum will discuss geographies of music and how these have developed, interconnecting with cultural practices, values and wider society, in keeping with the conference theme of landscapes. The social, legal, political, environmental, and economic geographies of music and sonic spaces offer many angles through which to explore the changing landscapes/soundscapes of the world.

Potential topics include:

Music festivals and gigs
Music subcultures and scenes

Music as resistance or protest
The night time or gig economy
Leisure spaces and music consumption
Drugs, drink and music scenes
City-based or regional sounds
Music and politics and/or legislation
Music Pilgrimage
Music Festivals and Gender

Accounts and reflections on research and fieldwork, alongside embodied experiences, are encouraged. We invite empirical and theoretical papers around these themes and others related to musical landscapes, including alternative forms of presentation.

Convened by Eveleigh Buck-Matthews
(Coventry University, UK),
Heather Jeffrey (Middlesex University, UK) and Kris Vavasour
(ARA Institute of Canterbury, New Zealand).
(Royal Geographical Society, 2018b)

Geographers at the University of California at Berkeley made a valuable, early contribution to the study of landscape. The publication of *The Morphology of Landscape* (Sauer, 1925) signalled a move away from environmental determinism with recognition of the role of human activity in the production of landscape. This was emphasised by the statement that 'culture is the agent and the natural area is the medium' (Sauer, 1925: 4). The imprint of human intervention led Lewis (1979) to describe landscape as an unwitting autobiography, a repository of social values and ideals. As a text, it can be read to reveal information beneath the surface and to learn more about the authors of the landscape (Duncan and Duncan, 1988). In the case of tourism landscapes, it has been proposed that 'they too are texts set within particular genres by the very fact that these landscapes are imagined, constructed, shaped and manipulated to meet particular expectations of the audience and to support particular interpretations' (Rickly-Boyd, Knudsen and Braverman, 2014: 6). This implies that landscapes are made for particular purposes (Greer, Donnelly and Rickly, 2008) and any reading must take account of ideology and power relations. Although interpretations will be subjective (Davis, 2001), concordances, due to common socialisation processes, will mean that there will be certain similarities in readings (Knudsen, Soper and Metro-Roland, 2008).

A visual bias towards the study of landscape has included recognition of scenic beauty and the aesthetic of the picturesque (Rickly-Boyd *et al.*, 2014). Aesthetic preferences impact a landscape observer's conscious experience (Ulrich, 1986) and according to Nohl (2001), an aesthetic experience of landscape involves four levels of cognition: sensual perception, expressive emotions, symptomatic associations and symbolic ideas. The experience will be determined by the extent to which the different levels are engaged by the viewer. As an artistic medium, specific perspectives may be presented by foregrounding certain attributes and the use of framing can turn the landscape into a prescribed sequence of views (Marshall, 2002). These ideas have drawn attention to the work of the French cultural theorist Michel Foucault who privileged sight as the most important human sense (Knudsen, Soper and Metro-Roland, 2008). Foucault (1977) describes how a vantage point allows a single prison guard to control all prisoners with an all-encompassing gaze. The idea of the gaze is an important concept in tourism and Urry suggests that it has caused 'the spectacularization of place' (1995: 139) with the tourism industry responsible for the production of symbols to be gazed upon and sites arranged for visual pleasure. Tourists read the landscape as semioticians, seek examples of typical scenes and are attracted by markers. According to Urry, the alienated observer pays more attention to the name of Rembrandt next to the painting rather than to the painting itself. An example of a tourist gaze is provided in **Framing the Swiss Landscape**.

FRAMING THE SWISS LANDSCAPE

The photograph (Figure 3.1) was taken from the Glacier Express as it travelled through Switzerland. The atmosphere onboard was conditioned by the sounds that accompanied the movement of the train and the sense of personal and social space within the compartment. Despite the cloudy conditions, the photograph shows a scenic environment. The contours direct the eye to the scene in the centre of the photo, to the building and the tower which stand on an elevated position. The light covering of snow enhances the visibility of the field pattern and the forestry activity on the surrounding mountains. There is evidence of natural processes and cultural practices that have created the landscape.

Figure 3.1 *View from the Glacier Express.*

Source: Graham Brown

The scene is framed and reflects a privileged gaze. Other photographs were taken from the train and, in combination, a particular view of the Swiss landscape was created. This was a product of personal meanings but also by the opportunities offered by the train and the system of which it was part. The train made the physical connection between the scenes in the photographs but it was not just providing a form of transport. The Glacier Express is promoted internationally and represents a prized part of the Swiss tourism industry. The journey from St Moritz to Zermatt takes eight hours and, according to literature promoting the Express, the tourist can 'experience Switzerland from within a single train'. For some passengers, an important part of the experience is the opportunity to learn about the scenes that are visible from the train and the historical events that have shaped the landscape. This is made possible by brochures that are placed on every seat. More detailed and timely interpretation is available on an audio programme that plays, at intervals, throughout the journey. It is accessed by individual headphones that create private experiential bubbles. It becomes evident who is following the recording when the commentary motivates people to stand and photograph a scene that is being described. At this time, the common behaviour indicates that space and cognitions are shared. The message directs attention to the world beyond the windows of the train and suggests particular meanings of the external environment. However, some passengers have an entirely internal orientation, exhibiting behaviour that responds to the train compartment as a service setting and a self-contained social world. The drinks that are served at regular intervals and the ritual associated with setting the table and eating lunch captures their attention and interest. At other times, conversation and the screens of mobile phones render the external environment largely irrelevant to these passengers. The spatial boundaries are very different for the two groups, as is the experience that is gained.

The work of phenomenological geographers such as Tuan (1974) sought to reorient interest: away from place being regarded as merely a location to it being a setting for experiences that is endowed with meaning. Distinctive features can give rise to a sense of place and the development of psychological bonds can result in place attachment that involves 'an interplay of affect and emotions in reference to place' (Low and Altman, 1992: 5). Early applications of place attachment focused on psychological connection with the home environment but a review of over 120 journal articles published in the last 40 years about people–place relations noted that 'one of the most visible new trends in studies of place attachment in the last decade is a growing interest in attachment to places other than permanent residences' (Lewicka, 2011: 213). Leisure researchers have examined the extent to which attachment to environmental settings makes it possible to achieve desired recreational outcomes (Bricker and Kerstetter, 2000; Hammitt, Backlund and Bixler, 2006; Kyle, Graefe, Manning and Bacon, 2003; Moore and Graefe, 1994), and the concept has been applied in tourism (Gross and Brown, 2008) and in event management (Smith, Brown and Assaker, 2017). An alternative analysis suggests that processes associated with increased mobility and globalisation have resulted in a loss of place uniqueness and consequently a greater sense of placelessness (Relph, 1976). Mobility also creates connections between places that are part of spatial networks, linking local and global operations (Massey, 1994). For Massey, 'what gives a place its specificity is not some long internalized history but the fact that it is constructed out of a particular constellation of social relations, meeting and weaving together at a particular locus' (1994: 28). Thus, a landscape contains places as points of encounter that offer potentially intimate local connections and access to global networks.

Massey's (1994) idea of relations coming together at particular places is similar to Hagerstrand's (1970) time-geography when landscapes become ordered according to certain practices and discourses and 'can be analysed as processes of negotiations, techniques and technologies of control and enactments of power' (Ek and Hultman, 2008: 224). Building on Hagerstrand's principles, it has been suggested that there can be 'pockets' of local orderings (Pred, 1984) and that topological space is stitched together by actor–network relations (Latham, 2002). Places are performed and in a continuous state of becoming (Ek and Hultman, 2008) but fixation (Adey, 2006) occurs with subjects attracted to 'sticky' places (Ek and Hultman, 2008) when 'hosts, guests, buildings, objects and machines are contingently brought together to produce certain performances in certain places at certain times' (Hannam, Sheller and Urry, 2006: 13). Using actor–network theory, Van der Duim has proposed that 'tourismscapes rely on the performance of countless workers in big and small enterprises connected through complex processes of ordering' (2007: 967) where 'material resources and technologies structure, define and configure interaction' (2007: 968) and the resulting networks can be interpreted through spatial analysis. 'Discrete tourism spaces are stabilizations of processes and relations and are the result of spatial practices in which people and things relationally are pooled into hotels, attractions, airports, resorts and national parks' (Van der Duim, 2007: 969). In a general sense, networks comprise relationships between mutually dependent actors whose behaviour is driven by policy initiatives or project outcomes (Van den Berg and Braun, 1999). In this context, events can be analysed as projects with an ordering process of actor–network relations where an eventscape represents the fixed, physical expression of stabilisations in time and space.

LANDSCAPES OF LEISURE

In 1972, Clare Gunn published *Vacationscape*, a text that has been recognised as one of the earliest examples of a book in English that made an international impact on the study of tourism (Kozak and Kozak, 2016). Gunn acknowledged the possible subliminal influence on his ideas of the writings about city planning in *Townscape* by Gordon Cullen (1961). The issues examined in this book are indebted to the insight about the tourism-land interface in *Vacationscape*. Gunn's contribution to the study and practice of tourism planning including his widely adopted text on Tourism Planning (Gunn, 1979), was partly driven by a question he posed in

Vacationscape: 'what do we as travellers see, smell, feel and hear as we travel, and are designers and developers sufficiently sensitive to our interests and reactions?' (Gunn, 1997: ix). Gunn's training as a landscape architect ensured that he stressed the role of design with the second edition making this explicit in the title. It became *Vacationscape: Designing Tourist Regions* (Gunn, 1988). The third edition was titled, *Vacationscape: Developing Tourist Areas* (Gunn, 1997) tracking the subtle evolution of Gunn's interests from understanding the landscape as the natural resource base of tourism, to the role of landscape design to sustainable approaches to tourism planning and development. The need for sensitive design remained at the forefront of his ideas and, in the third edition, he stated,

> tourism, by its very nature, tends to make all the world look the same. There is homogeneity in the chains and franchises proliferated by the business sector. Although seeking the unique characteristics of different areas, tourists tend to reduce the individuality of place by carrying their cultural baggage with them wherever they go. This is the paradox of tourism and therefore its design challenge.
>
> (Gunn, 1997: 106)

Very similar sentiments are expressed by Philip Cox, the celebrated Australian architect in **The Globalised Landscape**.

THE GLOBALISED LANDSCAPE

By Philip Cox

The characteristic urbanisation of the late twentieth century and the twenty-first century is globalisation and in architectural terms, a sameness of the international style that has replaced national identity on the macro scale and regionalism on the smaller scale.

The quest for travel, to explore other cultures, people and spaces is more usually directed to those places that are the very antithesis of internationalism. There is a quest for countries, cities, towns and villages that are different to one's own culture and where there are overt expressions of vernacular architecture and culture. The souvenirs of such popular tourist spots are generally related to their uniqueness of place and even though they may have been manufactured in China, they still express, and create memories of the place. The fascination of indigenous cultures has always been, since people began exploring the world seeking cultures that are different to their own in the expectation of finding new relevance to their own and the seeking out of ideas and inspiration that may lead to new avenues of thinking and exploration. As globalisation continues, there is little opportunity for national or regional identity. This is further exasperated by IT where information and culture are universal and instantly available.

Vernacular expression worked when information and culture were localised and shared between small groups and individuals. A vernacular architecture existed because of the availability of local materials and technology, so cities were either stone or brick, tile or slate, coloured or natural, all of which varied according to shared methods of building construction, know-how, local cultural values and creeds. There was a difference in the past between vernacular architecture and high style architecture that was designed for important buildings of state or religion that stood apart from the general urban configuration of the town or city. In general, the city remained a collection of buildings of like character, materials and expression, where interventions of square or place contained the major buildings of religion, state or government. These are the places we, as tourists, love to explore and examine, we love to feast upon the byways and the streets that lead through a maze of buildings of human scale and character to arrive at the centre of town with its square and cathedral or town hall. We delight at the public art, the textures and patterns of the buildings, the sculpture and the sensuous delight of colour, shade and shadow. How often do we delight in the point of discovery of reinterpreting the old in a new and interesting way and how often does history stir us to understanding our own evolution of civilisation?

Globalisation does not permit the realization of local cultures, it is bent on delivering a sameness that repeats models in different parts of the world with the result that the world now has a sameness. A city in India has much in common with a city in the USA or that of Malaysia or Africa. There is the same multi-storey building technology, the same steel or concrete frame with the same monotonous glass curtain wallpapering of the structure. The materials are the same, the same glass, aluminium, the same stone panel that may have originated in other parts of the globe, so the result is the usual urban porridge that leads to urban boredom. The same applies to the export of experts and consultants that are ambassadors for globalisation, spreading the good word and technology almost as quickly as IT spreads specific knowledge and communication. The results are inevitable as the celebration of local culture, art, architecture, music or literature is not possible unless localised, so the spread of sameness, the loss of national and regional identity is sealed.

There is no arrest of globalisation and the demise of the vernacular but there is still an appreciation of local cultures. Greek villages, Italian hill towns, Cotswold Villages, become increasingly visited as we witness the demise of urban identity within one's own environment. They become the places of pilgrimage in the tourist calendar. They are repeated in pastiche environments elsewhere on the globe as themed spaces. In Las Vegas, Venice can be explored in a motorised gondola where Venetian palaces are painted on stucco frames to the delight of the pleasure-seeking tourist. They become the new event spaces: places of the theatre of the pretend, the facsimile for whatever activity may have been organised.

Event spaces can be permanent such as stadia, both indoor and outdoor where the event may be sporting, games or rock concerts. Such spaces are adaptable for large crowds and depend upon the success of the stadium to bring a feeling of togetherness or oneness. It can be compared to theatre where the spectator and the performer have specific roles within the confines of space and the space is designed for expectation and excitement. Exhibition centres equally are purpose-made buildings for flexible gathering events and can range from crowds, convocation, banqueting to a wide variety of uses all of which can be staged for specific purpose. They remain as an important part of any major city and although the shell of the building may be fixed architecturally, the interior is entirely flexible and experimental. As marketing becomes more global as does entertainment, the uses of permanent buildings such as stadia and exhibition centres will become more prevalent. They will remain as adjuncts to major cities as did the market place of the medieval town.

The uniformity of tourist areas and the experiences they offer have been expressed in different contexts in the tourism literature. The rapid growth of charter flights and package holidays in the 1970s and 1980s was accompanied by the movement of large numbers of tourists from northern Europe to countries bordering the Mediterranean. This caused the development of what have been called 'identikit' destinations (Ashworth and Goodall, 1988). Similar problems have been expressed in relation to the more recent development of the cruise tourism industry in the 'touristed seascape' of the Caribbean where a consistent approach to facility development has made all the ports look alike (Momsen, 2005: 217). The spatial template for touristed seascapes was set in place at the time of the industrial revolution with the development of seaside resorts in the Britain. The private railway companies competed by encouraging people in the industrial towns to become tourists and travel to coastal towns that served as the termini of their emerging rail networks. Railway posters produced in this era needed to reflect the characteristics of the market with many people living in inland towns unaware what the sea looked like. Figures 3.2 and 3.3 clearly show the importance placed on the visual representation of the destination and the clarity of the message. The focus on the healthy coastal environments must have appealed to people working in polluted factories. The linear pattern of development is evident on the Blackpool poster that was produced in 1896. It looks like an aerial film with a sense of

Figure 3.2 *Poster: Midland Railway, 1896.*

Source: National Railway Museum Pictorial Collection/Science and Society Picture Library.

Figure 3.3 *Poster: Midland Railway, 1904.*

Source: National Railway Museum Pictorial Collection/Science and Society Picture Library.

movement in the sea. The Bridlington poster, from 1904, also offers an elevated perspective but it is closer to the ground with more detail, revealing the elegant clothes of the tourists. It also shows the different activity zones in the sea, on the sand, on the promenade and on the beachfront road where hotels and other tourist services are located. This spatial pattern remains the same today, even if the fashions in clothes and some of the activities have changed. The landscaped environment overlooking the beach with the pavilion, the bandstand and the ritual of genteel promenading can be regarded as an Edwardian eventscape.

Within a framework of landscape analysis, social and cultural geographers have sought to render leisure and tourism more 'visible, situated and placed within the rapidly evolving discourses of post-positivist or post-structuralist geographies' (Aitchison, MacLeod and Shaw, 2000: 1). In *Leisure and Tourism Landscapes* it is suggested that, over the last century, the geographies of leisure and tourism have downsized in spatial scope from an interest at the regional and national scale to microanalysis of everyday landscapes including the streetscapes of leisure. At the same time, the geographies have been subject to a tension between structural

and post-structuctural theories (Aitchison *et al.*, 2000). A structuralist perspective regards observed phenomena as representations of underlying
structures. For instance, Harvey (1985) sought to explain spatial patterns
and functional characteristics of cities according to Marxist interpretations
of labour market structures. In the case of tourism, production and consumption are mediated by a leisure industry with processes controlled by
professional and commercial interests (Adorno, 1993). A post-structuralist
perspective, drawing on phenomenological theory, endows consumers
with agency, offering scope for creativity and resistance and regards places
as continually evolving landscapes. The authors of *Leisure and Tourism
Landscapes* claim that their book seeks to examine 'the extent systematic
power exists in the creation of leisure and tourism landscapes and/or the
extent to which localised, contextualised and pluralised power relations
exert their influence on the landscape' (Aitchison *et al.*, 2000: 4).

As a reaction against the objectivity and spatial determinism associated
with positivist geography, cultural geographers were interested in sites and
sights of social inclusion/exclusion where spatial transformations result
from an interplay of structure and agency, 'dialectical struggles of power
and resistance among and between the diversity of landscape providers,
users and mediators' (Aitchison *et al.*, 2000: 19). The need to examine a
multiplicity of behaviours and meanings demands a dialogue with other
disciplines (Gregory, Martin and Smith, 1994) and an understanding of
theories that help explain social relations and the social construction of
landscape. As emphasised by Rose, 'whether written or painted, grown or
built, a landscape's meanings draw on the cultural codes of the society for
which it was made' (1993: 89). Aitchison, MacLeod and Shaw (2000)
refer to postmodernism's emphasis on signification where, according to
Lash, 'the signifier is a sound, image, word or statement; the signified is a
concept or meaning; and the referent is an object in the real world to which
the signifier and the signified connect' (1990: 5). They state that their book
'attempts to examine leisure and tourism landscapes as regimes of signification in which the production, representation and consumption of landscapes are mediated by sites and processes of leisure and tourism'
(Aitchison *et al.*, 2000: 4). This type of examination is valuable in the
context of eventscapes, which can be treated as polysemic objects, with
signifiers which are subject to multiple interpretations (Chalip, Green and
Velden, 2000). It offers a lens to consider the type of processes which
influence the production, representation and consumption of eventscapes.

A conscious attempt to 'complicate' the positions adopted by cultural geographers was made in *Seductions of Place* (Cartier and Lew, 2005) 'by
signaling multiple and shifting points of view in the context of leisure

economy production and consumption' (Cartier, 2005: 3). Fortunately, these complications provide additional insight about the operation of eventscapes within the leisure economy. Much of the book discusses tour-isted landscapes where place seductions involve situated subjectivities and emplaced experiences. There is an emphasis on embodied, multi-sensory experiences and an interest in 'the complexity of landscape formation, in who designs landscapes and why' (Cartier, 2005: 2). It is suggested that places in this landscape can be experienced as part of everyday life, by visitors and locals due to a dialectic of moving in and out of being a tourist. The view that tourism exists as a bubble of practice, detached from the rest of life is rejected (Crouch, 2005) and the reflexive subject is not conceived by mobility and displacement but by encounters with others in particular places (Oaks, 2005). Eventscapes qualify as an example of such places. For Crouch (2005), it is a tension between performative practices and the situational context, which creates landscape and the sharing of body–space and feelings of social connection serve to animate space. Ref-erence is made to the scope for imagination in spaces that offer intimacy (Kristeva, 1996) and playfulness (De Certeau, 1984). The city is presented as the most reliable place to find this type of touristed landscape due to the complexity of the scene, the difficulty of distinguishing between tourist and local culture and the ability to transition in moments and gestures from work to leisure (Crouch, 2005). Parts of the city where venues are located, which attract young people at night have been called 'playscapes' (Chat-terton and Holland, 2002). In these and other leisure settings, differences between everyday and tourism spaces have become blurred (Franklin, 2003), as is the case at many eventscapes that attract people from local and distant markets.

SPORTSCAPES

Some landscapes have become sportscapes, so momentous has been the impact of sport (Bale, 2003: 4).

The term sportscape has been central to geographical examinations of sport. It is closely associated with a body of work by the English geo-grapher John Bale (1993, 1994, 2000, 2003). In *Landscapes of Modern Sport* (1994), sport is regarded as part of the cultural landscape and his analysis of sportscapes benefits from a broad definition by including: 'everything we see around us, including people and buildings in a sport context; it is more or less synonymous with the scenery of sports' (Bale, 1994: 9). Although the visual dimension is central to this approach, it is firmly rooted in geographical analysis of 'the most human of landscapes'

(Bale, 1994: 9). He believes the symbolisms of these 'taken-for-granted landscapes of our daily lives' (Cosgrove, 1989: 131) are waiting to be decoded.

Bale (2000) acknowledges that the landscape as a text is susceptible to different interpretations and discusses the ambiguity of sportscapes, offering three different meanings that can be attributed to a sports stadium. In the first, drawing on the work of Foucault (1977), the stadium is seen through the lens of a prison. It is regarded as a container of docile bodies where everyone – players and spectators – occupy clearly defined spaces and exhibit controlled responses to the environment. In this depressing perspective, the sport spectacle is regarded as a mechanism of control. In the second, the stadium is seen as a manicured and scientifically managed garden or park that is devoted to specialised economic activities and revenue generation. Third, as a cathedral, the stadium is seen to be a place of rituals where sport and sport stars are worshiped. It may have a sacred quality, of overpowering significance, where people develop a strong sense of place. In this context, it is interesting to consider the risks associated with any transgression of strongly held beliefs about a venue. For instance, fans who venerate the integrity of a sports stadium may not wish spectators at a rock concert to set foot on the hallowed turf. In the same way, eventscapes will be subject to a range of interpretations and possible transgressions. This has been illustrated by using the categories proposed by Bale (1994) in ten views of the sports landscape and adapting them in the context of an eventscape (Table 3.1).

In an examination of the sport-place nexus, Bale stated that 'for many people, the most familiar features of sports are the places where they are played and watched' (2000: 9), citing the examples in England of Wimbledon, the home of Lawn tennis, and Wembley where the famous football stadium is located. This is also true for certain types of events and the term Hallmark event is applied to events such as the Carnival in Rio de Janeiro where the place and the event are intimately linked in the minds of many people. In *Sports Geography*, Bale (2003) describes how mental maps can be used to show the pattern of cognitive associations between sports and places. A map of the vernacular regions of British sport illustrates that golf is associated with Scotland, rugby with Wales and tennis with the south of England. Maps illustrating the relationship between events and place are absent from the event management literature but the use of maps to present event information is examined in Chapter 4 of this book.

The study of 'sensuous geographies' (Bale, 2000: 16) pays attention to the sights, sounds and smells that are experienced in sportscapes. It is

Table 3. 1 *Ten views of the eventscape*

Eventscapes and the natural landscape	The natural landscape features as part of the event experience. The landscape remains in a natural state after the event and has not been changed permanently into an eventscape.
Eventscapes as habitat	Nature is adapted and managed to offer a home for eventscapes, which become part of human habitat. The eventscape becomes a blending of humanity and nature.
Eventscapes as artefacts	Modern structures destroy evidence of nature. Event outcomes demand neutralisation of the natural world and its effects, as exemplified by indoor, air-conditioned, artificial venues.
Eventscapes as systems	Eventscapes are part of economic and physical systems to which they are both dependent upon and responsible for resource flows. Analysis can take the form of an input–output matrix.
Eventscapes as a problem	Eventscapes may be accompanied by social and environmental problems such as traffic congestion and pollution. This may lead to political contestation especially if, in addition to the problems, power is used to impose territorial exclusion.
Eventscapes as wealth	The eventscape is a factor of production, which can generate a financial return for investors and stakeholders such as corporate sponsors. New developments associated with an eventscape may attract new investment and increase land values.
Eventscapes as ideology	Messages implicit in the design of an eventscape may convey political or techno centric ideologies.
Eventscapes as history	The location and appearance of an eventscape may be a visible product of historical processes. Information about the authors and their world can be interpreted.
Eventscapes as place	The eventscape is a place, or a series of places, that directly influences the nature of the event experience of all participants.

(Continued)

Table 3. 1 *Continued*

Eventscapes as aesthetic	Observers will be predisposed, to varying degrees, towards the aesthetic qualities of eventscapes. The projection of representations in different forms will affect how the eventscape is perceived and interpreted by people attending an event and distant from it.

Sources: adapted from Bale (1994) and Brown, Lee, King and Shipway (2015).

suggested that a distinctive sensual experience affects the way people respond to the environment, their feelings about the place where the sport is held and the way it contributes to geographical memory and place identity. These reactions and psychological associations are no less significant in many types of eventscapes. With reference to Tuan's (1974) idea of topophilia and its application to sport settings, Bale (2003) suggests that a sense of place requires a playful domination by architecture and domination of the landscape with a human face. However, a recurrent theme in Bale's work concerns his belief that sportscapes are becoming increasingly placeless, as venues look the same as each other. This is attributed to factors associated with globalisation, the media and market expectations, which have produced a consistency in design and in the use of materials and technology. In the case of stadiums, this results in structures that are developed in the absence of locally embedded, historical associations with a physical form that denies visual connections with the surrounding environment (Bale, 2003). Bale (2000) expressed the view that sportscapes have become less attractive due to:

- The dominance of the achievement model in sport where display is more important than play.
- A greater separation of players from spectators where clearly marked spatial limits impose activity zones and exclusivity.
- The communication of territorial boundaries.
- The replacement of natural environments by artificial sites.
- Multifunctional facilities that are less identified with a particular sport.

The observation about multifunctional facilities is related to the integration of sport facilities with entertainment and other activities. Bale (2000) cites the example of the SkyDome in Toronto where a stadium, a hotel, a convention centre and restaurants are on the same site and where an integrated approach is adopted to the management of the different businesses. The need to spread costs and gain revenue from a mix of sources finds expression in multi-purpose property developments such as when new golf courses are built in conjunction with housing and leisure facilities. The organisation of local golf-orderings as part of a marketing strategy for the Scania region in Sweden produced a 'golfscape' that was described as a regional servicescape of golf activities (Ek and Hultman, 2008: 225).

Bale (1994) uses an analysis of spatial segmentation to identify the margins of the sports landscape. Drawing on the work of Tuan (1982) and cultural geographer Sack (1986), he refers to the process of 'territorialisation' (Bale, 1994: 14) and distinguishes between sports that have hard spatial boundaries to those with soft spatial limits. This typology is valuable when considering the boundaries of eventscapes and forms part of the analysis that is used in Chapter 4. It has been supported by recent territorological perspectives where 'fuzzy' places (Warnaby, Bennison and Medway, 2010) are shaped as much by 'symbols, social practice and consciousness as by "hard" territorial boundaries' (Warnaby, 2018). For Agnew (2009), territory is determined by the exercise of power over blocs of space and for Brighenti (2010), this is relative to a sphere of application or a domain of practice with the territory having both expressive and functional components. An event could be a domain of practice in this context. Warnaby concludes that territory results from active and dynamic endeavour: a 'product of human and institutional relations, having both spatial and relational implications' (2018: 64).

SERVICESCAPES

For as long as products have been displayed – in ancient markets or in modern shopping malls – the need to capture the attention of consumers and to facilitate the purchase process has demanded forms of environmental management. In certain settings, environmental practices need to address basic concerns about health and safety but increasingly design is part of attempts to stimulate emotional reactions to consumptive settings. Marketing scholars have drawn historical comparisons by noting the ability of imposing features such as cathedrals to inspire awe and elicit psychological responses (Kotler, 1973). A great deal of expertise and resources are invested to make retail settings attractive and competitive, to offer a wide range of experiences to consumers and to brand both products and places. Different types of scapes have been invoked to capture the particular characteristics of the processes or the places where they occur and the concept of servicescapes has attracted considerable interest from scholars in a number of disciplines and from practitioners operating in a wide range of physical settings.

Servicescapes share similarities with landscapes (Kumar, Parani and Sahadev, 2017) with both providing information cues that assist environmental understanding and exploration (Dogu and Erkip, 2000). Kumar *et al.* (2017) note that the structural properties that affect visual preferences of landscapes (Kaplan, 1987) are relevant to servicescapes. Kaplan's (1987) variables included coherence, complexity, legibility and mystery. Descriptions of these variables as well as novelty, proposed by Mehrabian and Russell (1974) and the extent to which they are most pertinent in hedonic or utilitarian service contexts are provided in Table 3.2. Hedonic services are associated with the provision of excitement and entertainment whereas utilitarian services are more functional and associated with problem solving. The application of a hedonic/utilitarian measurement scale developed by Voss, Spangenberg and Grohman (2003) categorised banks and hospitals as low-hedonic, high-utilitarian and restaurants and spas as high-hedonic, low-utilitarian services (Kumar *et al.*, 2017). Many eventscapes would be firmly located in the high-hedonic, low-utilitarian category.

In marketing, a servicescape is the physical setting where the service provider and the customer interact and where design seeks to influence consumer behaviour. As conceived by Bitner (1992), a servicescape consists of three elements; ambient conditions (temperature, air quality, sounds etc.), space and function (layout, furnishings etc.) and signs, symbols and artefacts (signage, personal artefacts, style of décor etc.). It draws on previous research in Psychology and particularly Environmental Psychology, on theories associated with information processing (Kaplan, 1987), the idea of a stimulus-organism-response (Mehrabian and Russell, 1974) and on the relationships between the environment and both cognitive and emotional behaviour (Maslow and Mintz, 1956; Stokols and Altman, 1987). According to the model proposed by Mehrabian and Russell (1974), the level of complexity and novelty present in an environment will generate pleasure or arousal which, in turn, affects attitudes towards the environment. Applications have been inspired by the proposition that stimulating environments generate levels of arousal leading to increased approach behaviour (Donovan and Rossiter, 1982; Kaplan and Kaplan, 1989). At the point of purchase, positive moods increase the likelihood of increased spending and establishing the right sort of cues is the key to controlling customers' moods (Newman, 2007). Visual arrangements direct peoples' evaluative processes (Orth and Crouch, 2014; Zeithaml and Bitner, 1996) and it has been shown that warm colours attract the attention of customers (Bellizzi, Crowley and Hasty, 1983) but music also impacts behaviour in service settings (Baker, Grewal and Parasuraman, 1994).

Table 3.2 *Environmental variables in service contexts*

Environmental stimulus	Sub-dimensions	Service context
Legibility Environmental features that facilitate understanding and way-finding	Clarity of layout and signage Presence of landmarks and walkways	Particularly valuable in task-oriented, utilitarian contexts
Mystery Information that is hidden or not readily accessible within a scene or setting	Level of lighting, Depth of view Visual permeability	Exploring in response to mystery may be an attractive part of hedonic experiences
Coherence Complementary arrangements of elements in a scene	Visual order Spatial balance Harmonious patterning	A sense of order may be valuable in both utilitarian and hedonic contexts
Complexity The number and diversity of features in an environment	Visual richness Mix of sensory stimuli Variety in shapes, colours, textures.	This may be associated with risk in utilitarian contexts but a source of excitement in hedonic contexts
Novelty An unfamiliar scene, perceived to be different from usual environmental settings	Atypical scene New features	Hedonic consumers may be most interested in unique experiences

Sources: adapted from Kaplan (1987); Kumar, Parani and Sahadev (2017); Mehrabian and Russell (1974).

Early studies about atmospherics had sought to identify the role played by variables such as window displays on purchase decisions and the amount of time spent in a store (Kotler, 1973) and designed commercial environments have been described as 'atmospheres of seduction' (Biehl-Missal and Saren, 2012). For the advertising industry, the urban landscape has a variable density of visibility metrics due to the spatial pattern of exposure to outdoor advertising. The time-space rhythm of promotional messages must be aligned with the rhythmic flows of urban residents (Cronin, 2010). The urban landscape is saturated with advertisements where there are temporary cessations in the flows of dense mobile passage (Cronin, 2006). Following a study of Fitzroy Square in London, Wunderlich claimed places in cities are symphonies of events where unique rhythms 'induced by recurrent stimuli, social practices and events of nature and physical space – orchestrate in time and space to shape the timescape of urban places' (2010: 54). With reference to the concept of flow (Csikszentmihalyi and Csikszentmihalyi, 1988), it was suggested that it is possible to become immersed in places such as Fitzroy Square and lose a sense of time. Lived time is fluid, slowing down to permit the calm appreciation of a special moment or imposing pressure when it propels to a fast approaching deadline or an exciting conclusion to an event. Our emotions are attuned to the episodic nature of kairotic time (Czarniawska, 2005) and Maguire and Geiger (2015) have discussed emotional reactions to experiences in servicescapes. They suggest that 'the passage of time in a service encounter provides ample space not just for a cognitive evaluation of the service received but also for consumer emotions to develop at various stages' (Maguire and Gieger, 2015: 211). Emotions respond to changing circumstances and the model of an emotional timescape is well suited to an examination of the temporal pattern of emotional responses when visiting an eventscape (Figure 3.4).

Servicescapes can be regarded as the product of two types of staging. Substantive staging is the physical creation of contrived environments and communicative staging refers to the ways in which the environment is presented and interpreted with the inclusion of performative and dramatic devices (Arnould, Price and Tierney, 1998). Arnould, Price and Tierney (1998) suggest that servicescapes may transcend purely commercial intent by offering a range of personal and social outcomes. They refer to the work of Brannen (1992) and use Disneyland in Tokyo as an example of a servicescape, which entertains and communicates information about Japanese culture and values. Disney gave the title 'imagineers' (Kirsner, 1998) to the corporation's designers and this led Wanhill (2003) to refer to the core of tourist attractions as imagescapes. His

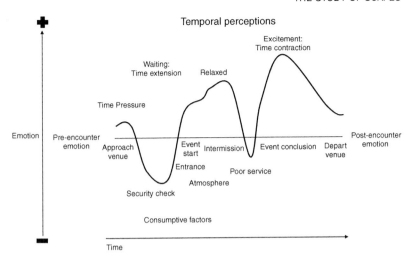

Figure 3.4 *Emotion in eventscapes.*

Source: Adapted from Maguire and Geiger, 2015.

model of the attractions product consists of tangible objects such as a thrill ride, which reflect the attraction's theme or imagescape and support services, which form the augmented imagescape. The term Imagineering has been used to describe creative engineering performed at mega-events by artists, architects, choreographers and articulators of the host city's atmospheres (Tzanelli, 2018). Operating in blends of filiative (ethno-national) and affiliative (professional) networks, the mobile imagineers are sought by governments to enhance the prestige of mega-events. They fuse art with technology to liberate society by 'rewriting practice, mate-riality and ideals on various humanscapes, such as those of a city' (Tzanelli, 2018: 32).

Casinos have been at the forefront of environmental design and, in places such as Las Vegas, they are examples of servicescapes. The shops, which line the canals of the Venetian and the Forum shopping mall which leads to Caesar's Palace, bring street scenes from Venice and ancient Rome to internal spaces in the Nevada desert. This is consistent with a postmodern manifestation of theatrification when realities are recrafted by juxtaposing phenomena separated from their substantial essence (Jirásek and Kohe, 2015). The architectural design of the buildings and the landscaping outside both Caesar's Palace and the Venetian set the scene for the internal servicescapes where there is very little confusion about behavioural scripts. An attractive external setting encourages an approach, as opposed to avoidance, form of response (Kaplan and Kaplan, 1989; Turley and

Milliman, 2000). The Olympic Museum in Lausanne, Switzerland is presented as an example of the relationship between external and internal environments in **The External Setting**. The scenery cannot be managed as part of the servicescape but buildings can be designed to blend into the landscape and it is possible to create a sense of integration between internal and external environments. In fact, this represents an opportunity for businesses of all sizes which can create a vernacular servicescape and a distinctive sense of place. There are limitless examples of how this can be achieved including the use of local materials and decorative colours, which invoke local scenery. In addition, the presence of furniture which bears the imprint of local craftsmen, the display of work by local artists and the sound of music linked to local cultural traditions reinforces the consistency of the environmental atmospherics.

A particular appeal of the concept of servicescapes is its potential to be applied in different types of settings by businesses, which occupy small, intimate spaces and others with more spacious surroundings. Studies have examined the servicescapes of casinos (Lucas, 2003), cafés (Hall, Tipler, Reddy and Rowling, 2010), restaurants (Ryu and Jang, 2007; Harris and Ezech, 2008; Kim and Moon, 2009), airports (Jeon and Kim, 2012; Newman, 2007), cruise ships (Lyu, Hu, Hung and Mao, 2017), sport facilities (Wakefield, Blodgett and Sloan, 1996) and convention centres (Siu, Wan and Dong, 2012). Location can be a key factor in the way a servicescape is managed. For instance, the desired experience of guests at a beachfront resort hotel will vary from that of guests staying at a business hotel in the centre of a city. Design decisions must reflect these differences and this can be achieved in relation to the type of look and feel that is created in the lobbies of the respective properties.

A servicescape should offer a harmonious environment where all design elements work in a consistent manner to reinforce a particular theme. A measure of the success of a servicescape is its ability to make customers feel comfortable in the spaces that have been designed to meet their needs. The comfort will be a product of evaluations about the extent to which the elements of the servicescape enhance the desired customer experience to include a feeling of being in the right place and understanding behavioural expectations where a script is readily identifiable and physical evidence and environmental cues offer a consistent message. It should be possible to move through the environment with ease and to identify places to linger, when required. Interactions with staff and fellow consumers should be enjoyable and rewarding in an environment that is inviting and welcoming to those who wish to return.

THE EXTERNAL SETTING

The external environment can be an integral part of a services-cape and the landscaped approach to the Olympic Museum in Switzerland offers a good example. It is located on the shore of Lake Geneva on the fringe of Lausanne. At the entrance by the road which borders the lake, water falls behind a sign showing the Olympic rings and the name of the museum. A path from the water feature becomes steps, leading to the building which houses the museum. Statues and sculptures depicting athletic performance rise from the grass on either side of the steps and, before passing through the doors, it is necessary to walk under a high jump bar, set at the height of the world record. This marks a symbolic entrance into the world of the Olympic Games. From inside the museum, windows offer views across the landscaped park to the mountains on the far side of the lake. This setting may be exceptional but the elevated position of the museum, the landscaping, the cultural and sporting artefacts and the interior layout take full advantage of the views. A harmonious connection between the external and internal environments creates an attractive, integrated servicescape.

Figure 3.5 *View from the Olympic Museum.*

Source: IOC (International Olympic Committee).

It may seem that servicescapes are associated with environmental determinism but there is scope for human agency and by using a servicescape's resources 'consumers transform it into a consumptionscape' (Venkatraman and Nelson, 2008: 1010). Similarly, a level of engagement is implicit in the creation of a brandscape, which is 'the material and symbolic environment that consumers build with marketplace products, images and messages' (Sherry, 1998: 112). Hall (2008) has noted that companies such as Starbucks create a symbolic retail space with which consumers gain familiarity making it possible for them to experience the brandscape no matter where they are in the world. Social interaction is considered to be an important part of the experiences gained in these environments and the idea of a social-servicescape (Tombs and McColl-Kennedy, 2003) was supported in a study of place branding in Christchurch, New Zealand. Hall (2008) found that an increase in visitation to the South of Litchfield (SOL) by people who shared lifestyle attributes helped develop a sense of belonging to the SOL brand. It was suggested that the development of a place brand in SOL depended on both *hardware*: architectural design and *software*: the use of marketing strategies. This is consistent with the idea that place branding is activated through material objects in combination with narrational cues which give meaning to a place (Leach, 2002).

New museums, art complexes and theatres, as grand cultural projects, are examples of hard branding which act as signifiers in post-modern cityscapes (Evans, 2003). However, Julier (2005) has warned of the dangers of 'me-too' copycat reproduction of architecture-led projects, which can lead to the homogenisation of city identities. He suggests that if landmark buildings are designed by famous international architects, a location may be distinguished as much by its civic patronage as by the building itself. Julier calls for the full range of design production and consumption to be considered in the creation of 'urban designscapes'. He uses this concept to analyse the dynamics of design and the network of activities and artefacts that produce place-identity within cities. With reference to the work of Lash (2002), Julier refers to the importance of the global sign economy and the role of design 'in the structuring of systems of encounter within the visual and material world' (Julier, 2005: 875). The designscape 'exists through a variety of aesthetic platforms ranging through brand design, architecture, urban planning, events and exhibitions' (Julier, 2005: 874) with producers, consumers and designers operating in a localised circuit of culture. Julier acknowledges the difficulty of achieving a coherent design aesthetic across a city (Molotch, 1996) and believes this is partly due to the impossibility of coordinating activities in a programmatic way. It is also suggested that agreement about an urban narrative will require the acquiescence of stakeholders, acknowledging the importance of value systems and power relations.

> Any form of '-scape' involves a privileged position in terms of what it defines for viewing. – Within the term 'designscapes', I infer an extended system that engages not just spatial attributes, but also issues of taste, practice and the circulation of design that are nonetheless still inflected by power mechanisms.
>
> (Julier, 2005: 875)

O'Dell (2005) used the term experiencescapes to describe strategically planned, stylised landscapes to which consumers are attracted in the search for enjoyable experiences. They are everyday 'spaces of pleasure, enjoyment and entertainments' (O'Dell, 2005: 16). The broad range of settings for these experiences confirms that environmental management can be applied far beyond internal environments (Clarke and Schmidt, 1995; Rosenbaum and Massiah, 2011) and Hall has stated that 'the conscious design and manipulation of the physical environment – is being extended to the fabric of space itself and the aesthetic experiences and social interactions that occur within it' (2008: 237).

An early example of servicescape research was conducted in a wilderness area and examined the communicative staging practices of white water rafting businesses operating in river canyons that flow through the Dinosaur National Monument on the Colorado–Utah border in the USA (Arnould *et al.*, 1998). In contrast with more traditional settings in built environments, providers and consumers enter the servicescape together from the outside and there was limited managerial control over the substantive staging of the site where preservation was privileged above consumer needs. In addition, service outcomes were moderated by situational factors such wildlife sightings and weather and river conditions (Arnould *et al.*, 1998). A spatially expansive approach towards servicescapes has been adopted in more recent studies when winescapes have been examined as 'a context-specific service environment' (Bruwer and Lesschaeve, 2012: 615). A winescape involves the integration of winemaking and wine tourism within a viticultural setting (Patriquin, 2005) and there may be a symbiotic relationship between the service encounter and the environmental experience (Clarke and Schmidt, 1995). Differences in scale have seen the analysis of wine regions and of individual wineries (Bruwer and Gross, 2017). Both natural and cultural resources were included in a 25-item scale, with five constructs, that was found to be a reliable and valid instrument to measure the winescape of the McLaren Vale region of South Australia. The constructs were infrastructure and socio-economic environment, natural and cultural resources, atmosphere and social setting, layout and signage and people (Bruwer and Gross, 2017).

In another expansive application of the servicescape concept, Lee, Lee, Lee and Babin (2008) examined the impact of seven dimensions of a festivalscape on the relationship between consumer satisfaction and programme content, staff service, facilities, food, souvenirs, convenience and information. There was a strong focus on intangible service elements but the role of the physical environment was not included. Similarly, a study by Chou, Huang and Mair (2018) of the 2016 Taipei Lantern Festival sought to examine the role of a festivalscape on local residents' co-creation behaviours and subjective well-being. It was stated that 'context is essential to determine the dimensions of a festivalscape' (Chou *et al.*, 2018: 409) and the role of environmental cues were claimed to be fundamental to how people respond to a festivalscape. But, strangely, no relevant environmental measures were included in the study. The festival environmental cues were programme content, staff, information, facility, souvenir and convenience. The facility dimension included one general question about the size of the site. In a study of a festival in Italy, it was stated that food and wine events are hedonistic and 'become polysensorial experiential units through the mise-en-scene' (Mason and Paggiaro, 2012: 1329). The authors considered the festivalscape to be physical elements related to the environment and so it is surprising that, once again, environmental measures did not feature in their operationalisation of the construct. Using measures for food (such as food quality), fun (such as live entertainment; time of events) and comfort (such as cleanliness of restrooms; number of seats), it was found that the effect of the festivalscape on future behaviour was mediated by satisfaction (Mason and Paggiaro, 2012). A more complete discussion of the role of the environment as part of the festivalscape was offered in a study of two music festivals in Australia (Gration, Arcodia, Raciti and Stokes, 2011). Interviews with festival organisers and focus groups with festival-goers were held and it was found that 'the natural contours of the land, the bush, the smell, and the scents of the natural environment blend with the man-made and social constructs to form these two blended festivalscapes' (Gration *et al.*, 2011: 355).

EVENTSCAPES

In comparison with festivalscapes, eventscapes have rarely been the subject of academic research and the term has appeared infrequently in the academic literature. It has been used loosely and interchangeably with festivalscapes (Shaw, 2014). Although Ferdinand and Shaw use the term in relation to place marketing, it was mentioned in the context of 'media-oriented festivalization' that has tended to celebrate 'universal as opposed to place-specific references' (2012: 13). It has also been used without definition in conjunction with builtscapes and artscapes when discussing an event precinct in Singapore (Chang and Huang, 2005) and Furman (2007) discussed the use of streets to create temporary eventscapes. An applied perspective was provided in a book chapter with the title 'Creating the Eventscape' (Tattersall and Cooper, 2014), which provided guidance about how to develop and implement a set of competencies to create events. It made the case that an interest in eventscapes is a logical progression from studies of atmospherics and servicescapes and defined an eventscape as 'a combination of the tangible elements which shape the event environment and therefore influence the emotional responses and experiences of attendees, event staff, and other involved stakeholders' (Tattersall and Cooper, 2014: 142). Consistent with the applied orientation of the chapter, Tattersall and Cooper (2014) provide a checklist of variables to be considered in the design of an eventscape under the headings of external variables (e.g. exterior signs, height/size/colour of building, surroundings), internal variables (e.g. staging, seating, colour schemes), human variables (employee uniforms, employee-attendee engagement), layout and design (e.g. space allocation, placement of equipment, flow and queuing) and event specific elements (e.g. programme content, point of purchase displays).

A very different analysis of an eventscape treated an expansive landscape as an environmental resource where a series of places were temporarily connected and transformed by an event. The eventscape of the Tour Down Under cycle race was shaped by the selection of routes, the location of services and the spatial pattern of spectator and community activities (Brown, Lee, King and Shipway, 2015). It has been recognised that key stakeholders make an impression on eventscapes, particularly at mega-events as reflected in Traganou's use of the term 'Olympic sponsor-scape' (2016: 203).

In an approach similar to that adopted in this book, Smith drew attention to the many types of scapes that are relevant to an analysis of events and suggested that, in public spaces, 'eventscapes represent instances where events are used to construct, capture and circulate a specific urban imaginary; a staged and enlivened cityscape that simultaneously provokes memorable experiences and spectacular media images' (2016: 176). This book seeks to identify the spatial pattern of these imaginaries and examine how they are constructed. Smith reviewed clearly defined processes before describing relevant case studies. With reference to Lefebvre (1991), he noted trends leading to the consumption of city spaces and discussed the role of events in the restructuring of urban environments. The process of festivalisation was described as 'the use of festivals, events and entertainment to generate economic and symbolic capital' (Smith, 2016: 34). Smith refers to Jacob's (2013) assertion that festivalisation has become an important planning tool and Colomb's (2012) observation that it is the city itself that is 'staged' as various places become the location for events and dramatisations of urban phenomena. Positive changes to the identity of urban spaces occurs through 'eventilisation' that involves animating spaces and encouraging new uses whereas 'eventification' refers to the effects of events in associated with commercialisation, privatisation and securitisation (Smith, 2016). These detrimental aspects are similar to the way 'sportification' has been described as the transfer of superficial elements of sport phenomena beyond the sporting realm with signs, rather than substantive connections, used to infer sporting associations (Jirásek and Kohe, 2015). Jacob defines eventification as 'the process with which the consumption of products and space is turned into an event' (2013: 449) with space itself transformed into an aestheticised place of consumption. The process is used to advance urban and economic development, consumer experiences and city images and her case study of the event-based art scene in New York's SoHo district revealed the role played by local artists in the transformation of the locale through the development of collaborative networks. However, it was recognised that there can be significant costs associated with eventification, listing the diversion of resources from areas such as health, education and housing and the creation of conflict and division between people and sub-areas of the city (Jacob, 2013).

Eventscapes: a conceptual model

The processes described in the literature reviewed in this chapter make possible the development of a conceptual model that describes the key characteristics of eventscapes. It is proposed that eventscapes are spaces of encounter which attract local engagement and global flows where stabilisation is imposed by event-related design and programmatic consistency in event-affected settings. Drawing on Amin's (2015) discussion of animated space, an eventscape is the setting for multiple happenings, a composite ecology of human and non-human interactions where geographies of association and attachment course through the space. The aesthetic effect is part of a creative narrative that provides opportunities for identity formation and network development. The model, as illustrated in Figure 3.6, recognises the fundamental role of behaviour–environment and event–place relationships and the tensions that may exist between local practices and global processes. It incorporates ideas about servicescapes (Bitner,

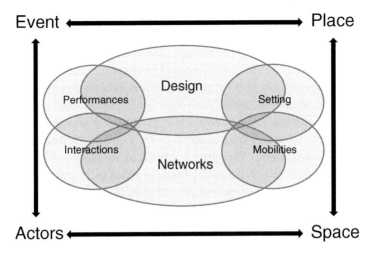

Event ◄————————————————► Place

Design
Performances
Setting
Interactions
Mobilities
Networks

Actors ◄————————————————► Space

Figure 3.6 *Eventscapes: a conceptual model.*

Source: Graham Brown

1992) and the production of designscapes (Julier, 2005) and the actor–network system of relationships as described by authors such as Van der Duim (2007).

SUMMARY

An extensive and diverse literature was reviewed in this chapter and certain themes are prominent across a number of disciplines. An analysis of visual representations in art, design and landscape determined them to be used as a mechanism to impose social order. This drew attention to the need for critical interpretations of texts written in the landscape, to reveal the objectives of the artists, and the authors to better understand to whose expectations they are responding. The techniques and related management objectives were more explicit in the context of servicescapes. It was important to note the expansion of servicescape horizons as there has been a movement away from the confines of indoor settings such as retail spaces to environments such as winescapes that include outdoor spaces. When examined at a regional scale, mechanisms for connections between places become important.

There were frequent references to the relative importance of agency and structure and to tensions between local and global forces. It was noted in relation to architecture, tourism, sport and various forms of cultural production that the power of globalisation has produced placeless environments. Creative design represents a potential counter to this power but the difficulty of coordinating activities and achieving coherence across different settings were identified. In this context, events offer the potential to stabilise spatial relationships and develop partnerships. This is made possible by the distinctive characteristics of events, as outlined in Chapter 2. They direct activities to a time-specific deadline but require only temporary commitments that can be reassessed after an event. They often attract political support and goodwill from a diverse range of community and business groups. Significantly, they offer a clearly defined opportunity for creativity in design and other forms of engagement. The chapter concluded by providing a conceptual model of eventscapes as the setting for these activities. Examples of the form and spatial pattern of eventscapes are examined in Chapter 4.

REFERENCES

Adey, P. (2006). If Mobility is Everything Then it is Nothing: Towards a Relational Politics of Mobilities. *Mobilities*, 1(1): 75–94.

Adorno, T. (1993). *Dialectics*. London: Routledge.

Agnew, J. (2009). Territoriality. In: D. Gregory, R. Johnson, G. Prat, M. J. Watts and S. Whatmore, eds, *The Dictionary of Human Geography*, 5th edn. Chichester: Wiley-Blackwell, 744–745.

Aitchison, C., MacLeod, N. E. and Shaw, S. J. (2000). *Leisure and Tourism Landscapes: Social and Cultural Geographies*. London: Routledge.

Amin, A. (2015). Animated Space. *Public Culture*, 27(2): 239–258.

Appadurai, K. (1996). *Modernity at Large: Cultural Dimensions of Globalisation*. Minneapolis, MN: University of Minnesota Press.

Arnould, E. J., Price, L. L. and Tierney, P. (1998). Communicative Staging of the Wilderness Servicescape. *Service Industries Journal*, 18(3): 90–115.

Ashworth, G. and Goodall, B. (1988). *Marketing in the Tourism Industry: The Promotion of Destinations and Regions*. London: Routledge.

Baker, J., Grewal, D. and Parasuraman, A. (1994). The Influence of Store Environment on Quality Inferences and Store Image. *Journal of the Academy of Marketing Science*, 22(4): 328–339.

Bale, J. (1993). *Sport, Space and the City*. London: Routledge.

Bale, J. (1994). *Landscapes of Modern Sport*. London: Leicester University Press.

Bale, J. (2000). *Sportscapes*. Sheffield: The Geographical Association.

Bale, J. (2003). *Sports Geography*, 2nd edn. London: Routledge.

Bellizzi, J. A., Crowley, A. E. and Hasty, R. W. (1983). The Effects of Color in Store Design. *Journal of Retailing*, 59: 21–45.

Biehl-Missal, B. and Saren, M. (2012). Atmospheres of Seduction: A Critique of Aesthetic Marketing Practices. *Journal of Macromarketing*, 12(2): 168–180.

Bitner, M. J. (1992). Servicescapes: The Impact of Physical Surroundings on Customers and Employees. *Journal of Marketing*, 55(April): 57–71.

Böhme, G. (2016). *The Aesthetics of Atmospheres*, edited by J.-P. Thibaud. London: Routledge.

Brannen, M. Y. (1992). 'Bwana Mickey': Constructing Cultural Consumption at Tokyo Disneyland. In: J. J. Tobin, ed., *Re-Made in Japan*. New Haven, CT: Yale University Press, 216–234.

Bricker, K. S. and Kerstetter, D. L. (2000). Level of Specialization and Place Attachment: An Exploratory Study of Whitewater Recreationists. *Leisure Sciences*, 22: 233–257.

Brighenti, A. M. (2010). On Territorology: Towards a General Science of Territory. *Theory, Culture & Society*, 27(1): 52–72.

Brown, G., Lee, I. S., King, K. and Shipway, R. (2015). Eventscapes and the Creation of Event Legacies. *Annals of Leisure Research*, 18(4): 510–527.

Bruwer, J. and Gross, M. J. (2017). A Multilayered Approach to Conceptualizing the Winescape Construct for Wine Tourism. *Tourism Analysis*, 22: 497–509.

Bruwer, J. and Lesschaeve, I. (2012). Wine Tourists' Destination Region Brand Image Perception and Antecedents: Conceptualization of a Winescape Framework. *Journal of Travel & Tourism Marketing*, 29: 611–628.

Cartier, C. (2005). Introduction: Touristed Landscapes/Seductions of Place. In: C. Cartier and A. A. Lew, eds, *Seductions of Place: Geographical perspectives on Globalization and Touristed Landscapes*. London: Routledge, 1–19.

Cartier, C. and Lew, A. A. (2005). *Seductions of Place: Geographical perspectives on Globalization and Touristed Landscapes*. London: Routledge.

Chalip, L., Green, B. C. and Velden, L. V. (2000). The Effects of Polysemic Structures on Olympic Viewing. *International Journal of Sports Marketing and Sponsorship*, 2(1): 29–47.

Chang, T. C. and Huang, S. (2005). Recreating Place, Replacing Memory: Creative Destruction at the Singapore River. *Asia Pacific Viewpoint*, 46(3): 267–280.

Chatterton, P. and Holland, R. (2002). Theorising Urban Playscapes: Producing, Regulating and Consuming Youthful Nightlife City Spaces. *Urban Studies*, 39(1): 95–116.

Chou, C. Y., Huang, S.-C. and Mair, J. (2018). A Transformative Service View on the Effects of Festivalscapes on Local Residents' Subjective Well-Being. *Event Management*, 22: 405–422.

Chronis, A. (2005). Constructing Heritage at the Gettysburg Storyscape. *Annals of Tourism Research*, 32(2): 386–406.

Clarke, I. and Schmidt, R. A. (1995). Beyond the Servicescape: The Experience of Place. *Journal of Retailing and Customer Services*, 2(3): 149–162.

Cohen, S. (2012). Urban Musicscapes: Mapping Music-Making in Liverpool. In: L. Roberts, ed., *Mapping Cultures*. Basingstoke: Palgrave Macmillan, 123–143.

Colomb, C. (2012). *Staging the New Berlin: Place Marketing and the Politics of Urban Reinvention Post-1989*. Abingdon: Routledge.

Cosgrove, D. (1985). Prospect, Perspective and the Evolution of the Landscape Idea. *Transactions of the Institute of British Geographers*, 10: 45–62.

Cosgrove, D. (1989). Geography is Everywhere: Culture and Symbolism in Human Geography. In: D. Gregory and R. Walford, eds, *Horizons in Human Geography*. London: Macmillan, 118–153.

Cronin, A. (2006). Advertising and the Metabolism of the City: Urban Space, Commodity Rhythm. *Environment and Planning D: Society and Space*, 24: 615–632.

Cronin, A. M. (2010). *Advertising, Commercial Spaces and the Urban.* Houndmills: Palgrave Macmillan.

Crouch, D. (2005). Flirting with Space: Tourism Geographies as Sensuous/Expressive Practice. In: C. Cartier and A. A. Lew, eds, *Seductions of Place: Geographical Perspectives on Globalization and Touristed Landscapes.* London: Routledge, 23–35.

Cullen, G. (1961). *Townscape.* London: Architectural Press.

Csikszentmihalyi, M. and Csikszentmihalyi, I. S., eds (1988). *Optimal Experience: Psychological Studies of Flow in Consciousness.* Cambridge: Cambridge University Press.

Czariawska, B. (2005). On Time, Space, and Action Nets. *Organization*, 11(6): 773–791.

Davis, J. (2001). Commentary: Tourism Research and Social Theory – Expanding the Focus. *Tourism Geographies*, 3(2): 125–134.

De Certeau, M. (1984). *The Practice of Everyday Life.* Berkeley, CA: University of California Press.

Dogu, U. and Erkip, F. (2000). Spatial Factors Affecting Way Finding and Orientation: A Case Study in a Shopping Mall. *Environment and Behavior*, 32(6): 731–755.

Donovan, R. J. and Rossiter, J. R. (1982). Store Atmosphere: An Environmental Psychology Approach. *Journal of Retailing*, 58: 34–57.

Drebin, D. (2016). *Dreamscapes.* Kempen: teNeues Publishing.

Duncan, J. and Duncan, N. (1988). (Re)reading the Landscape. *Environment and Planning D: Society and Space*, 6(2): 117–126.

Edensor, T. (2015). Light Design and Atmosphere. *Visual Communication*, 14(3): 331–350.

Edensor, T. and Lorimer, H. (2015). 'Landscapism' at the *Speed of Light*: Darkness and Illumination in Motion. *Geografiska Annaler: Series B Human Geography*, 97(1): 1–16.

Ek, R. and Hultman, J. (2008). Sticky Landscapes and Smooth Experiences: The Biopower of Tourism Mobilities in the Oresund Region. *Mobilities*, 3(2): 233–242.

Evans, G. (2003). Hard-Branding the Cultural City – from Prado to Prada. *International Journal of Urban and Regional Research*, 27(2): 417–441.

Evans, G. (2015). Rethinking Place Branding And Place Making Through Creative and Cultural Quarters. In: M. Kavaratzis, G. Warnaby and G. J. Ashworth, eds, *Rethinking Place Branding: Comprehensive Brand Development for Cities and Regions.* New York: Springer, 135–158.

Ferdinand, N. and Shaw, S. J. (2012). Events in Our Changing World. In: N. Ferdinand and P. Kitchin, eds, *Events Management: An International Approach.* London: Sage, 135–158.

Foucault, M. (1977). *Discipline and Punish: The Birth of the Prison*. Harmondsworth: Peregrine.

Franklin, A. (2003). *Tourism: An Introduction*. London: Sage.

Furman, A. (2007). The Street as a Temporary Eventscape. *The International Journal of the Humanities*, 5(9): 77–84.

Gandy, M. (2017). Urban Atmospheres. *Cultural Geographies*, 24(3): 353–374.

Giordano, E. and Ong, C.-E. (2017). Light Festivals, Policy Mobilities and Urban Tourism. *Tourism Geographies* 19(5): 699–716.

Gration, D., Arcodia, C., Raciti, M., and Stokes, R. (2011). The Blended Festivalscape and its Sustainability at Nonurban Festivals. *Event Management*, 15: 343–359.

Greer, C., Donnelly, S. and Rickly, J. M. (2008). Landscape Perspectives for Tourism Studies. In: Daniel C. Knudsen, Michelle M. Metro-Roland, Anne K. Soper and Charles E. Greer, eds, *Landscape, Tourism and Meaning*. Aldershot: Ashgate Publishing, 8–17.

Gregory, D., Martin, R. and Smith, G. (1994). *Human Geography: Society, Space and Social Science*. Basingstoke: Macmillan.

Gross, M. and Brown, G. (2008). An Empirical Structural Model of Tourists and Places: Progressing Involvement and Place Attachment into Tourism. *Tourism Management*, 29(6): 1141–1151.

Gunn, C. (1972). *Vacationscape*. Austin, TX: University of Texas.

Gunn, C. (1979). *Tourism Planning*. New York: Crane Russak.

Gunn, C. (1988). *Vacationscape: Designing Tourist Regions*, 2nd edn. New York: Van Nostrand Reinhold.

Gunn, C. (1997). *Vacationscape: Developing Tourist Areas*, 3rd edn. Washington, DC: Taylor & Francis.

Gyimothy, S. (2005). Nostalgiascapes: The Renaissance of Danish Countryside Inns. In: T. O'Dell and P. Billing, eds, *Experiencescapes: Tourism, Culture and Economy*. Copenhagen: Copenhagen Business School, 111–126.

Hagerstrand, T. (1970). What About People in Regional Science? *Papers of the Regional Science Association*, 24(1): 6–21.

Hall, C. M. (2008). Servicescapes, Designscapes, Branding, and the Creation of Place Identity: South of Litchfiel, Christchurch. *Journal of Travel & Tourism Marketing*, 25(3–4): 233–250.

Hall, C. M., Tipler, J., Reddy, R. and Rowling, K. (2010). Coffee Servicescapes: The Design of Café Culture in New Zealand. In: L. Jolliffe (ed.), *Coffee Culture, Destinations and Tourism*. Bristol: Channel View, 23–40.

Hammitt, W. E., Backlund, E. A. and Bixler, R. D. (2006). Place Bonding for Recreation Places: Conceptual and Empirical Development. *Leisure Studies*, 25: 17–41.

Hannam, K., Sheller, M. and Urry, J. (2006). Editorial: Mobilities, Immobilities and Moorings. *Mobilities*, 1(1): 1–22.

Harris, L. C. and Ezech, C. (2008). Servicescapes and Loyalty Intentions: An Empirical Investigation. *European Journal of Marketing*, 42(3/4): 390–422.

Harvey, D. (1985). *The Urbanisation of Capital*. Oxford: Basil Blackwell.

Ingold, T. (1993). The Temporality of the Landscape. *World Archaeology*, 25(2): 24–174.

Iveson, K. (2012). Branded Cities: Outdoor Advertising, Urban Governance, and the Outdoor Media Landscape. *Antipode*, 44(1): 151–174.

Jacob, D. (2013). The Eventification of Place: Urban Development and Experience Consumption in Berlin and New York City. *European Urban and Regional Studies*, 20(4): 447–459.

Jeon, S. and Kim, M. (2012). The Effect of the Servicescape on Customers' Behavioural Intentions in an International Airport Service Environment. *Service Business*, 6(3): 279–295.

Jirásek, I. and Kohe, Z. (2015). Readjusting Our Sporting Sites/Sight: Sportification and the Theatricality of Social Life. *Sport, Ethics and Philosophy*, 9(3): 257–270.

Julier, G. (2005). Urban Designscapes and the Production of Aesthetic Consent. *Urban Studies*, 42(5–6): 869–887.

Kaplan, S. (1987). Aesthetics, Affect and Cognition Environmental Preference from an Evolutionary Perspective. *Environment and Behaviour*, 19(1): 3–32.

Kaplan, S. and Kaplan, R. (1989). Environmental Preference – A Comparison of Four Domains of Predictors. *Environment and Behaviour*, 21(5): 509–530.

Kim, W. G. and Moon, Y. J. (2009). Customers' Cognitive, Emotional, and Actionable Response to the Servicescape: A Test of the Moderating Effect of Restaurant Type. *International Journal of Hospitality Management*, 28: 144–156.

Kirsner, S. (1998). Hack the Magic: The Exclusive Underground Tour of Disney World. *Wired*, March, 162–168, 186–189.

Knudsen, D. C., Soper, A. K. and Metro-Roland, M. M. (2008). Landscape, Tourism and Meaning: An Introduction. In: Daniel C. Knudsen, Michelle M. Metro-Roland, Anne K. Soper and Charles E. Greer, eds, *Landscape, Tourism and Meaning*. Aldershot: Ashgate Publishing, 1–7.

Kolamo, S. and Vuolteenaho, J. (2013). The Interplay of Mediascapes and Cityscapes in a Sport Mega Event: The Power Dynamics of Place Branding in the 2010 FIFA World Cup in South Africa. *International Communication Gazette*, 75(5–6): 502–520.

Kolodney, Z. (2012). Between Knowledge of Landscape Production and Representation. *Journal of Architecture*, 17(1): 97–118.

Kotler, P. (1973). Atmospherics as a Marketing Tool. *Journal of Retailing*, 49(4): 48–64.

Kozak, M. and Kozak, N. (2016). Institutionalisation of Tourism Research and Education: From the 1900s to 2000s. *Journal of Tourism History*, 8(3): 275–299.

Kristeva, J. (1996). *The Portable Kristeva*. New York: Columbia University Press.

Kumar, D. S., Parani, K. and Sahadev, S. (2017). Visual Service Scape Aesthetics and Consumer Response: A Holistic Model. *Journal of Services Marketing*, 31(6): 556–573.

Kyle, G. T., Graefe, A., Manning, R. and Bacon, J. (2003). An Examination of the Relationship Between Leisure Activity Involvement and Place Attachment

Among Hikers Along the Appalachian Trail. *Journal of Leisure Research*, 35: 249–273.

Lash, S. (1990). *Sociology of Postmodernism*. London: Routledge.

Lash, S. (2002). *Critique of Information*. London: Sage.

Latham, A. (2002). Retheorizing the Scale of Globalization: Topologies, Actor–Networks, and Cosmopolitanism. In: A. Herod and M. W. Wright, eds, *Geographies of Power: Placing Scale*. Oxford: Blackwell, 115–144.

Leach, N. (2002). Belonging: Towards a Theory of Identification with Space. In: J. Hillier and E. Rooksby, eds, *Habitus: A Sense of Place*. Aldershot: Ashgate, 281–298.

Lee, Y.-K., Lee, C.-K., Lee, S.-K. and Babin, B. J. (2008). Festivalscapes and Patrons' Emotions, Satisfaction, and Loyalty. *Journal of Business Research*, 61: 56–64.

Lefebvre, H. (1991). *The Production of Space*. Oxford: Blackwell.

Lefebvre, H. (2004). *Rhythmanalysis: Space, Time and Everyday Life*, trans. S. Elden and G. Moore. London: Continuum.

Lewicka, M. (2011). Place Attachment: How Far Have We Come in the Last Forty Years? *Journal of Environmental Psychology*, 31: 207–230.

Lewis, P. (1979). Axioms for Reading the Landscape. In: D. W. Meinig, ed., *The Interpretation of Ordinary Landscapes*. New York: Oxford University Press.

Low, S. M. and Altman, J. (1992). Place Attachment: A Conceptual Enquiry. In: J. Altman and S. M. Low, eds, *Place Attachment*. New York: Plenum Press, 1–12.

Lucas, A. F. (2003). The Determinants and Effects of Slot Servicescape Satisfaction in a Las Vegas Hotel Casino. *UNLV Gaming Research & Review Journal*, 7(1): 1–17.

Lyu, J., Hu, L., Hung, K. and Mao, Z. (2017). Assessing Servicescape of Cruise Tourism: The Perception of Chinese Tourists. *International Journal of Contemporary Hospitality Management*, 29(10): 2556–2572.

McQuire, S. (2008). *The Media City: Media, Architecture and Urban Spaces*. London: Sage.

Maguire, L. and Geiger, S. (2015). Emotional Timescapes: The Temporal Perspective and Consumption Emotions in Services. *Journal of Services Marketing*, 29(3): 211–223.

Marshall, D. (2002). The Problem of the Picturesque. *Eighteenth-Century Studies*, 35(3): 413–437.

Maslow, A. L. and Mintz, N. L. (1956). Effects of Aesthetic Surroundings. *Journal of Psychology*, 1(41): 247–254.

Mason, M. C. and Paggiaro, A. (2012). Investigating the Role of Festivalscape in Culinary Tourism: The Case of Food and Wine Events. *Tourism Management*, 33(6): 1329–1336.

Massey, D. (1994). *Space, Place and Gender*. Minneapolis, MN: University of Minnesota Press.

Mehrabian, A. and Russell, J. A. (1974). *An Approach to Environmental Psychology*. Cambridge, MA: MIT Press.

Molotch, H. (1996). L.A. as a Design Product: How Art Works in a Regional Economy. In: A. J. Scott and E. W. Soja, eds, *The City: Los Angeles and Urban Theory at the End of the Twentieth Century*. Berkeley, CA: University of California Press, 225–275.

Momsen, J. H. (2005). Uncertain Images: Tourism Development and Seascapes of the Caribbean. In: Carolyn Cartier and Alan Lew, eds, *Seductions of Place: Geographical Perspectives on Globalization and Touristed Landscapes*. Abingdon: Routledge, 209–221.

Moore, R. L. and Graefe, A. R. (1994). Attachment to Recreation Settings. *Leisure Sciences*, 16: 17–31.

Nadeau, J., O'Reilly, N. and Heslop, L. A. (2015). Cityscape Promotions and the Use of Place Images at the Olympic Games. *Marketing Intelligence & Planning*, 33(2): 147–163.

Newman, A. J. (2007). Uncovering Dimensionality in the Servicescape: Towards Legibility. *The Service Industries Journal*, 27(1): 15–28.

Nohl, W. (2001). Sustainable Landscape Use and Aesthetics Perception – Preliminary Reflections On Future Landscape Aesthetics. *Landscape and Urban Planning*, 54(1–4): 223–237.

Oaks, T. (2005). Tourism and the Modern Subject: Placing the Encounter Between Tourist and Other. In C. Cartier and A. A. Lew, eds, *Seductions of Place: Geographical Perspectives on Globalization and Touristed Landscapes*. London: Routledge, 36–55.

O'Dell, T. (2005). Experiencescapes: Blurring Borders and Testing Connections. In: T. O'Dell and P. Billing, eds, *Experiencescapes: Tourism, Culture and Economy*. Copenhagen: Copenhagen Business School, 11–33.

Orth, U. R. and Crouch, R. C. (2014). Is Beauty in the Aisles of the Retailer? Package Processing in Visually Complex Contexts. *Journal of Retailing*, 40(4): 524–537.

Patriquin, J. L. (2005). *Winescape: An Architecture of Place* (MR741). Calgary, AB: University of Calgary.

Pred, A. (1984). Place as Historically Contingent Process: Structuration and the Time-Geography of Becoming Places. *Annals of the Association of American Geographers*, 74(2): 279–297.

Relph, E. (1976). *Place and Placelessness*. London: Pion.

Rickly-Boyd, J. M., Knudsen, D. C. and Braverman, L. C. (2014). *Tourism, Performance and Place: A Geographical Perspective*. Aldershot: Ashgate Publishing.

Rose, G. (1993). *Feminism and Geography: The Limits of Geographical Knowledge*. Cambridge: Polity Press.

Rosenbaum, M. S. and Massiah, C. (2011). An Expanded Servicescape Perspective. *Journal of Service Management*, 22(4): 471–490.

Rosenfield, G. H., Fitzpatrick-Lins, K. and Johnson, T. L. (1987). Stratification of a Cityscape Using Census and Land Use Variables for Inventory of Building Materials. *Annals of Regional Science*, 21(1): 22–33.

Royal Geographical Society (2018a). Chairs Theme. *RGS-IGB Annual International Conference 2018.* www.rgs.org/WhatsOn/ConferencesAndSeminars/Annual+International+Conference/Chairs+theme.htm.

Royal Geographical Society (2018b). Call for Papers *RGS-IGB Annual International Conference 2018.* http://conference.rgs.org/CAllForPapers/View.aspx?heading=Y&session=286bc6a1-0bb2-499e-9be-7-f84479f113d6.

Ryu, K. and Jang, S. S. (2007). The Effects of Environmental Perceptions on Behavioral Intentions Through Emotions: The Case of Upscale Restaurants. *Journal of Hospitality and Tourism Research*, 31(1): 56–72.

Sack, R. (1986). *Human Territoriality.* Cambridge: Cambridge University Press.

Sauer, C. O. (1925). The Morphology of Landscape. In: J. Leighly, ed., *Land and Life: A Selection from the Writings of Carl Ortwin Sauer.* Berkeley, CA: University of California Press.

Schlor, R. (1998). *Nights in the Big City.* London: Reaktion.

Shakespeare, W. (1992). *A Midsummer Night's Dream.* New York: Dover Publications.

Shakespeare, W. (1998). *The Taming of the Shrew.* New York: Dover Publications.

Shaw, S. (2014). Faces, Spaces and Places: Social and Cultural Impacts of Street Festivals in Cosmopolitan Cities. In: S. Page and J. Connell, eds, *The Routledge Handbook of Events.* Hokoben, NJ: Taylor & Francis, 401–414.

Sherry, J. F. (1998). The Soul of the Company Store: Nike Town Chicago and the Emplaced Brandscape. In: J. F. Sherry, ed., *Servicescapes: The Concept of Place in Contemporary Markets.* Lincolnwood, IL: Nike Town Chicago Business Books, 109–150.

Siu, N. Y.-M., Wan, P. Y. K. and Dong, P. (2012). The Impact of the Servicescape on the Desire to Stay in Convention and Exhibition Centers: The Case of Macao. *International Journal of Hospitality Management*, 31(1): 236–246.

Smith, A. (2016). *Events in the City: Using Public Spaces as Event Venues.* Oxford: Routledge.

Smith, A., Brown, G. and Assaker, G. (2017). Olympic Experiences: The Significance of Place. *Event Management,* 21: 281–299.

Stokols, D. and Altman, I. (1987). *Handbook of Environmental Psychology.* New York: John Wiley & Sons.

Takacs, C. (2018). *Dreamscapes: Inspiration and Beauty in Gardens Near and Far.* South Yarra: Hardie Grant Books.

Tattersall, J. and Cooper, R. (2014). Creating the Eventscape. In: L. Sharples, P. Crowther, D. May and C. Orefice, eds, *Strategic Event Creation.* Oxford: Goodfellow, 141–165.

Tombs, A. and McColl-Kennedy, J. R. (2003). Social-Servicescapes Conceptual Model. *Marketing Theory*, 3: 447–475.

Traganou, J. (2016). *Designing the Olympics: Representation, Participation, Contestation.* New York: Routledge.

Tuan, Y.-F. (1974). *Topophilia: A Study of Environmental Perception, Attitudes and Values.* Englewood Cliffs, NJ: Prentice Hall.

Tuan, Y.-F. (1982). *Segmented Worlds and Self.* Minneapolis, MN: University of Minnesota Press.

Turley, L. W. and Milliman, R. E. (2000). Atmospheric Effects on Shopping Behavior: A Review of Experimental Evidence. *Journal of Business Research*, 49: 193–211.

Tzanelli, R. (2018). *Mega Events as Economies of the Imagination: Creating Atmospheres for Rio 2016 and Tokyo 2020.* London: Routledge.

Ulrich, R. S. (1986). Human Responses to Vegetation and Landscapes. *Landscapes and Urban Planning*, 13: 29–44.

Urry, J. (1995). *Consuming Places.* London: Routledge.

Van den Berg, L. and Braun, E. (1999). Urban Competitiveness, Marketing and the Need for Organizing Capacity. *Urban Studies*, 36(5): 987–999.

Van der Duim, R. (2007). Tourismscapes: An Actor–Network Perspective. *Annals of Tourism Research*, 34(4): 961–976.

Venkatraman, M. and Nelson, T. (2008). From Servicescapes to Consumption-scape: A Photo-Elicitation Study of Starbucks in the New China. *Journal of International Business Studies*, 39: 1010–1026.

Vickery, V. (2015). Beyond Painting, Beyond Landscape: Working Beyond the Frame to Unsettle Representations of Landscape. *Geo Humanities*, 1(2): 321–344.

Voss, K. E., Spangenberg, E. R. and Grohman, B. (2003). Measuring the Hedonic and Utilitarian Dimensions of Consumer Attitude. *Journal of Marketing Research*, 40(3): 310–320.

Wakefield, K. L., Blodgett, J. G. and Sloan, H. J. (1996). Measurement and Management of the Sportscape. *Journal of Sport Management*, 10(1): 15–31.

Wanhill, S. (2003). Interpreting the Development of the Visitor Attraction Product. In: A. Fyall, B. Garrod and A. Leask, eds, *Managing Visitor Attractions: New Directions.* Oxford: Butterworth Heinemann, 16–35.

Warnaby, G. (2018). Taking a Territorological Perspective on Place Branding? *Cities*, 80: 64–66.

Warnaby, G., Bennison, D. and Medway, D. (2010). Notions of Materiality and Linearity: The Challenges of Marketing the Hadrian's Wall Place Product. *Environment and Planning A*, 42(6): 1356–1382.

Wrightson, K. (2000). An Introduction to Acoustic Ecology. *The Journal of Acoustic Ecology*, 1(1): 10–13.

Wunderlich, F. M. (2010). The Aesthetics of Place-Temporality in Everyday Urban Space: The Case of Fitzroy Square. In: T. Edensor, ed., *Geographies of Rhythm: Nature, Place, Mobilities and Bodies.* London: Routledge, 45–56.

Zeithaml, V. A. and Bitner, M. J. (1996). *Service Marketing.* New York: McGraw-Hill.

Plate 1 Rio 2016: visual identity.
   The Olympic logo – mapped by Sugar Loaf mountain (top) and designed to connect people (middle). The lush colours as displayed at Volleyball House (bottom).

Credit: Tátil.

Plate 2 *Byron Bay Bluesfest.*
Transformation in northern NSW, Australia.

Credit: Even Malcolm.

Plate 3 *Mysteryland, Holland.*
Adding colour to the landscape.

Credit: ID&T.

Plate 4 *The stage at Mysteryland.*
An explosive atmosphere at night.

Credit: ID&T.

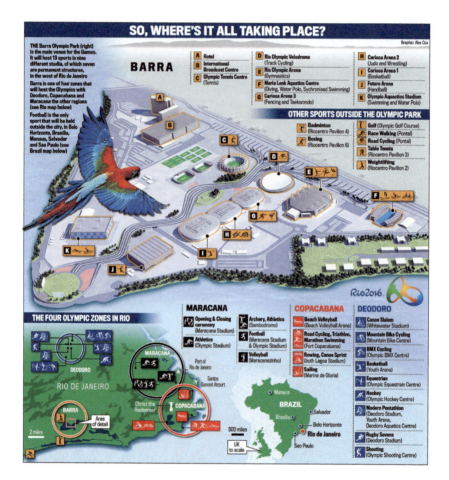

Plate 5 Mapping the 2016 Games.

Locating Brazil, Rio's Olympic zones and venues at the Barra Olympic Park.

Source: Daily Mail, 2016.

Plate 6 *Interacting with the eventscape.*
Searching for knowledge about Rio and the Olympic Games.

Credit: Fiasco Design.

Plate 7 *Salt Lake City skyline.*
Sporting images and monumental wrapping.

Credit: Fusion Imaging.

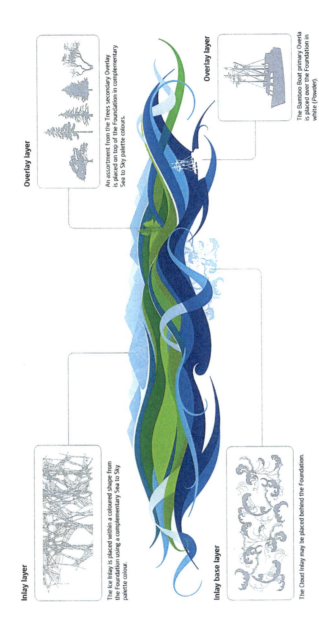

Inlay layer

The Ice Inlay is placed within a coloured shape from the Foundation using a complementary Sea to Sky palette colour.

Overlay layer

An assortment from the Trees secondary Overlay is placed on top of the Foundation in complementary Sea to Sky palette colours.

Overlay layer

The Bamboo Boat primary Overlay is placed over the Foundation in white (*Powder*).

Inlay base layer

The Cloud Inlay may be placed behind the Foundation.

Plate 8 *Vancouver 2010: constructing the core graphic. Creating a storyline for British Columbia.*

Source: VANOC, 2009.

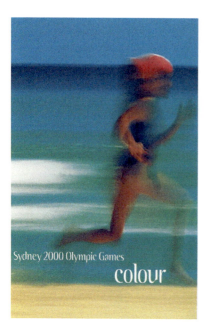

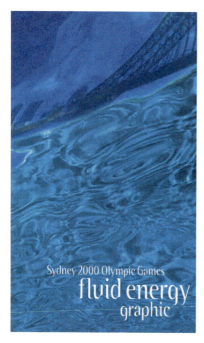

Plate 9 *Sydney 2000: colour, movement and the fluid graphic.*
Inspiring the Olympic 'look'.

Credit: SOCOG, 1998. Copyright: Sydney Olympic Park Authority.

Plate 10 *Sydney 2000: iconic setting.*
      Stage design.

Credit: Jamie Squire/Getty Images.

Plate 11 *London 2012: venue design.*
Applying the colour palette.

Credit: FutureBrand.

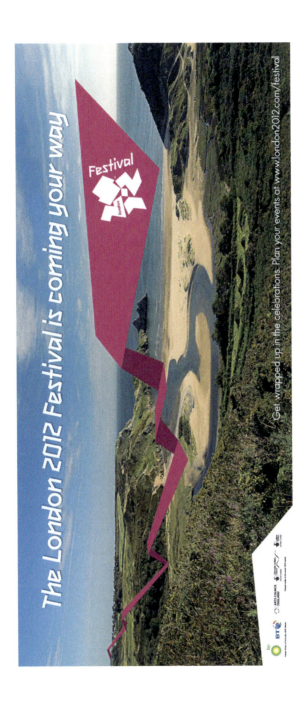

Plate 12 *London 2012 Festival.*
Communication and spatial connections.

Credit: FutureBrand.

Plate 13 *Starry Night over the Rhône.*
Vincent van Gogh's vision of heaven and earth.

Credit: photo © RMN-Grand Palais (Musée d'Orsay) / Hervé Lewandowski.

Plate 14 *Vivid Sydney.*
Reflections across Sydney Harbour.

Credit: Destination NSW.

Plate 15 *Supertrees in Singapore.*
The nightly light show that transforms the Gardens by the Bay.

Credit: Gardens by the Bay.

Plate 16 *Strengthening communities through culture. A model for visual storytelling.*

Credit: Allan Sumner.

4 Eventscapes

INTRODUCTION

An attempt to categorise eventscapes must be sufficiently flexible to accommodate analysis at different spatial scales and the many types of relationship that exist between events and the physical environment. The relationship may be permanent or temporary and the environmental anchors for events may be natural or artificial, fixed or fluid, in rural or urban locations, at single or multiple sites and at locations that are in public or private ownership. This variability will be illustrated by describing different types of eventscapes with attention directed to the way events are managed and experienced. It will be demonstrated that events transform the place where they are held but that they are also functionally and, often, symbolically dependent on their environmental setting. After considering resource issues, the chapter discusses the different types of eventscapes and their presentation on maps.

THE RESOURCE BASE

Local resources, both environmental and cultural, are used in event management to gain a competitive advantage and deliver unique experiences. Bidding to host mega-events can be very competitive and environmental protection and sustainability have become important criteria in recent years. Cities emphasise positive geographical characteristics and, in the case of the 2010 Winter Olympics, Vancouver's Bid Document stated, 'In its setting for the Sea to Sky Games, Vancouver and Whistler offer a compelling theatre for sport: a world class stage that combines the oceanfront allure of Vancouver with the breathtaking alpine setting of Whistler' (Vancouver 2010, 2002). During the Games, design features were added to this 'stage' to create a desired Olympic 'look' and those who took the journey from Vancouver to Whistler were travelling through an eventscape. In a very different environmental context, the Birdsville Big Red Bash in Australia is promoted as the world's most remote music festival. A 40-metre high red dune is the setting for the event with a stage handbuilt into the sand. The dune serves as a viewing platform to watch the sun rise and set across the desert and it is a playground for activities such as sand boarding. Part of the attraction of the event is what is described as the epic outback road trip to reach the site, which is 1,600 km west of Brisbane and 2,000 km north-west of Sydney (Donovan, 2018).

Distance is not an impediment in the pursuit of unique event experiences as enthusiasts travel across the globe to witness events such as a solar eclipse and remote locations with expansive vistas and dark skies offer ideal viewing conditions (Hartman and Brown, 2004). In England, at the time of the two solstices, English Heritage makes special provision for people to walk between the stones at Stonehenge. Access is denied at other times in order to protect the World Heritage Site. The sunrise on 1 January 2000 was eagerly anticipated around the world and, in Australia, large numbers of people travelled to Cape Byron to celebrate the new Millennium. The Cape is Australia's most easterly point and the place where the light first touches the continent. In response to the expected demand, a special event was organised as the clifftop at the Cape presented both opportunities and dangers. Special measures had to be taken to ensure safety as people arrived in the dark after celebrating New Year's Eve in traditional fashion at nearby Byron Bay (Brown, 2000a).

Even if events are based on resources that are place-specific, there is still variability in the way they are managed. The beach at Coolangatta at the southern end of the Gold Coast in Queensland, Australia hosts events that use the resources of sand and surf. As the venue for the Quicksilver pro surfing event, Coolangatta was described as 'the epicenter of the Australian surf scene. The Superbank at Snapper Rocks is the preeminent stage, supplying waves that allow surfers to showcase the highest caliber of performance surfing just yards away from thousands of cheering fans' (Gold Coast Event Guide, 2018). In September 2017, the opera *Aida* was performed on the same sands, recreating Egyptian scenes at Coolangatta. It required 18 months of planning and took more than ten days to build the set, but Louise Robertson, the Executive Producer, maintained that 'If you're not an opera fan, you'll still get a lot out of it as the environment makes the show' (Simonot, 2017). In the following year, the same location was the setting for the beach volleyball competition at the 2018 Commonwealth Games. A temporary stadium was constructed on the beach and spectators watched the game and the surf rolling in from the Pacific. A similar experience was offered at the 2016 Olympic Games when a beach volleyball stadium was constructed at Copacabana in Rio de Janeiro. The eventscape that was created on the sand of the famous beach can be seen in Figure 4.1. It is sandwiched between the surf and Avenida Atlantica with a large area of support facilities on the beach to the side of the stadium. The cityscape and mountains provided a layered, visual backdrop. The contrast is remarkable between this eventscape and what had been created for the beach volleyball tournament at the previous Olympics in London (Figure 4.2). The photographs demonstrate the transportability of sport (Hinch and Higham, 2011) and the way eventscapes can emerge from and transform very different environmental settings.

An online report by a journalist provided a colourful description of the atmosphere at the beach volleyball games at the London Olympics. It described the music, the entertainment and the sporting spectacle at the beach that had been created amid the city's most historic sites. It was reported that the players were taking photos everyday with frequent reference made to the contrast between the site as 'the coolest venue in Olympic history' with that of its traditional role as a venerable parade

Figure 4.1 *Beach volleyball, Rio 2016 Olympic Games: Copacabana Beach.*

Source: Graham Brown

Figure 4.2 Beach volleyball, London 2012 Olympic Games: Horse Guards Parade.

Source: IOC (International Olympic Committee).

ground where the Queen traditionally inspects the troops on her birthday (Cable, 2012). Cultural heritage added a significant dimension to the Olympic experience at Horse Guards Parade. The resource base for an equestrian event in St Moritz, Switzerland is a frozen lake. The event experience is augmented by the town's historical associations with winter sports and its reputation as an exclusive Alpine resort. These relationships are explained in **Event Marketing at St Moritz**.

EVENT MARKETING AT ST MORITZ

By Martin Berthod, Director Sport & Events, Tourism St Moritz

The winter sport image of St Moritz has a long heritage. It is synonymous with Alpine and Nordic skiing and approximately 50 per cent of our guests take part in these sports. St Moritz hosted the Winter Olympic Games in 1928 and 1948 and will host events as part of the Youth Olympic Games in 2020. It has held the World Ski Championships on five occasions in 1934, 1948, 1974, 2003 and, most recently, in 2017. The

Men's Downhill World Championship attracts about 40,000 spectators.

British visitors started to arrive at St Moritz in the mid-nineteenth century following a bet with a hotel owner who told them they would enjoy the 'short sleeve' winter climate on the terraces of St Moritz. These early tourists introduced a number of winter sports such as curling that was brought from Scotland and skeleton which started in 1884 and continues to take place on the famous Cresta Run to this day. In 1897, the St Moritz bobsleigh club was created and each year races are held on a natural ice run. The 1.7-kilometre track is built by hand by 14 men in early December and is maintained until World Cup races have been held in mid-January and other events which use the track finish towards the end of February. More than 30 World Championships have been held on this track. It is fascinating to watch the track take shape as this form of construction is unique to St Moritz.

In 1908, horse races were held for the first time on the frozen lake and, 110 years later, it is an important part of our event calendar. It is also unique to St Moritz and appeals to a special clientele – people who like sport and animals, enjoy betting on horses and like to stay in five-star hotels. It is an ideal match for the high-class image of St Moritz. The event depends on the most important thing we can sell – our natural environment. The whole climate has to be just right for ice to form to a minimum thickness of 25–30 centimetres – not just cold temperatures but still conditions as wind creates waves which stop ice forming. We have to use amphibious machinery when the ice is forming to create the infrastructure for the 10,000–15,000 people who will be on the lake during the races. This infrastructure includes grandstands, tents and betting cabins. Similar facilities are used by people who attend the polo event that has been held since 1985.

I have been in this role since 1981 and I can say that event marketing is crucial to the promotion of St Moritz. It makes it possible for us to speak directly to the people we want to communicate with. Importantly, events attract a remarkable level of media interest. Print advertising is very expensive but we have been able to attract a full page of coverage about cricket on ice in the prestigious Swiss newspaper *Neue Zurich Zeitung*. About 30 years ago, when working with Mark McCormac to license the St Moritz brand, we established a cricket on ice tournament on the lake. The resulting film about the tournament, produced by TWI, attracted 200 million television viewers. This year we will have the first ice cricket competition featuring professional players from different countries. It will be organised by an Indian company and a media conference about the competition, held in Delhi, produced an immense level of interest.

We continue to develop more events on the ice including a Swiss speed skating championship and ice hockey, which will feature matches between Canadian teams. However, we have to be careful as you can have too many events. We hold nearly 200 events each year in St Moritz but this is only possible due to the fantastic support of the host community. We have a permanent resident population of only 5,000 but regularly call on 200 or 300 people to act as volunteers at events. This has not been a problem as local people want to be involved in the events that are such an important part of life in St Moritz.

The St Moritz Polo World Cup attracts an impressive list of partners including Cartier, which has been a sponsor since the event started in 1985. The 2018 Snow Polo brochure claimed that the success of the event was based on 'the location: St Moritz is the sumptuous snow glamour capital of the world – (and) the actual venue: the frozen lake that is home to the White Turf racing and nestles in the magnificent Engadine Valley' (Hine, 2018: 14). The White Turf event has been held since 1907 and features a series of races over three Sundays in February: Flat Races, Trotting races (with horses pulling small sleighs) and Skikjoring. In Skikjoring, drivers on skis are pulled by unmounted thoroughbred horses at speeds of up to 50 km/hour. A tent city built on the frozen lake includes art displays, concerts, restaurants, shops, a children's funfair and exclusive hospitality spaces where the guests of sponsors are entertained. When the tent city is dismantled, no physical evidence of the event remains and the landscape returns to normal. Looking at the blue water of the lake in the summer, it would be difficult to imagine it as the setting for White Turf. Martin Berthod's description of the construction each year, by hand, of the ice track for the Cresta Run is an excellent example of the finely balanced relationship between the natural environment and the rhythms of local life. In contrast with the Palio horse race in Siena (see Chapter 2), it does not involve the conservation of a public place, but requires a commitment to maintain cultural traditions and, in so doing, to create a space at the same location each year so the event can be staged.

SPATIAL PATTERNS

Single sites

Drawing on Max Weber's (1978) *ideal types* framework, Wynn (2015) presents three models which describe the spatial pattern of music festivals. The patterns are citadel, core and confetti. His analysis is related to urban settings in the USA at Austin, Nashville and Newport but it has wider application. He suggests that with a citadel pattern, events are isolated within a single, bounded space. This means that resources must be brought to the site but it allows organisers to exert control over activities within the boundary (Wynn, 2015). The Byron Bay Bluesfest serves as an example of a citadel pattern.

The aerial photograph of the site (Plate 2) where the Bluesfest is held clearly shows the presence of the event as a prominent feature in the landscape of northern New South Wales, Australia. The site is located between the Pacific Ocean to the east and mountains in the World-Heritage listed hinterland to the west. The colours of the temporary structures stand in marked contrast with those of the surrounding natural environment. It is an example of an eventscape with a citadel pattern, which emerges from and temporarily transforms a single, green field site.

The Byron Bay Bluesfest is an annual music festival that attracts an audience of 100,000 people. It has been held over the Easter long weekend since 1990 and, after using a number of different sites in Byron Bay, moved to a permanent home of 120 hectares at a Tea Tree Farm just north of the town in 2010. The site includes camping for 6,000 people and up to 200 performances are held on seven stages. Ownership of the land by the company that runs the event makes it possible to conduct year-round maintenance to improve the physical capacity of the site as an event venue and to engage in environmentally sustainable practices. 'Greening the Blues' includes initiatives to reduce soil erosion, improve waste management and preserve the natural fauna of the site which has a population of resident koalas (Meek, 2018).

The festival is firmly embedded in a physical environment. But it is also benefits from the distinctive culture of northern New South Wales. Byron Bay, in particular, is famous for its youthful, relaxed, alternative and beach lifestyle. The accommodation mix in the town reflects Byron Bay's diverse tourist market which ranges from camping sites and hostels full of international backpackers to spiritual resorts and expensive apartments that serve as retreats for city executives and film stars. The local culture is an integral part of the Bluesfest's brand and is used strategically. Promotional communications reinforce positive local associations and feature imagery of surfing and the Cape Byron lighthouse, which commands spectacular views from Australia's most easterly headland. The mix of musical performances, the environmental setting and the local culture is clearly illustrated on the Bluesfest's 2017 highlights video (www.youtube.com/watch?v=uG9rS5VfRGQ).

The eventscape of the Byron Bay Bluesfest is similar to that of many outdoor music festivals that are held around the world. The **Mysteryland** Case Study discusses the development of music festivals in Europe and describes the eventscape at Mysteryland's Floriade site in Holland.

MYSTERYLAND: THE WORLD'S LONGEST RUNNING ELECTRONIC DANCE MUSIC FESTIVAL

By Rosanne Janmaat, Director, International, ID&T, Holland

The company

ID&T was founded in Holland in 1992 by **I**rfan van Ewijk, **D**uncan Stutterheim and **T**heo Lelie.

The three friends organised a party for 400 people at a local village followed by a celebration to mark their final year at school. 'The Final Exam' attracted 13,000 people to the Utrecht Conference Centre in 1993. After transforming the electronic dance music scene throughout Europe, ID&T have been responsible for organising some of the world's largest music events, operating in over 45 countries and attracting millions of visitors. The company offers licensing agreements for existing brands and works with local partners to identify opportunities globally to develop new music festivals.

Festivals and music culture

Among the most famous festivals organised by ID&T are *Thunderdome, Sensation* and *Tomorrowland* which started as a joint venture in 2005.

Thunderdome was first organised in June 1993, when more than 10,000 people attended the event. It has been held annually in large indoor venues in Holland. What started as a celebration of hard-core music became a brand and a movement with a cult-like following.

Sensation, another indoor event, was held for the first time in the Amsterdam Arena in 2000 – the first electronic dance music event ever to be held in a stadium. It has become an international phenomenon and has toured to 45 countries, attracting more than two million people who wear white clothes to the events. The 'be part of the night, unite in white' tradition started in 2001 as a tribute to the brother of one of ID&T's founders who had died that year. The dress code went viral and became a tradition at all *Sensation* events helping it to win awards in countries such as Germany, Australia, Brazil and Denmark. The concept combines performances by world-famous DJs with extraordinary stage designs and state-of-the-art light shows. In 2014, *Sensation* was held outdoors for the first time in Dubai and India.

Tomorrowland, which is now owned by Michel and Manuel Beers, has been held annually in Boom, Belgium since 2005 and is the largest electronic music festival in the world. In 2008, it was held on 26 and 27 July and the number of visitors exceeded 50,000. A record of 120,000 visitors attended in 2010 and the festival expanded to three days in 2011 when it was voted the best festival of its kind in the world at the International Dance Music Awards. In 2012, 400 DJs played on 15 stages each day and 185,000 people from over 75 countries were in attendance. *Tomorrowland* partnered with Brussels Airlines to provide exclusive travel packages from over 15 cities around the world. Thirty-five thousand visitors stayed in Dreamville, *Tomorrowland*'s campsite. Dreamville is a vibrant city that welcomes tens of thousands of festival visitors after an exuberant day at *Tomorrowland*. To celebrate the tenth anniversary of *Tomorrowland*, the 2014 edition was held over two weekends: 18–20 July and 25–27 July.

The success of ID&T's festivals reflects a timely response to social trends that affected European youth before sweeping around the world. The scale of mass participation means the events have helped shape these trends. The festivals offer a combination of artist-driven and concept-driven experiences which appeal to people who appreciate the emerging genres of electronic dance music. People who wish to share experiences in settings that offer an escape from their daily lives. These young people bring to the events a mental state that is receptive to an expressive, party atmosphere celebrated with friends and feelings of being united in the moment with like-minded people from the around the world. The environmental setting and the way it is designed create the atmosphere and facilitate the festival experiences.

Mysteryland

Mysteryland started in 1993, which makes it the world's longest running electronic music festival. It is a full-weekend festival with four days of camping in the on-site village and attracts over 100,000 festivalgoers. In addition to offering a melting pot of electronic music genres, it is famous for its elaborate décor, interactive art installations and extraordinary stage designs.

The first edition of *Mysteryland* was held at a racetrack in Lelystad in the Netherlands and for several years, it moved from site to site with the government providing access to park locations in different parts of the country. In 2002, the festival found a permanent home at the former Floriade site near Amsterdam. Site design is an integral part of the event experience at this attractive location. The setting offers two parts – one natural and the other more landscaped. Plate 3 shows the landscaped part of the *Mysteryland* site with the bridges which cross the prominent water features and the elevated land which looks onto one of the 18 stages. Plate 4 shows the transformation at night with one of the main stages alive with colour.

Changes are made each year to the design of the stages, food stands and bars which make a large footprint on the site. The visual creativity expressed at the bars and, particularly, at the stages provides decorative surprises for people returning to the festival. These innovative changes are combined with a sense of consistency related to the setting and the brand values. In many ways, the look is the brand – from the first visual encounter on a website or a poster to the decorative greeting at the entrance to the site and the subsequent festival experience.

Music festivals that have achieved international recognition include the Glastonbury Festival in England and the Coachella Valley Festival in California, which is attended by over 90,000 people each day of the festival. The fame attached to these events is partly a product of their size and the media coverage they attract. With longevity, tangible symbols have become important and the pyramid stage at Glastonbury is considered to be the most instantly recognisable stage in the world. It is now in its third incarnation. The first stage was built in 1971 using temporary material in the belief that a pyramid is a very powerful shape with the apex projecting energy upwards while energy from the stars and sun are drawn down to earth. In 1981, a permanent structure came to symbolise the magic of the Festival before it was destroyed by fire in 1994. In 2000, the phoenix rose from the ashes as a glittering 30 m steel structure.

It can be difficult to find sites that are able to accommodate large numbers of visitors in urban areas as events often require parts of the city to be closed when an eventscape is being established, used and dismantled. However, some places such as Hyde Park in London have become synonymous with events with the Park's reputation as the setting for large outdoor events firmly established by the 'Stones in the Park' concert on 5 July 1969. It was a free event that attracted an estimated crowd of 500,000. However, the suitability of Hyde Park as a venue for large gathering had been established over 100 years earlier when the Great Exhibition was held in 1851. This event helped to democratise Hyde Park symbolically and legally. It was the first time that many of the millions of people who came to the event had mingled in public with people of other social classes and it was linked to the Crown Lands Act (1851), which transferred the management of London's Royal Parks from the monarch to the government (Smith, 2016).

Precincts

A precinct where multiple venues are located on a single site equates to Wynn's (2015) core pattern. The prefix of sporting or cultural may be attached, if permanent structures associated with particular types of activities dominate the use of a precinct. This type of eventscape forms part of the urban fabric and can be found in many cities around the world. In Australia, the South Bank precinct in Brisbane, which was developed on the site of the 1988 Expo, is discussed in **An Evolving Eventscape**. Within a generation, the status of the South Bank changed from being a site that was largely irrelevant to the life of the city, to being a key part of the answer to the question, what is Brisbane? It has a sense of place that shapes how the city is perceived by both residents and visitors. As the case explains, this transformation has happened in stages, stimulated by Expo and reinforced by the development of art and cultural venues. The location, separated from the CBD by a bridge over the river, has become particularly significant as the city has grown and the river has become an increasingly important asset. More people now use river transport to access different parts of the city and many places along the riverbank have become leisure spaces. There is a cognitive relationship between the rhythms of the South Bank precinct and those associated with the high-rise buildings in the CBD that can be seen on the other side of the river.

AN EVOLVING EVENTSCAPE

By Chris Krolikowski

South Bank in Brisbane is considered to be one of the most successful urban tourism precincts in Australia. A legacy of Expo '88, it incorporates design elements of the event and builds on the festive and leisurely atmosphere that emerged during the event. On a broader level, the South Bank precinct is symbolic of the transformation of Brisbane. It is difficult to conceive of Brisbane without South Bank. This relationship between the eventscape and the broader city is fundamental to understanding the transformative effect of events.

Expo '88

In 2018, when Brisbane and Queensland celebrated the thirtieth anniversary of hosting the World Expo, the reflection about the long-term legacy of the event became central to assessing its impact. Much of the rationale behind the decision to stage Expo was associated with a desire to internationalise the state and its capital city (Sanderson, 2003). As declared by Sir Llew Edwards, Chairman of the Expo Authority, Expo '88 was to become a 'catalyst for a significant change in our lifestyle' (cited in Sanderson, 2003: 66). At the closing ceremony, on 30 October 1988, it was already apparent that Expo '88 was a transformative event, whose legacy would be felt long after the event. It was widely reported as a 'coming of age' for Brisbane and Queensland (Sanderson, 2003: 66).

The idea to host Expo '88 was first floated in 1976 by the architect James MacCormick who considered potential ways of activating the southern shores of the Brisbane River, around Kangaroo Point (Cheng, 2018). As was the case with other similar events, the resource provided by the water-based location was an important consideration when developing the concept. The post-industrial area of South Brisbane, located on the southern banks of the Brisbane River, offered a convenient site that was both proximate to the CBD, yet sufficiently demarcated from the city centre. The rationale presented to state and federal governments to obtain financial support emphasised the potential of the event for the regeneration of the site and the intention to increase the importance of the Brisbane River. The management bodies responsible for staging Expo '88, the Expo Ministerial Council and the Brisbane Exposition and South Bank Redevelopment Authority (BESBRA), were established in 1984 and tasked with the transformation of a significant area of South Brisbane into the South Bank site for the Expo (Davies, 1990).

The event opened in April 1988 and lasted for half a year. Brisbane's Expo adopted a casual design, reflecting the relaxed atmosphere of Queensland and the tropical climatic conditions of the state. A series of eight tent-like 'sun sails' were erected along the Brisbane River and were used as canvases for lights and images projections. They resembled circus tents and evoked the image of a carnival and accentuated the festive, temporary nature of the event (Cheng, 2018). People were encouraged to explore the outdoor spaces as well as the pavilions. The World Expo Park that was part of the site, provided a theme park environment containing a rollercoaster, car rides and futuristic attractions such as 'orbitron', 'supernova' or 'alien encounter'. Connecting the entire area of Expo was a 2-kilometre monorail loop that transported visitors between the northern and the southern ends of the exhibition.

An artificial 'Pacific Lagoon' in the southern part of Expo was an attractive water feature that created a central point from which visitors were able to access diverse attractions and exhibitions. The Amphitheatre, Piazza and the River Stage, located in different parts of the Expo, produced important public space and meeting places and areas to host events. The linear shape of the site paralleled the Brisbane River and offered views of the cityscape, juxtaposing the formality of the city and the fun offered at the Expo site. The overall environment of Expo '88 reflected the main theme of the event: 'Leisure in the Age of Technology', and highlighted the symbiosis between the two, leisure and technology in what was transformed into an attractive and convenient riverbank area (Bennett, 1991)

When it ended, Expo '88 was already considered highly successful. Visitation levels were almost double those initially expected, reaching approximately 15 million. Exhibitors included 52 governments and 48 corporations (Foundation Expo '88, 2004). With a total cost of approximately AUS$600 million, it was estimated to have contributed AUS$1 billion to the economy (Our Brisbane, 2009). The main success of the event, however, was attributed to the changes that it triggered in the level of confidence of the people of Brisbane and Queensland (Bennett, 1991; Sanderson, 2003). Following six months of outdoor activities, outdoor dining and exposure to international visitors and trends, Expo '88 had left Brisbane 'hungry' for the new leisure opportunities. The effect of Expo '88 was profound, as it altered the identity of the host city and its community, and ultimately led to the rewriting of the prevailing perceptions of Brisbane. The direct material legacy of Expo '88, the South Bank precinct which evolved on the event site, was integral to this process. It expressed the new identity of Brisbane, while allowing the community to enjoy the kinds of leisure opportunities that were rehearsed during Expo '88.

The evolving legacy: the South Bank precinct

Following the completion of the Expo '88, the evolution of South Bank illustrates the lasting effects of the event and the way the eventscape has transformed the city. The initial plans for the site included the construction of a large number of residential developments to accommodate the growing population of the city. Having been accustomed to using South Bank during the Expo as a public leisure space, large sections of the local community opposed these plans and a new master plan was developed to accommodate the need for community leisure space.

When the South Bank precinct opened in 1992, it was apparent that the concerns of the local community had been addressed through radical rethinking of the experiential space of the new precinct. While new commercial developments have been incorporated, they were complemented by a park and open space that allowed the focus to be on leisure and relaxation. Many of the elements of Expo '88 were retained in the new South Bank while new additions drew inspiration from the event. The artificial beach area, a butterfly garden and a series of 'Venetian' water canals through which visitors were able to discover the precinct aimed to evoke an association with fun and spectacle. Structures, such as the Boardwalk, and a Nepalese pagoda had been part of Expo.

The precinct has been progressively reshaped by successive master plans, which have gradually altered the form and uses of the precinct. The first revision of the original master plan took place only four years after the opening of South Bank, when its development stalled (Noble, 2001: 89). The new master plan, shaped by Denton Corker Marshall, included a range of changes, particularly with respect to increasing the precinct's connectivity with the surrounding West End and with the city centre (Noble, 2001: 89). This was particularly important in the early stages of South Bank's existence, as the physical separation between the CBD and the precinct was limiting access to the site. Over the years, access to the precinct has significantly improved with the addition of major transport nodes (bus and train). Pedestrian and bike accessibility have been developed with new bridges linking the northern and southern edges of the precincts with the CBD. Connectivity has improved via the ferry that links South Bank with other parts of the city.

South Bank, under the control of the South Bank Corporation, has seen a continual evolution of its form with ongoing facilities development. The Queensland State Library and the Gallery of Modern Arts have been added to the northern border of the precinct, reflecting the growing significance of culture and the creative industries. New commercial facilities, including accommodation, shops and restaurants have been added, while the Brisbane Convention and Exhibition Centre and a range of educational institutions have also been incorporated. The expansion of the Arbour, which acts as a pedestrian spine weaving through the different parts of the precinct, has been a successful attempt to spatially integrate the precinct, link the diverse sections and create a coherent experience. The continuing existence of the Rainforest Walk, the Nepalese Pagoda and the tropical beach lagoon allows the precinct to maintain its image of a park and enables the visitors to appreciate the unique contrast that exists between South Bank and the Brisbane's cityscape.

South Bank represents a case of an evolving urban space, which, despite being purposefully designed and 'artificial', remains a popular space. It has been embraced by the local community and by visitors. Building on the experience of Expo '88 which delivered a festive leisure space, South Bank allows for a comparable feeling of respite to be experienced while being in a busy metropolis. By employing facilities management, urban and landscape design, an attractive environment which facilitates ease of movement and a relaxed atmosphere has been created. South Bank is a key urban space for Brisbane.

There are two major precincts in Melbourne: Melbourne Park, which includes the Melbourne Cricket Ground and Tennis Park, where the Australian Open is held, and the Southbank which is an entertainment area centred on the large Star Casino complex. A river or body of water is a common feature at precincts and this is true at the Adelaide Riverbank

Figure 4.3 *Riverbank precinct, Adelaide.*

Source: Graham Brown

precinct – an open space in the centre of the city through which flows the River Torrens. The precinct contains a number of event venues with the Adelaide Oval, sport stadium located on one side of the river. It is connected to the other venues by a bridge that is an attractive feature of the precinct. Figure 4.3 shows the Adelaide Convention Centre, to the right, the tall Intercontinental Hotel and part of Adelaide Festival Centre, a theatre and multi-purpose arts complex. The Adelaide Casino and the Festival Plaza are located behind the Festival Centre. Clearly visible, in the foreground, is the floating Palais that is built as a temporary venue for events during the Adelaide Festival that is held each year in March. This demonstrates that, although permanent buildings dominate urban precincts, as an eventscape, they adapt to a city's rhythms. The temporary changes respond to the pattern of iterative events and their resource needs. Some urban precincts respond to seasonal changes by adding temporary ice rinks during winter months that become the focus of Christmas events in the northern hemisphere. The success of precincts requires integrated management between the businesses, which share the site with events planned in ways that complement rather than compete with each other. This is described in the **Adelaide Riverbank Precinct**.

THE ADELAIDE RIVERBANK PRECINCT

A Riverbank Entertainment Precinct Advisory Committee (REPAC) was established by the recently elected Liberal government in South Australia in 2018. The membership comprised a Chair and a representative from each of the Sky City

Casino, the InterContinental Hotel, Adelaide Convention Centre, Adelaide Festival Centre, the Adelaide Oval Stadium Management Authority, the Adelaide City Council and Renewal SA. Reporting directly to the Minister for Transport, Infrastructure and Local Government, REPAC was tasked to provide advice about major projects and strategic direction with economic development and job creation key objectives. The successful operation of the precinct depends on coordinated management between the key precinct partners and discussions were held with the Chief Executive Officers of the Adelaide Convention Centre, the Adelaide Festival Centre, the Adelaide Oval and the Sky City Casino. There was considerable consistency in the views that were expressed and perceptions about the role of the precinct.

The precinct was considered to be the heart of the city: a scenic attraction with open, green spaces on the edge of the city centre. The river and water frontage were integral to the business plans of all the CEOs with frequent reference to the benefits of venues facing the water and the visual amenity of the water and the way it reflects light. The precinct was described as a 'go to place' with the current level of investment giving it the potential to become a world-class destination. It was explained that the precinct offers environmental affordances; spaces for quiet relaxation and other spaces which excite and energise, especially as settings for events. This makes it appeal to people of all ages and to different types of uses. From a management perspective, the spaces outside the venues make it possible for people to vacate the venues quickly and, in the case of the Oval, people can sit on the grass outside listening to a concert. The CEO of the Oval suggested the venue is the 'anchor tenant' as it hosts events for over 40,000 people on 40 occasions each year and attracts a total of 1.8 million people to the precinct. The investment in lighting to create a 'sparkling' icon symbolises the 'anchor' status.

The benefits of coordination encompass operational practices, marketing and management. Some of this is forced by the need to share road access for deliveries and drop-offs. Sharing information about future bookings and jointly planning event calendars helps avoid negative impacts while identifying collaborative opportunities. The Casino offers packages that include tickets to shows at the Festival Centre to replicate what is available in Las Vegas, 'under one roof'.

The precinct needs to be a safe, attractive environment where people can gather, stop and stroll and crowds can flow. Features such as the walk of fame outside the Festival Centre increase the 'stickiness' of that part of the precinct. In the daytime, shading and water features are needed while, at night, lighting assists wayfinding and safety and creates colourful illuminations across the bridge and on the buildings. All of the venues benefit from well-planned infrastructure in the precinct which enhances their ability to attract consumers and encourage repeat visitation.

It was interesting to note the significance of different spatial horizons, radiating from the venues, across the precinct to places beyond, extending connections to other parts of the city. This was expressed in terms of the proximity of the precinct to the railway station and to trams but it also reflected the vision of Adelaide as a walkable city and the plans to encourage movements between the Riverbank and the Food Market at King William Square. The latter is regarded as the other heart of the city, as enshrined in William Light's original plans for Adelaide. The current plans involve making the laneways between the River and the Square more attractive. As a walking route, it will offer multiple experiences as pedestrians pass through interesting streets between the city's two key and complementary nodes.

When precincts stage events such as the Olympic Games or an Expo, the scale of development has a major impact on even the biggest cities in the world. Expos are held for six months and have been used to make statements about the host city's position in the world. The first Expo, in 1851, declared the pre-eminence of London at that time and it was felt that Expo 2010 marked 'Shanghai's coronation as the next great world city' (Minter, 2010). The Great Exhibition, held in Hyde Park in 1851, was a celebration of culture, industrial technology and design and displayed the achievements of Victorian Britain at the height of its Imperial power. The construction of the massive Crystal Palace, which housed much of the

Exhibition, represented a tangible expression of these achievements. It was regarded as a triumph of engineering and the impact of physical structures is a recurrent theme at Expos. The Eiffel Tower was built as a gateway to the Expo in Paris in 1889 and both architecture and landscape design were important features at the Chicago Columbian Exposition that was held in 1893 and celebrated the 400th anniversary of Christopher Columbus's arrival in the New World. Life-size reproductions of Columbus's three ships were built in Spain and sailed to America where they became popular attractions at the event. The Exposition covered more than 2.4 km², included canals and lagoons and nearly 200 buildings that were designed in an ornate, neoclassical style. They were painted white, resulting in the fair site being referred to as the White City. The fairgrounds were created by Frederick Law Olmsted, who designed Central Park in New York. Forty-six nations participated in the Chicago Expo, which was the first to have national pavilions.

The pavilions have served as architectural signifiers of place identity (Julier, 2005) and at the Expo in 2010 each national pavilion made a statement based on its size, design and location in the eventscape. The Saudi Arabian pavilion cost $146 million and covered an area of 6,000 m². The largest theatre screen in the world showed images of the meeting between King Abdullah and Chinese president Hu Jintao to symbolise the friendship between the two nations. The event in Shanghai was the largest and most expensive Expo with 189 countries participating. It took over eight years to clear the 5.3 km² site requiring the demolition of 18,000 homes. It was divided into four zones, on either side of the Hangpu River. Journalists were eager to identify what was communicated by the eventscapes paying particular attention to the position and size of the China Pavilion. MacKinnon commented that:

> at 63 meters high, the inverted crimson pyramid hangs over Shanghai's waterfront, dwarfing the 200 other newly built structures around it. Designed to resemble an ancient crown, the China Pavilion in the centre of the sprawling Expo 2010 grounds along the Hangpu River is very much the powerful host surrounded by rings of anxious-to-please guests.
>
> (MacKinnon, 2010)

Similarly, it was noted that:

> the politics are sometimes comically obvious: the China pavilion practically hangs over the Hong Kong, Macau and Taiwan pavilions; meanwhile the U.S. and Japanese pavilions are exiled to the far ends of the Expo site, as far from the China pavilion as physically possible.
>
> (Minter, 2010)

Figure 4.4 *The Olympic Green, Beijing.*
Source: Sassaki.

Symbolism is very important in Chinese culture and is incorporated in event design. The opening ceremony of the 2008 Olympic Games in Beijing started at 8 pm on the 8/8/2008 as 8 is considered to be an auspicious number. It was held in the National Stadium, known as the Birds Nest which, together with the Aquatic Centre, known as the Water Cube, have become famous icons that rival the Great Wall and the Forbidden City as national symbols (Meyer, 2009). Hosting the 2008 Olympic Games marked China's arrival on the world stage (de Lisle, 2009) and the construction of stadiums created an 'architectural language to narrate national ambitions' (Ren, 2008: 175). Beijing's identity was branded 'materially through the construction of landmark buildings – (which) showcased the city's productive capacity and modernization achievements' (Zhang and Zhao, 2009: 248). The Bird's Nest and the Water Cube were key components of the Masterplan for the Olympic precinct that was prepared by the Boston firm, Sasaki Associates (Figure 4.4). The 1135 ha, Olympic Green occupied a key location within the city and exhibited design features that were both symbolic and functional (Brown and Huang, 2015). It was located on the city's central axis, to the north of the Forbidden City and the Temple of Heaven and, at the southern entrance to the Green, the Bird's Nest was located to the east of the axis and the Water Cube to the west. The contrasting shapes of these key structures are consistent with the idea of yin and yang in Chinese philosophy which believes that seemingly contradictory forces may be complementary and interdependent. According to Zou and Leslie-Carter, the Water Cube is blue against the stadium's red, water v. fire, square vs. round, male vs. female, heaven vs earth. – The Water Cube Aquatic Centre design portrays the way in which humanity relates to water and the harmonious coexistence of humans and nature which in Chinese culture is life's ultimate blessing.

(Zou and Leslie-Carter, 2010: 176)

The flow of water through the Olympic Green and around the Bird's Nest reflected the incorporation of landscape features associated with feng shui which uses natural energy to create harmony.

Olympic parks stand as impressive symbols of the commitment made by host cities to fulfil Olympic expectations. They are crowded, colourful eventscapes during the Games but present problems in terms of their long-term relationship with the city. As large precincts in the heart of rapidly changing urban environments, many Olympic parks have been unable to generate demand for the facilities they offer and maintenance costs become an ongoing financial burden. If allowed to decline in use and appearance, they can be a cause of embarrassment rather than pride. For these reasons, the case study of the **Munich Olympic Park** provides valuable insight about the factors that have made the Park successful in its post-Olympic life.

MUNICH OLYMPIC PARK

By Nicola John

The Olympic Park in Munich can be considered a role model for the successful ongoing operation of an Olympic precinct. The park was constructed for the 1972 Summer Olympics but remains an integral component of Munich's urban landscape and is popular with both tourists and local citizens. A retrospective examination of the park demonstrates a link between favourable preconditions, future-oriented actions and its present-day status.

When Munich applied for the 1972 Olympic Games in 1966, all the city could offer in terms of sports venues was two stadiums and one swimming pool (Münchner Olympiapark GmbH, 1982). However, they were considered too small for a major sporting event and hosting the Games demanded building a whole new Olympic precinct for Munich, and the district of

Oberwiesenfeld was considered to be ideal. It was approximately three square kilometres in size, mainly waste ground and only four kilometres away from the city centre, making it possible to realize the concept 'Spiele der kurzen Wege' – the desire for all venues to be in close proximity (Münchner Olympiapark GmbH, 1982: 22). It was also the intention to host the Games in a green environment to provide a scenic backdrop for the festivities (Vogel, 1969a). Following a national competition, Behnisch and Partner were selected as the architects for the project. Unlike other entrants, their concept emphasised the integration of architecture and landscape, of buildings and nature (Münchner Olympiapark GmbH, 1982). The extensive project converted the *Oberwiesenfeld* into a parkland and included the extension of a pre-existing canal into an artificial lake as well as the transformation of a rubble mountain into a permanent hill. These architectonic elements reflected Munich's surrounding area and the alpine upland. The sports stadiums and other venues were then embedded into this landscape (Vogel, 1969b). To create a fit of these artificial buildings with the surrounding parklands, the architectural team designed a tented roof, which became and remains one of the city's main landmarks (Figure 4.5). It was built over the

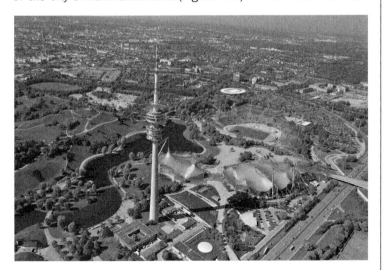

Figure 4.5 *Olympic Park, Munich.*

Source: Olympiapark München GmbH

Olympic Stadium, the Olympic Hall, the Olympic Swimming Pool as well as parts of the footpaths connecting them. According to Schall, on the one hand the tent structure 'was designed to make the big buildings appear lighter and free, to connect them, and create a look of structures in flight' (2002: 25). On the other hand, its shape was intended to be in line with the hilly parklands and to correspond with the alpine panorama that can be seen from the Olympic Hill in good weather (Schall, 2002). Another important concept was for the Games to be on a human scale (Schall, 2002). Significantly, there was recognition of the need to plan for future use of the park and its facilities with sustainability taking precedence over gigantism (Münchner Olympiapark GmbH, 1982).

According to Munich's former mayor, Dr Hans-Jochen Vogel, the role of the 1972 Olympics in Munich was to demonstrate a new Germany with different values and views than those presented during the Berlin Olympics in 1936. Instead of claims about power and monumentality, the Munich Olympics were intended to convey democracy, openness and worldliness (cited in Valentien, 2013). In terms of the park design, these modern and tolerant values were expressed through the open and transparent tented roofs, the extensive accessible green areas as well as the soft transitions between the individual architectonic elements.

The communication of this new attitude was supported by the visual design of the Olympics. Otl Aicher, who was one of Germany's most pioneering graphic designers, and his colleagues managed to realize what has become known as 'Corporate Design' (Schall, 2002: 22). Consistency in the application of colours, fonts, paper formats, pictograms and other design elements created a uniform appearance that 'successfully conveyed a sense of the Federal Republic as a modern and well-organized, yet informal and easy-going society' (Schiller and Young, 2010: 1). These central ideas of the 1972 Olympics ran like a common thread through planning and the realization of the Games. Besides being a venue for the sporting competitions, the park also functioned as a gathering place for everything that happened around the Games. The extensive cultural events, including music and street theatre, enabled the different cultures to compete on a non-sporting basis and promoted international understanding in a playful manner (Münchner Olympiapark GmbH, 1982). Unfortunately, on 5 September 1972, the Games were overshadowed by the fatal attack of a Palestinian terrorist group on the Israeli Olympic team.

The basis for a successful post-Games life for the venues was established in the early planning phase of the park. The *Olympiapark München GmbH*, the agency responsible for managing the park after the Games, was founded in 1970, two years ahead of the event. As soon as the Olympics were finished, there was a seamless transition to staging other events and competitions. The Olympic Stadium became the home stadium of Munich's famous soccer team *FC Bayern Munich* until they moved to a new stadium in 2005. It has been used for other sporting events, including the 2002 European Athletics Championships and the *X-Games Munich in 2013*, and concerts of renowned international artists are held in the stadium. The adjacent Olympic Hall is nowadays used for a variety of events, including congresses and concerts. At these venues, visitors predominantly take the role of spectators but the park also offers places for active participation in sport such as the Olympic Ice Sport Centre and the Olympic Swimming Pool, which are open to the public. Moreover, the natural setting of the park allows for a variety of outdoor activities. There is an outdoor cinema, short- and long-term festivals, Ski World Cups on the Olympic Hill and wakeboard events in the Olympic Lake. The Olympic Village has been used as a residential area, while the television and broadcasting station was transformed into a sport campus of the Technical University Munich and a centre for university sports. Although recreational activities play an increasing role in the park, professional sports are still firmly established, and the Bavarian elite track and field athletes have their primary training venue in the Olympic Park.

In the more than 45 years of post-games life the park has been subject to some modifications, but its overall appearance has not changed significantly. This is partly because the entire park has been protected as a historic monument since 1997, and the scope for modifications of the buildings are limited.

However, a new Sea Life aquarium was opened in 2006, the Olympic Ice Sporting Centre was extended, and later a part of it was converted into the SoccArena, an indoor soccer area open to the public. The relevance of recreational activities in the park was also emphasised by the construction of new venues, for example, the beach volleyball courts of the centre for university sports, which opened in 2017. The restoration of the Olympic Stadium will start in 2022, just after the fiftieth anniversary of the park (Abendzeitung, 2018).

The Olympic Park is not only one of Munich's most visited tourist attractions, but it is also an important resource for local residents. The outdoor areas provide an environment for a variety of sporting activities, which is well suited to the active lifestyle of Munich citizens. People go mountain biking on the hilly parklands, jogging around the Olympic Lake or sledding down the Olympic Hill in winter. Due to its proximity to the city centre and accessibility by public transport, the park serves as an everyday haven to many people who seek a healthy balance in their lives. Those who don't want to get physically active take the chance to picnic or just relax under the sun on the abundance of green areas. The variety of uses underlines the park's ongoing significance for the city.

Protection of the park's architecture will remain one of its priorities, and a first step regarding an application for it to be listed as a UNESCO World Heritage site has already been made by the city council (Presse- und Informationsamt der Landeshauptstadt München, 2018). This status would provide benefits, but may also present challenges. 'I am sure, the park would profit in terms of popularity', states Benedikt Happe, Project Manager of the *Olympiapark München GmbH* since 2010, in a personal interview on 10 December 2018. Nevertheless, he emphasises that the park's main idea has always been to function as a sports precinct instead of an open-air museum. Therefore, a challenge would be to maintain the balance between the protection of the architecture on the one hand and its appeal and relevance as a sports and events venue on the other hand.

Multiple settings

Wynn's (2015) third spatial model of events is a confetti pattern where a great variety of locations are used. He suggests that the involvement of so many actors is inevitably accompanied by a loss of control for event organisers but, at open access events, such as the **Adelaide Fringe**, control is less important than facilitating high levels of participation and creative engagement. This event encourages venues, big and small to 'pop up' throughout the city as platforms for any artists who wish to share their work (Adelaide Fringe, 2017).

THE ADELAIDE FRINGE

By Heather Croall, Director and Chief Executive, Adelaide Fringe

There are over 300 Fringe festivals in the world and Adelaide is the second largest – second only to the Edinburgh Fringe, which is over 70 years old. The Adelaide Fringe was founded in 1960 and runs from February–March each year. Most Fringe festivals do not have the audience numbers or ticket sales that the Adelaide Fringe has, nor do they transform their entire city the way Adelaide Fringe does. Adelaide also has the incredible summer weather, a month of warm, balmy nights with thousands of people out enjoying wild Fringe fun under the big South Australian starry skies. It is a magical wonder-land that is enjoyed by people across an extremely wide demo-graphic. In 2018, the spread across age groups was under 18: 8 per cent; 18–27: 11 per cent; 28–37: 18 per cent; 8–47: 20 per cent; 48–57: 24 per cent; and 58+: 19 per cent. The size of the audience (2.7 million, in 2018) has been built over many decades, growing every year since the beginning. Some people who came to Fringe shows 40 and 50 years ago are still attending, coming with their (now adult) children and their grandchildren!

In 2018, 705,761 tickets were sold and the Adelaide Fringe is responsible for 40 per cent of ALL tickets sold at multi-art form festivals in Australia. Sales have grown by almost 10 per cent every year for the last few years. Over 1,200 shows from around Australia and the world were held in over 400 venues including a few massive outdoor hubs such as the Garden of

Unearthly Delights, Gluttony and the Royal Croquet Club that take over parklands and riverbanks with multiple tents and bars. Each of those super outdoor hubs sells in excess of 100,000 tickets. The other, more than 400 venues, range from 20-seater converted basements to 1,000-seat, fully functioning theatres and everything in between. The venues are magical spaces – big and small – where artists, covering a wide range of genres, present their work:

Genre	Number of shows
Comedy	341
Music	260
Theatre	128
Cabaret	127
Children's	96
Visual Art	77
Events	73
Circus/Physical Theatre	36
Dance	33
Interactive	25
Magic	22
Film and Digital	13

The Adelaide Fringe is not curated – the programme is created at a grass-roots level by the artists and venues who choose to be a part of it. As festival director, I'm here to drive the overall vibe of the festival, to set a vision that makes an impact and brings the city alive – we are one of the few Fringe festivals in the world that fully transforms a whole city. The only way we can do this is with the help from all our artists, venues, funders, sponsors and partners. The vibrancy in the city is underpinned by this ecosystem all working together.

The Adelaide Fringe Box Office sold $16.6 million worth of tickets in 2018 and, after ticketing fees, this is handed to the artists. That's the model of an open access Festival. The Artist (in a split with their venue) earns their own box office as opposed to curated festivals that normally offer the artist a guaranteed fee regardless of ticket sales. It means around $15 million dollars is injected into the arts sector each year as a result of the Adelaide Fringe. Of course not every show sells out but there are many ways an artist can walk away happy from the Fringe.

In 2018, 6,929 artists participated in the Fringe and, late at night, they gather at the famous Adelaide Fringe Club to perform to one another and have fun. Behind the scenes, there is a lot going on for artists that you might not notice at first glance. One thing is the Adelaide Fringe Artist Fund. We give out grants to Australian Artists to help them put on their shows in the Fringe. It is a wonderful way for us to foster new talent. To be able to give out these grants, we need to do some fundraising. We hold fundraising events that raise around $20,000 a year and we have micro-donations at point of ticket purchase that raises about $30,000. We also have a Friends of the Adelaide Fringe Artist Fund and these donors give $1,000 each. Then we give out the grants. This year we gave out $84,000 of grants and we also paid artists in other ways such as tickets for disadvantaged groups to attend Fringe shows thanks to the Artist Fund.

We also run a marketplace for artists behind the scenes at the Fringe. Buyers, Festival Directors and Programmers from around the country and the world descend on Adelaide scouting for new shows to book for the future. An Adelaide Fringe artist might finish the season with tours booked for the year ahead as a result of Honey Pot. The Honey Pot is a hidden gem; it's a marketplace where Fringe artists can do deals with the range of buyers from across the world. In 2018, 349 shows registered to be part of Honey Pot and 204 delegates came from 25 countries to discover new shows and talent. Of the deals that were completed, 78 per cent were booking for Australian artists and 48 per cent were for international tours. The marketplace is great for artists. It is also a great boost for the South Australian economy and our audiences. Attracting more buyers in the marketplace – local, national and international – means we attract more artists and attract more visitors who inject more money into the arts and into the South Australian economy. The 20,244 visitors to the state to attend the Fringe in 2018 generated 97,941 bed nights.

Finally, an important objective of the Adelaide Fringe is to develop young audiences and we run a Fringe Schools programme called YEP!. Many schools come out and see shows via the YEP! programme. YEP! is how we can build the Fringe audience of the future. Overall, the Adelaide Fringe was built on risk and innovation. The WOW! of the Fringe is made by the participants at every level – the artists, the venues, the audience and more! Everyone takes a risk and that is what gives Adelaide Fringe its edge and its energy.

The Adelaide Fringe occurs during what has become known as 'Mad March' when the Adelaide Festival and a number of other major events are held. During this time, much of the city is transformed by sounds and scenes that are absent during the rest of the year. Large banners that are hung above streets state that the Fringe is 'the party that defines a city'. The crowds that throng the streets late into the night are surrounded by musicians, magicians and clowns shouting directions to venues where their shows will be performed. Cafés become theatres, pubs stage comedy festivals and churches offer space for art displays. The venues and artists promote their shows by distributing leaflets on street corners. Small shipping containers and water tanks are dropped into position where pedestrians congregate and disappear under a mass of promotional messages. An annual competition is held to design the Fringe Poster and the winner provides a visual identity for the event. The most dramatic transformation occurs when the 'Garden of Unearthly Delights' and 'Gluttony' take over part of the city's Parklands. The trees in the normally quiet parks provide the backdrop for coloured lights as the grass disappears beneath tents, marquees, outdoor stages, food stalls and the crowds of people. An atmosphere of joyful excitement pervades the sites and extends into much of the city. The boundaries of the eventscape are fluid and are largely determined by the circulation of people as they move between event venues and visit cafés and bars. This is facilitated by street closures and the provision of additional space for outdoor dining and drinking. It is a very popular event where the spatial arrangements provide endless opportunities for local artists and local residents to participate. This contrasts with the tendency for many art events to privilege tourists and exclude residents (Quinn, 2005).

Routes

When an event follows a predetermined route it produces a spatial pattern that does not conform to any of Wynn's (2015) models. Parades usually follow a route through a city and many, such as Christmas pageants, encourage interaction between spectators, particularly children, and performers. Royal events are more formal and, in Britain, spectators are kept at a distance from the Queen and members of the Royal family. The Mall is London's famous ceremonial route, running from Buckingham Palace, through Admiralty Arch to Trafalgar Square. It has a synthetic surface that gives the appearance of a red carpet and is closed to traffic on Sundays, Public Holidays and ceremonial occasions when it is decorated with Union flags. At Trooping the Colour, the Royal procession arrives at Horse Guards Parade precisely as the clock strikes 11 and the Queen takes the Royal salute. The Royal processions are respected in Britain as an expression of tradition, discipline and practised precision.

The Queen's Diamond Jubilee in 2012 was marked with a pageant of 1,000 boats travelling along the River Thames, though the heart of London. A wealth of information about the event, the pageant boats and attractions along the route was provided on a website prepared by London-Town (see www.londontown.com/London/Thames-Diamond-Jubilee-Pageant). It included a link to download a hand-drawn infographic by Katherine Baxter whose work is discussed later in this chapter in the section on mapping eventscapes. A web page by Les Enfants – a children's event planning company, included a map prepared by Nikon that suggested the best places to view the pageant and gave advice about taking photographs of the event. Nikon also sponsored a competition that was published in the *Daily Telegraph* newspaper that encouraged photographers to capture 'the spirit of the Diamond Jubilee and the best of British' (Daily Telegraph, 2012). An online report by the BBC gave interesting information about the size of the event, the importance of the setting, cultural connections (historical, artistic and sporting), the role of the Royal Family, the dedication of, 'rain soaked' spectators and activities that augmented the event (Thomas, 2012). Celebratory parties were held around the country and overseas, demonstrating that a widely dispersed pattern of activities accompanies significant Royal events.

The formality of Royal processions is in marked contrast to many other type of parades such as those held during carnivals. In the case of the Venice Carnival, informality and the celebration of life's pleasures have been enjoyed in the days before Lent since the fifth century and it was mentioned in a Doge's charter as early as 1094. A time of disguise behind masks offers an opportunity to criticise and make fun so, during carnival, the aristocratic Republic became a democracy of laughter and joy (Visit-Venice-Italy, 2018). The Venice Carnival includes a Water Parade in which people wearing costumes travel in a flotilla of decorated gondolas and boats from the Punta della Dogana in St Mark's Basin, along the Grand Canal to the Rio di Cannaregio (Martin, 2017).

Carnivals are held in many places around the world, including countries throughout the Caribbean and in Brazil, where the blocos move through the streets of cities such as Salvadore and Recife. The events in these cities in the north-east of Brazil are famous throughout the country but do not have the international recognition that is attached to the Rio Carnival. The cost of tickets at the 90,000-seat Sambadrome in Rio and at Carnival Balls exclude many Brazilians from attending but locals flock to the street parties which are free. Information about the work of the Samba Schools and the life on the streets in Rio during the Carnival is provided on the Carnival website. The variety of experiences is evident in the descriptions of some of the most popular blocos. The Banda de Ipanema bloco parades along the beach at sunset and is popular with drag queens. Most people wear a veil as the Carmelitas bloco winds through the streets of the Santa Teresa district, celebrating a nun who left her convent to join the Carnival. The Cordão do Boitatá bloco parades through the historical quarter and is popular with families as it celebrates Brazilian folk traditions about a fire snake (Rio Carnival, 2018).

The displays on the streets of Rio during the Carnival are produced by community groups that live in favelas and neighbourhoods that are dispersed throughout the city. People spend much of the year working on carnival projects: writing songs, designing dance routines and making the elaborate costumes for the local samba school. Many hours are spent practising and perfecting the performances. An analysis of where these activities take place would produce a picture of an extensive spatial network of activities without which the Carnival would not exist. In December, the samba schools begin holding technical rehearsals at the Sambadrome. The official Carnival parades take place just before the start of Lent. They are held for four consecutive nights, during which the schools parade one after another from 8 pm until the morning. Each school is allocated 85 minutes to parade along the length of the Sambadrome in front of the judges. The *A Series* samba schools perform on Friday and Saturday, and the elite *Special Group* schools perform on Sunday and Monday.

The Sambadrome is a particularly interesting eventscape. Built in 1984, it is 700 metres long and 13 metres wide with grandstands on each side and a square at the end where an arch, designed by Oscar Niemeyer, serves as a symbol of the Carnival. It was used as the venue for archery and for the closing stages of the marathons in the 2016 Olympics and concerts are held in the square from time to time. But, for most of the year, the Sambadrome stands as an empty concrete expanse until, during four nights in February each year, it can lay claim to being the most colourful place on earth. The atmosphere is completely transformed and the bland background is lost beneath the colours of the parade.

Environments are transformed by events in many ways and not always for the better. On most days in the summer, in Notting Hill, London, the shop fronts along streets such as Westbourne Grove bring colour with flower displays and umbrellas above tables for outdoor dining. During the Carnival, everything is removed and shop windows disappear behind ugly boards covered in graffiti. However, the attention of the crowds is directed to the streets, as the parade passes by, not towards the boarded windows. When the Carnival is over, the litter is removed and the streets are cleaned, the boarding comes down and life returns to normal. The disruption associated with events can be beneficial, providing a boost to psychic income. The dedication in *Four Magical Days in May* states, 'This book tells the story of an extraordinary few days in May 2006 when a work of art turned a great capital city into a playground and London changed forever' (Webb, 2006: 2). The work of art featured a 40-foot-high elephant and an 18-foot-high girl, operated as mechanical puppets (Figure 4.6). The story, about a time-travelling elephant, was written by Royal de Luxe, a French theatre company, to mark the Jules Verne centenary. More than a million spec-

Figure 4.6 *Sultan's Elephant in the Mall, London.*

Source: Sophie Laslett

tators witnessed the puppets as they moved through the streets of London. The event was performed by Royal de Luxe and was produced by Artichoke, an arts charity, based in London that specialises in large, outdoor art productions in public spaces. After working on events at the Salisbury Festival, Artichoke approached the opportunity to produce events in London with considerable enthusiasm.

> We'd learnt huge lessons about transcending territories; the power of artists to transform familiar landscapes, – experiences that change lives forever. – that work that is highly professional, created by extraordinary imaginations, but also free and accessible, is just as important as anything taking place in a gallery, theatre or concert hall.
>
> (Marriage, 2006)

Four Magic Days in May was produced by Artichoke and includes photographs that capture the scale and atmosphere of the event. It also includes observations by people from a range of personal and professional backgrounds who witnessed the event. Quotes taken from *Four Magical Days in May* provide evidence that the joyous experience needed no instrumental justification and that London became a new city in terms of how it was used and perceived. So, Webb's (2006) 'changed forever' comment refers partly to the attitude of Londoners towards using spaces in the city as a performance playground and not just a setting for ceremonial pageants. It is of interest to note that this type of performance theatre grew in popularity in France during the 1980s, where cultural traditions encouraged the use of outdoor spaces for community activities and socialist national and local governments encouraged artistic creativity and provided financial support to make art accessible. This contrasted with a political climate in Britain at the time where economic rationalism required cultural organisations to be self-funding (Taylor, 2006).

FOUR MAGICAL DAYS IN MAY

A theatre critic:

> Ambling through the capital, the magnificent beast and his entourage changed forever the British idea of street theatre, and what it is to be in a crowd. It made Londoners look freshly at what they see every day; it created a new map of the city – it was a revelation, about the capital and about yourself, to watch with others as familiar landmarks changed their meaning before your eyes.

The Executive Director of Arts Council London:

> I know I'll never look at the National Gallery again without seeing the image of the elephant coming out of Haymarket and appearing, trunk first, against the backdrop of that building which seemed dwarfed by the elephant's presence. – I felt absolutely overjoyed at being in London – and loving the city which loved the elephant, and became a completely different place for all of us.

During the House of Lords debate on the Arts:

> I spent a large part of last Friday in the elephant's company along with an amazingly disparate crowd of others, and I can honestly say that it was one of the most uplifting, joyous, life enhancing days I have ever spent.

A journalist:

> If art is about transformations, there's no more transforming experience than *The Sultan's Elephant*. This is a show that disrupts the spectacle of everyday life and transforms the city from an impersonal place of work and business into a place of play and community.

At some sport events, the pattern of eventscapes is dictated by the routes taken by competitors. Mass participation events became a global phenomenon in the 1980s and marathons, held in cities such as Boston, New York and London, continue to attract large numbers of runners and an international television audience. The Great North Run started in 1981 and follows a route in north-east England, from the centre of Newcastle-upon-Tyne, across the Tyne Bridge and on to South Shields at the mouth of the river Tyne. Participants are attracted to the event for health reasons: making training part of a fitness regime, but the profile of the event and its popularity in the local community helps shape the social and place identities of 'Geordies' on Tyneside. Many events of this type have strong links with local charities, which benefit from event-related donations.

In rural areas, events such as car rallies see parts of forests transformed into eventscapes and professional cycling events are particularly interesting from the perspective of eventscape formation and impact. The Tour de France is the most celebrated of the Union Cycliste Internationale (UCI) series of races and ends with cyclists completing several laps along the

Champs-Élysées in Paris. The race has been described by Lamont and McKay as 'a fluid sporting phenomenon that traverses the French landscape' (2012: 314) which offers participants a 'kinesthetic submergence in the sportscape' (2012: 324). The affordances of the eventscape can be both challenging and visually stimulating for competitors due to the variability of the natural environment. This characteristic distinguishes this type of eventscape from many others where, as far as possible, consistent conditions are sought by those responsible for managing competitive environments.

The Santos Tour Down Under (TDU) is an excellent example of an event which moves through landscapes, connecting spatially dispersed natural and cultural resources. The TDU has been held annually in South Australia since 1999 and it was the first race outside Europe to be given UCI World Tour status. Over ten million spectators have watched the race in its 20-year history (TDU, 2018). It is owned and managed by Events South Australia, the major events division of the South Australian Tourism Commission (SATC) on behalf of the Government of South Australia. It is the largest cycling festival in the southern hemisphere and attracted 810,000 spectators in 2018 with 46,000 event-specific visitors from interstate or overseas (TDU, 2018). It is very popular with local residents with people of all ages participating in charity cycling events and street parties. The Hilton Adelaide in the centre of the CBD acts as the race headquarters and the City of Adelaide Tour Village is created for the duration of the event in Victoria Square opposite the Hilton. There is a street circuit held in the city and six stages of racing that takes competitors to regional locations, passing through wine areas and along the coastal fringe. The spectator experience and media coverage of the event are enhanced by the visual appeal of the scenic backdrops. The route that was held for Stage Five in 2019 is shown in Figure 4.7. The eventscape is created by the selection of routes, the location of support services and the behaviour of spectators and local businesses. Where there are soft spatial limits (Bale, 1994), spectators can move freely and find places where they can best view the race or socialise at pre- and post-race events. By doing so, they help define the boundaries of the eventscape which are extended when local businesses such as restaurants and entertainment venues offer event-related activities and services. These behaviours help create the event atmosphere and provide symbols that help define it. Communities located on the route are temporarily integrated by the event and can benefit through association with event stakeholders (Brown, Lee, King and Shipway, 2015). The landscape acts as an environmental resource but in most places a direct relationship between place and event is brief due to the speed of the peloton.

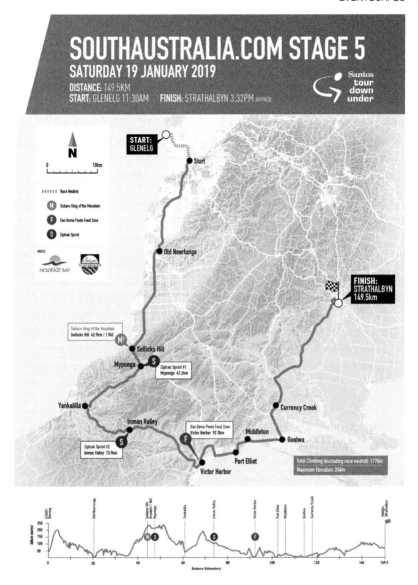

Figure 4.7 *Tour Down Under, Stage Five, 2019.*

Source: South Australian Tourist Commission

Cycle races are not the only type of event-related activity that moves through a landscape and the Olympic Torch Relay is a strategic initiative that is the product of detailed spatial planning. It attempts to connect as many communities as possible in the host country with the Olympics. The excitement and national pride generated by the Torch Relay is clearly demonstrated in two videos which show highlights of the 2010 Vancouver Olympic Games (see www.youtube.com/watch?v=nQDGgmufBI4; and www.youtube.com/watch?v=7v0o27BPIIk). In 2012, the torch visited 1,000 villages, towns and cities in Britain as it travelled from Land's End to the Olympic stadium in London (Lee and Brown, 2017). Route planning takes account of media interest and includes visits to scenic locations, important cultural sites and tourist attractions. The relay becomes a platform to promote the host country as a tourism destination and a unique type of eventscape is created. **The Sydney 2000 Torch Relay** demonstrates that it can be used to achieve a wide range of objectives.

THE SYDNEY 2000 TORCH RELAY

AMP, a financial services company based in Sydney, was the presenting partner for the Torch Relay at the 2000 Olympic Games. It was assisted by two other Team Millennium Olympic Partners: Ansett Australia, the official airline for the Games and the media organisation, News Limited. These Australian companies stimulated interest in the relay and encouraged engagement by community members at places visited by the Torch.

In 1999, AMP organised the *Ignite the Dream Tour* to 143 locations around Australia. It featured the Olympic mascots and an exhibition of Olympic torches from previous Games and served as a trial run for the Torch Relay. It provided an opportunity to work with the company's 1,500 advisors throughout the country who recommend AMP products. AMP's advisor-based distribution model made the Tour an important part of the company's leveraging strategy (Brown, 2000b).

After being lit in Olympia on 10 May, the torch made a tour of 12 countries in Oceania. On 8 June, it was brought from New Zealand to Uluru by Ansett Australia to start the journey around the host country. Media coverage of the arrival of the torch helped Ansett gain recognition for its role as the official airline for the Games. This was important to counter a widely held perception that its rival, Qantas Airways, was acting in this capacity (Brown, 2000b). Ansett provided flights and accommodation and purchased the Torch for employees who took part in the relay. Other staff benefited from the emotion and atmosphere created on planes and in airport lounges when torches and their bearers were travelling on Ansett flights (Brown, 2002). An employee recognition programme operated by AMP, named 'Champions' included opportunities for 200 staff and 150 advisors to carry the flame. This was part of an internal marketing campaign that sought to motivate staff during the period of the company's sponsorship. It involved a comprehensive communication strategy that included Olympic-themed information and motivational stories about the Games in newsletters and the provision of Olympic merchandise that was only available to AMP employees (Brown, 2007). Advantage was taken of the popularity of Olympic pin collecting with a three-part puzzle pin that was offered to staff in 1998, 1999 and 2000 (Brown, 2000b). 'Fun Days' for employees and their families were held when the torch arrived in the communities where they lived (Brown, 2002).

The Torch Relay included community celebrations and tangible products to make it possible for as many people as possible to share the spirit of the Sydney 2000 Olympic Games. Communication was critical and this was facilitated by local editions of News Limited newspapers, which gave information about the route, the date the torch would arrive in towns and the timing of activities. The style was motivational, featured local interest stories and encouraged children to collect Olympic pins. A pin album was available from News Limited, which included a map, identifying places along the relay route to which pins could be attached. Cauldron pins with the name of the town where celebrations where were held were particularly popular as tangible evidence of a place's connection to the event. In a similar way, AMP established a permanent, tangible connection with the communities that hosted celebrations by donating the cauldron that was used at each site. The backdrop of each cauldron showed a montage of photographs of local residents that had been taken during the *Ignite the Dream Tour* (Brown, 2002).

As tourism destinations, places on the relay route hoped to benefit from media coverage. The Australian Tourist Commission invited international journalists to participate in the Torch Relay to broaden the geographical scope of their

Games-related coverage. A particularly creative initiative was organised by an inbound tour operator, which encouraged people from the sister cities of places on the relay route to visit Australia. Many of the cities responded by sending groups of up to 180 people and, in total, 4,000 visitors travelled on regional tours after taking part in these torch celebrations (Brown, 2007).

The Torch Relay establishes spatial relationships at different geographical scales. At the 2000 Games, it created links between Olympia, countries in the South Pacific and Australia and, at a national scale, it was expressed as pins collected and placed on a colourful map in thousands of albums.

MAPPING EVENTSCAPES

A 'spatial turn' in a number of disciplines has been accompanied by an increased interest in maps among scholars in film and literary studies, art and visual culture, anthropology, cultural studies, architecture and popular music (Roberts, 2012). Missing from this list is event studies which is surprising as maps are an essential aid to event planning and are used to support stories about events in the media (Field, 2012). They help visitors make travel arrangements and orient their movements both to and within event sites. Maps that provide accurate information about spatial relationships help identify the location of venues, the routes of parades and the best place to view events such as cycle races which move through the landscape (see Figure 4.7). Recent technologies have made it possible for maps to offer connections to systems of information, creating link-ages to data about activities held in different places and at different times. Other maps present a graphic representation of the event environment in ways that affect the imageability of the host city (Hospers, 2009). In the context of festivalisation, globally transparent maps make territory legible (Tzanelli, 2018), turning land into landscape (Urry, 2004). Maps inform creative processes of ontological genesis (Roberts, 2012) and, using the language employed by Woods (2010), can bring an eventscape into being.

The information and imagery on maps is highly selective and, as early as the sixteenth century, Saxton's county maps in England were considered to be instruments of Tudor power (Cosgrove, 1985). They bear the imprint of contemporary social, cultural and political processes (Woods, 2010) and their preparation is pervaded by ideology (Harley, 2001). Positive features are accentuated while negative features are shrouded in darkness (Short, 1999) and Harley (2001) considered 'cartographic silence' to be a form of censorship. An emphasis on visually appealing characteristics has been compared with approaches adopted in place branding (Warnaby, 2015).

Koeck and Warnaby (2015) discuss the distinction between cartography and chorography. The authors refer to the analysis of Plato's *Timaeus* by Pérez-Gómez (1994) in which Plato's explanation of human space is seen as being a combination of *topos* (natural place) and *chora*. The Greek astronomer and geographer Ptolemy introduced the concept of chorography as the portrayal of a local area. Stylistically, it has been associated with a subjective and aesthetic orientation which incorporates elements of landscape painting (Casey, 2002). Adopting a 'celebratory' form (Cosgrove, 2008), chorography was commonly employed during the European Renaissance to prepare town portraits in profile or from an oblique perspective. The former provided a low, distant viewpoint with some of the space occupied by the sky. In contrast, the *pianta prospective* placed man, like God, at the circumference of Renaissance space, offering a bird's-eye view with the city revealed as a theatre (Cosgrove, 1985, 2008). Cosgrove (1985) cites the example of Barbari's 1500 map of Venice as an example of this perspective, describing it as an expression of urban dominion with sweeping panoramas in the style of landscapes by Bruegel and Titian. An Elizabethan map that was published in 1598 showed three people in front of an oblique rendering of the city of London. It included three-dimensional drawings and a relationship between people and place that was described as 'urban spectatorship' (Keock and Warnaby, 2015). From the Enlightenment, projections of the globe made cartographers 'set designers' for the expanding appropriation of space (Cosgrove, 1985: 46). In the 1860s, the cartographical imagination was expanded by the French pioneer of photography Nadar, who used a tethered balloon to experiment with aerial views of Paris (Gandy, 2017). A 'rhetoric of practicality' (Cosgrove, 2008) saw the production of functional maps at different scales that monitored and made legible the growth of cities.

Recent trends in mapping, with space broken into themes are indicative of a return to a more chorographic approach that can be seen in guides and tourist maps. Isometric projections have been used to highlight important buildings and the most striking visual features, 'echoing the work of a caricaturist' (Warnaby, Keock and Medway, 2017: 105). In addition, satellite and digital technologies make it possible to move from aerial to three-dimensional ground-based perspectives with a menu of information accessible via mobile portals. Consequently, the importance and relevance of maps for place representation widens out to an amalgam of visual forms (photographs, pictures, graphic design, symbols) and characteristics (colour, lighting, shading), which translates easily to the ocular vehicles of printed (leaflets, brochures, billboards) and screen-based media channels (TV, cinema, mobile, tablet and PC).

(Warnaby *et al.*, 2017: 105)

An interactive map of the Vancouver 2010 Olympic Games offered the flexibility to move from an aerial view of mountain scenery to an immersive, ground-level experience. By clicking on a date, a list was provided of events held on that day and a sport icon gave details of the venue where the event was held. In a review of the use of maps at the London 2012 Olympics, it was claimed that cartography was 'showcased exceptionally well during the Games' (Field, 2012: 281). Field (2012) described how the graphic requirements associated with the official look and the branding of the Games affected the design of maps produced by Transport for London and by the Geographers' A–Z Company that produced a range of Olympic maps under license to the organising committee. Stamen Design were contracted to build maps for the LOCOG website which, prior to the Games, provided geo-coded articles and imagery to encourage engagement. During the Games, they were modified to act as a navigable tool for the event schedule (Field, 2012). Field was particularly impressed by 'a visually stunning map of the Olympic venues' (2012: 284), produced by Katherine Baxter for Londontown (Figure 4.8). It adopted an isometric projection with 'superb hand-drawn renderings of the key buildings and landmarks' (Field, 2012: 284). Selectivity is clearly evident but the familiarity of the landmarks enhanced the city's legibility and made it the type of map, which becomes an emotionally charged artefact to which people make connections (Palmer and Lester, 2013). A transformative function is illustrated by Field's comment that Baxter's map 'certainly gives a sense of the city being taken over by the Games and displaying the venues in such close proximity on the map, while distorting reality, suggests London itself as the Olympic village' (Field, 2012: 284). This echoed newspaper articles in 2005, which announced that London had won the bid to host the 2012 Games. A map of London published in the *Evening Standard* at this time identified the location of event venues and it was used to claim that the whole of the city would have 'the chance to live the experience of the Games' (Evening Standard, 2005: 10).

Field (2012) suggests that there has been a digital mapping revolution that has produced a landscape that is unrecognisable from that of 2005, when Google Maps was introduced. His article includes a large number of

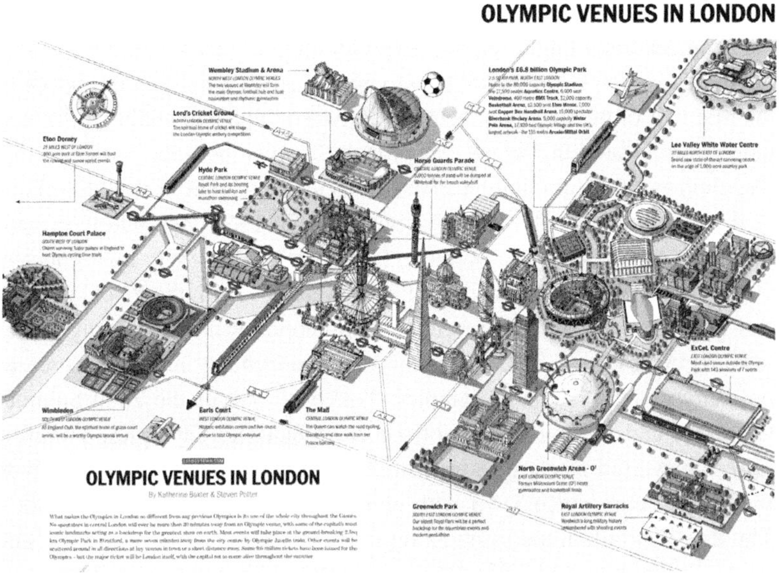

OLYMPIC VENUES IN LONDON

Figure 4.8 *Artistic cartography at London 2012.*

Source: Katherine Baxter

colourful figures to illustrate the wide range of Olympic-related information that is presented on maps. The official LOCOG website provided a map of the Torch Relay, which showed the route and gave detailed information about places along the route. An interactive 'Route and Pub Finder' map, designed for Coca-Cola, one of the sponsors of the Torch Relay, showed pubs that were located close to the relay route (Field, 2012). The Royal Mail produced a web map showing the location of postboxes that had been painted gold near the home of gold medal-winning athletes. By clicking on the box, information was given about the athlete and their medal-winning performance. Another map using a cartogram design showed which counties in the UK had produced Olympians from 1896 to 2012 (Field, 2012). It supported the Games 'Inspire a Generation' initiative as identifying with local sporting heroes has been found to encourage people to take part in sport (Brown, Essex, Assaker and Smith, 2017).

Maps published by media organisations take advantage of opportunities to provide contextual, particularly historical, information. A map of the world, in *The Economist*, gave information about the countries that have participated in each of the modern Olympiads. By clicking on the first button, 14 countries were highlighted on the map as participants in the

Games held in Athens in 1896. Fifty-nine countries were highlighted on the map for the London Games in 1948 and 208 countries for the Rio Olympics in 2016. Almost all the Olympic Games were held in Europe in the first half of the twentieth century. Between 1908 and 1952, all the host cities were located in Europe except in 1932 when both the Summer (Los Angeles) and Winter Olympics (Lake Placid) were held in the USA. Four of the seven Summer Olympic Games between 1968 and 1996 were held in North America (1968: Mexico; 1976: Montreal; 1984: Los Angeles; 1996: Atlanta) and the Winter Olympics were held in Lake Placid in 1980 and in Calgary in 1988. A recent shift in geopolitical and sporting power towards Asia has seen the selection of Pyeongchang in South Korea as host city of 2018 Winter Olympics, Tokyo as host of the 2020 Summer Olympics and Beijing as host of the 2022 Summer Olympics. The *New York Times* used Dorling cartograms to show the number of medals won by each country since 1896 with animations revealing annual statistics. The use of proportional symbols on maps produced in the *Guardian* and the *Daily Telegraph* identified the impact of factors such as population size on medal success. A map published in the *Huffington Post* that was commended for its design and attention to detail, allowed users to explore the medal count for individual sports, by country and GDP (Field, 2012).

Counter-mapping is used to challenge and modify hegemonic spatial formations (Roberts, 2012) and famous symbols provide a powerful medium to communicate alternative visions. A map that used the Olympic rings to show levels of inequality in the five regions of the world became a 'viral infographic' (Field, 2012). Transport for London created a special Olympic Legends Underground Map to celebrate the London 2012 Games on which the names of the 361 tube stations were changed to the names of Olympic athletes (Degun, 2012). The map, designed by a BBC sports journalist and a sports historian, provided an opportunity for countries to draw attention to the recognition accorded to their athletes. A webpage of the Australian Olympic Committee highlighted the large number of Australian athletes that featured on the map and the fact that Oxford Circus had become Ian Thorpe (Australian Olympic Committee, 2012). In another example, Beck's Underground map was distorted to show lines in the shape of the Olympic rings with stations named after Olympic sponsors (Figure 4.9). Information above the rings stated that the stations would not be operating during the Games due to 'profiteering works' (Pablo, 2012). This is an example of using graphic imagery to raise awareness of geopolitical indignities (Amin, 2008). During personal communication in 2018, the designer of the map commented that he thought the map made a valuable observation at the time but he is now a little embarrassed by it and wishes the

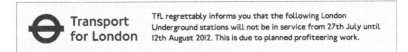

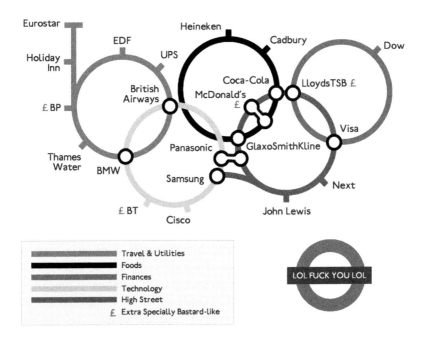

Figure 4.9 *Disruptive cartography at London 2012.*

Source: Harper/telekin

country could go back to the social and economic situation that existed in 2012. The fame of the London Underground map and its ability to connect people with the city had been exploited in the handover section of the Closing Ceremony at the Beijing Olympics. The introduction of the next host city included an animation in which a London bus passed iconic landmarks such as Big Ben and St Paul's Cathedral while morphing in and out of a tube map.

Prior to the 2016 Olympic Games in Rio de Janeiro, a map was published in the *Daily Mail* giving information at three spatial scales (Plate 5). The top half offered a bird's-eye view of venues located at the Olympic Park, showing a colourful parrot flying above the Aquatic Stadium. Below, a map showed the location of the Olympic Park in the Barra zone and the three other Olympic zones at Deodora, Maracanã and Copacabana. The sports staged at the venues in each zone were indicated by icons and a key.

To the right, maps of Brazil and the UK indicated the relative size of the countries and the location of Brazil's main cities including Rio de Janeiro. Maps employ techniques to increase levels of engagement and a colourful interactive map by Fiasco Design showed many of Rio's famous landmarks and included sound effects and animated features such as moving cable cars and flying parrots (Plate 6). It also included a treasure hunt that encouraged people to enter into the landscape. Exploration was facilitated by clicking on places on the map to reveal information about the city, its people and history as well as facts about the 2016 Olympic Games. A photo taken by NASA's Terra satellite just prior to the opening ceremony of the 2016 Games showed a 378 kilometre view of Brazil with Rio clearly visible in the centre. Next to the photo, a map with measures of aerosol optical depth was superimposed over the image to show the amount of air pollution recorded above the host city.

The examples of event mapping demonstrate what Ingold (2000) has called a totalising vision of cartography. A global perspective is facilitated by technologies which deliver images of the world as past and present geographies which can be distributed instantaneously. With an increase in participative practices and the use of a wide range of media and visual styles, there has been a loosening of cartographic definition (Crouch and Matless, 1996) and a blurring of the boundaries between maps and images (Roberts, 2012). Maps continue to attract visitors, encourage mobility and assist wayfinding but they do much more. By adopting the categories outlined by Roberts (2012), an eventscape map can be:

- *Iconographic*, when using famous landmarks to create an image of the event and a symbol of the host environment.
- *Ethnographic*, if the framing reflects social practices embedded at an event.
- *Performative*, when places to play and spaces of performance at an event are identified.
- *Psychographic*, when the viewer is invited to imagine the potential of the eventscape as a malleable space and a dynamic assemblage.
- *Mnemonic*, when it serves as a memory map and a vehicle to revisit experiences gained in the eventscape.

SUMMARY

It is difficult to categorise eventscapes due to the variability in the spatial form of these environments. However, Wynn's (2015) 'ideal types' model provides a valuable framework for the analysis of eventscapes and the examples discussed in this chapter help understand the factors that affect their development and their impact on event management and event experiences. The resource base influences the feasibility of holding events in particular locations but the flexibility of events, their transportability and their ability to attract people to almost any environment was illustrated by the contrasting examples of an eventscape at a large sand dune in outback Australia and another on a frozen lake in Switzerland. Photographic images can make dramatic statements and this was demonstrated by the photos of the Beach Volleyball eventscapes at the Olympic Games: at Horse Guards Parade in London in 2012 and on Copacabana beach in Rio de Janeiro in 2016.

The success of eventscapes depends on spatial relationships and organisational networks. A single site may have the advantage of delivering a self-contained experience but its market position and the cognition of attendees are inevitably placed in a broader socio-cultural context. This was demonstrated in many of the cases including the Byron Bay and Mysteryland music festivals. The evidence of conative relationships was strong at parades and 'confetti' eventscapes such as the Adelaide Fringe, when the spatial pattern is determined by people moving between venues and performing connections with cafés, bars other businesses en route. In the case of precincts, there needs to be coordination between the managers of the different venues at the precinct and, as a management group, they benefit from partnerships with businesses in the surrounding environment. The connectivity created by an event is particularly significant at fluid events such as cycle races that move through an expansive landscape.

The representation of spatial relationships is fundamental to map design and those included in this chapter show the location of activity zones and the artistic depiction of purposefully selected landmarks. It is surprising that this subject is largely absent from the event management literature. It may be that familiarity breeds contempt as there is endless variety in the type of event information that is displayed on maps: on billboards, in printed form and, increasingly, as electronic data. There is scope for research which seeks to interpret the ideological bias of event maps and to analyse the visual techniques they employ.

REFERENCES

Abendzeitung (2018). *Olympiastadion für zwei Jahre dicht.* www.abendzeitung-muenchen.de/inhalt.sanierung-ab-herbst-2022-olympiastadion-fuer-zwei-jahre-dicht.3f4ef736-0c6c-47a2-9a8f-24f5c6784619.html.
Adelaide Fringe (2017). *About Us: Adelaide Fringe.* www.adelaidefringe.com.au/about-us.

Amin, A. (2008). Collective Culture and Urban Public Space. *City*, 12(1): 5–24.

Australian Olympic Committee (2012). Olympians Take Over London Underground. *News*, 29 March. http://corporate.olympics.com.au/news/olympians-take-over-london-underground.

Bale, J. (1994). *Landscapes of Modern Sport*. Leicester: Leicester University Press.

Bennett, T. (1991). The Shaping of Things to Come: Expo '88. *Cultural Studies*, 5: 30–51.

Brown, G. (2000a). Revisiting the Millennium: The Marketing of Sunrise 2000. *Journal of Vacation Marketing*, 7(3): 247–258.

Brown, G. (2000b). Emerging Issues in Olympic Sponsorship: Implications for Tourism. *Sport Management Review*, 3: 71–92.

Brown, G. (2002). Taking the Pulse of Olympic Sponsorship. *Event Management*, 7: 187–196.

Brown, G. (2007). Sponsor Hospitality at the Olympic Games: An Analysis of the Implications for Tourism. *International Journal of Tourism Research*, 9: 315–327.

Brown, G., Essex, S., Assaker, G. and Smith, A. (2017). Sport Involvement, Event Satisfaction and Behavioural Intentions: Examining the Impact of the London 2102 Olympic Games on Participation in Sport. *European Sport Management Quarterly*, 17(3): 331–348.

Brown, G. and Huang, S. (2015). Interpreting Tourism at Olympic Sites: A Cross-Cultural Analysis of the Beijing Olympic Green. *International Journal of Tourism Research*, 17(4): 364–374.

Brown, G., Lee, I. S., King, K. and Shipway, R. (2015). Eventscapes and the Creation of Event Legacies. *Annals of Leisure Research* 18(4): 510–527.

Cable, J. (2012). Volleyball Venue is Party Central. *ESPN*, 31 July. www.espn.com.au/skiing/summer/2012/espnw/story/_/id/8213773/undefined.

Casey, E. S. (2002). *Representing Place: Landscape Painting and Maps*. Minneapolis, MN: University of Minnesota Press.

Cheng, L. (2018). *Brisbane's Expo 88 Celebrates 30th Anniversary*. https://architectureau.com/articles/brisbanes-expo-88-celebrates-30th-anniversary/.

Cosgrove, D. (1985). Prospect, Perspective and the Evolution of the Landscape Idea. *Transactions of the Institute of British Geographers*, 10: 45–62.

Cosgrove, D. (2008). *Geography and Vision: Seeing, Imagining and Representing the World*. New York: I. B. Tauris.

Crouch, D. and Matless, D. (1996). Refiguring Geography: Parish Maps of Common Ground. *Transactions of the Institute of British Geographers* 21(1): 236–255.

Daily Telegraph (2012). Battersea Park Diamond Jubilee Photo Competition. *Daily Telegraph*, 30 May. www.telegraph.co.uk/culture/photography/9300691/Battersea-Park-Diamond-Jubilee-Photo-Competition.html.

Davies, R. (1990). Urban Redevelopment: A Case Study of the Impact of the World Expo 88. In: R. Ritchie, ed., *Australian Geography: Current Issues*. Sydney: McGraw-Hill.

Degun, T. (2012). Tube Map Stops Named after Olympic Icons to Celebrate London 2012. *Inside the Games*, 29 March. www.insidethegames.biz/articles/16412/tube-map-stops-named-after-olympic-and-paralympic-icons-to-celebrate-london-2012.

De Lisle, J. (2009). After the Gold Rush: The Beijing Olympics and China's Evolving International Roles. *Orbis*, 53(2): 179–204.

Donovan, G. (2018). Birdsville Big Red Bash. Submission to the 2018. *Australian Event Awards.*

Evening Standard (2005). We've Won It. *The Evening Standard Olympic Special*, 7 July.

Field, K. (2012). Mapping the London Olympics. *The Cartographic Journal*, 49(3): 281–296.

Foundation Expo '88 (2004). *About World Expo '88: Attendance.* www.foundation expo88.org/aboutattendance.html.

Gandy, M. (2017). Urban Atmospheres. *Cultural Geographies*, 24(3): 353–374.

Gold Coast Event Guide (2018). www.worldsurfleague.com/posts/91989/quiksilver-pro-roxy-pro-gold-coast-guide.

Harley, J. B. (2001). Silences and Secrecy: The Hidden Agenda of Cartography in Early Modern Europe. In: J. B. Harley. *The New Nature of Maps: Essays in the History of Cartography*. London: Johns Hopkins University Press, 83–107.

Hartman, L. and Brown, G. (2004). The 30 Second Tourism Event – A Total Eclipse of the Sun in Outback Australia. In: P. Long and M. Robinson, eds, *Festivals and Tourism: Marketing, Management and Evaluation*. Sunderland: Business Education, 101–114.

Hinch, T. and Higham, J. (2011). *Sport Tourism Development*, 2nd edn. Bristol: Channel View.

Hine, R., ed. (2018). Snow Polo History. *Brochure Snow Polo World Cup*, 26–28 January, St. Moritz. Bishops Norton: The Polo Magazine.

Hospers, G.-J. (2009). Lynch, Urry and City Marketing: Taking Advantage of the City as a Built and Graphic Image. *Place Branding and Public Diplomacy*, 5(3): 226–233.

Ingold, T. (2000). *The Perception of the Environment: Essays in Livelihood, Dwelling and Skill*. London: Routledge.

Julier, G. (2005). Urban Designscapes and the Production of Aesthetic Consent. *Urban Studies*, 42(5–6): 869–887.

Keock, R. and Warnaby, G. (2015). Digital Chorographies: Conceptualizing Experiential Representations and Marketing of Urban/Architectural Geographies. *Architectural Research Quarterly*, 19(2): 183–191.

Lamont, M. and McKay, J. (2012). Intimations of Postmodernity in Sports Tourism at the Tour de France. *Journal of Sport & Tourism*, 17(4): 313–331.

Lee, I. S. and Brown, G. (2017). Sport Event Management. In: T. Bradbury and I. O'Boyle, eds, *Understanding Sport Management: International Perspectives*. Abingdon: Routledge, 243–258.

Mackinnon, M. (2010). Expo 2010 Confirms How China has Moved to World's Centre Stage. *The Globe & Mail.* First published 30 April. www.theglobeand

mail.com/news/world/expo-2010-confirms-how-china-has-moved-to-worlds-centre-stage/article1381254/.

Marriage, H. (2006). Foreword. In: N. Webb, ed., *Four Magical Days in May: How an Elephant Captured the Heart of a City*. London: Artichoke Trust.

Martin, J. (2017). This Year's Stunning Venice Carnival Launches a Colourful Water Parade. *Lonely Planet*, 13 February. www.lonelyplanet.com/news/2017/02/13/venice-carnival-launches-colourful-water-parade/.

Meek, B. (2018). Personal communication with the Event Manager, Byron Bay Bluesfest.

Meyer, M. (2009). One World, One Dream One Year Later. *Sports Illustrated*, 111(4): 66–72.

Minter, A. (2010). China Rules the World at Expo 2010. *The Atlantic*, 29 April. www.theatlantic.com/international/archive/2010/04/china-rules-the-world-at-expo-2010/39566/.

Münchner Olympiapark GmbH (1982). *Der Münchner Olympia-Park: Geschichte – Gegenwart – Daten*. Munich: Heyne.

Noble, L. (2001). South Bank Dreaming. *Architecture Australia*, 90: 86–93.

Our Brisbane (2009). *Expo 88 Remembered*. www.ourbrisbane.com/see-and-do/expo-88-remembered.

Pablo, K. (2012). The Olympic Semiosphere. *The Disorder of Things*, 10 August. https://thedisorderofthings.com/tag/olympic-games/.

Palmer, C. and Lester, J.-A. (2013). Maps, Mapping and Materiality: Navigating London. In: C. Scarles and J.-A. Lester, eds, *Mediating the Tourist Experience: From Brochures to Virtual Encounters*. London: Routledge, 237–254.

Pérez-Gómez, A. (1994). Chora: The Space of Architectural Representation. In: A. Pérez-Gómez and S. Parcell, eds, *Chora 1: Intervals in the Philosophy of Architecture*. Montreal: McGill University Press, 1–34.

Presse- und Informationsamt der Landeshauptstadt München. (2018). Olympiapark als UNESCO-Weltkulturerbe: Stadtrat stellt weichen. *Rathaus Umschau*, 74: 3–4.

Quinn, B. (2005). Arts Festivals and the City. *Urban Studies*, 42(5–6): 927–943.

Ren, X. (2008). Architecture and Nation Building in the Age of Globalization: Construction of the National Stadium of Beijing for the 2008 Olympics. *Journal of Urban Affairs*, 30(2): 175–190.

Rio Carnival (2018). Street Parties. *Rio Carnival*. www.riocarnival.net/rio-carnival/street-parties.

Roberts, L. (2012). Mapping Cultures: A Spatial Anthropology. In: L. Roberts, ed., *Mapping Cultures: Place, Practice, Performance*. Basingstoke: Palgrave Macmillan, 1–25.

Sanderson, R. (2003). Queensland Shows the World: Regionalism and Modernity at Brisbane's World Expo '88. *Journal of Australian Studies*, 65–75: 229–230.

Schall, U. (2002). *Olympiapark München. Das Dach der Welt – Sport und Vergnügen für Millionen*. Munich: Olympiapark München GmbH.

Schiller, K. and Young, C. (2010). Motion and Landscape: Otl Aicher, Günther Grzimek and the Graphic and Garden Designs of the 1972 Munich Olympics. *Urban History*, 37(2): 272–288.

Short, J. R. (1999). Urban Imagineers: Boosterism and the Representation of Cities. In: A. E. A. Jonas and D. Wilson, eds, *The Urban Growth Machine: Critical Perspectives Two Decades Later*. New York: State University of New York Press, 37–54.

Simonot, S. (2017). Coolangatta Beach Egyptian-Themed Opera Spectacular Aida to Run from Next Week. *Gold Coast Bulletin*, 15 September. www.goldcoast bulletin.com.au/entertainment/coolangatta-beach-egyptianthemed-opera-spectacular-adia-to-run-from-next-week/news-story/324956372b8b969d29053 ebea90d388e.

Smith, A. (2016). *Events in the City: Using Public Spaces as Event Venues*. Abingdon: Routledge.

Taylor, E. (2006). The Great Divide. In: N. Webb, ed., *Four Magical Days in May: How an Elephant Captured the Heart of a City*. London: Artichoke Trust, 65–67.

Thomas, P. (2012). Diamond Jubilee Thames Pageant Cheered by Crowds. *BBC News*, 3 June. www.bbc.com/news/uk-18312403.

Tzanelli, R. (2018). *Mega Events as Economies of the Imagination: Creating Atmospheres for Rio 2016 and Tokyo 2020*. London: Routledge.

TDU (Tour Down Under) (2018). 2018 Santos Tour Down Under Attracts Record Number of Visitors to South Australia. *Santos Tour Down Under News*, 15 May. www.tourdownunder.com.au/news/2018/may/15/2018-santos-tour-down-under-attracts-record-number-of-visitors-to-south-australia.

Urry, J. (2004). Death in Venice. In: M. Sheller and J. Urry, eds, *Tourism Mobilities*. London: Routledge, 205–215.

Valentien, C. (2013). Günther Grzimek als Landschaftsarchitekt und Hochschullehrer. In: S. Hennecke, R. Keller and J. Schneegans, eds, *Demokratisches Grün: Olympiapark München*. Berlin: Jovis Verlag GmbH, 128–136.

Vancouver 2010 (2002). *The Sea to Sky Games*. Vancouver 2010 Bid Corporation.

Visit-Venice-Italy (2018). History of the Carnival in Venice. *Visit Venice*. www. visit-venice-italy.com/history_of_the_carnival_in_venice.htm.

Vogel, H. (1969a). Foreword. In: H. Weitpert, ed., *Olympia in München*. Munich: Münchner Leben GmbH, 8–9.

Vogel, H. (1969b). Investitionen von bleibendem Wert. In: H. Weitpert, ed., *Olympia in München*. Munich: Münchner Leben GmbH.

Warnaby, G. (2015). Rethinking the Visual Communication of the Place Brand: A Contemporary Role for Chorography? In: M. Kavaratzis, G. Warnaby and G. J. Ashworth, eds, *Rethinking Place Branding: Comprehensive Brand Development for Cities and Regions*. New York: Springer, 175–190.

Warnaby, G., Keock, R. and Medway, D. (2017). Maps and Tours as Metaphors for Conceptualizing Urban Place Representation for Marketing/Branding Purposes. In: M. Kavaratzis, G. Massimo and M. Lichrou, eds, *Inclusive Place Branding: Critical Perspectives on Theory and Practice*. London: Routledge, 96–110.

Webb, N. (2006). *Four Magical Days in May: How an Elephant Captured the Heart of a City*. London: Artichoke Trust.

Weber, M. (1978). *Economy and Society: An Outline of Interpretive Sociology.* Berkeley, CA: University of California Press.

Woods, D. (2010). *Rethinking the Power of Maps.* New York: Guilford Press.

Wynn, J. (2015). *Music City. American Festivals and Placemaking in Austin, Nashville, and Newport.* Chicago, IL: University of Chicago Press.

Zhang, L. and Zhao, S. (2009). City Branding and the Olympic Effect: A Case of Beijing. *Cities*, 26: 245–254.

Zhou, P. X. W. and Leslie-Carter, R. (2010). Lessons Learned from Managing the Design of the 'Water Cube' National Swimming Centre for the Beijing 2008 Olympic Games. *Architectural Engineering and Design Management*, 6(3): 175–188.

Transformations by 5 design

INTRODUCTION

This chapter examines the visual transformation of eventscapes by focusing on the impact created by graphic design. Of particular interest is the importance placed on the development of a distinctive look that seeks to capture the relationship between an event and the environment where it is held. A visual identity seeks to communicate with a wide range of stakeholders and to enhance event experiences. It should also express values associated with the event and the host environment. There are similarities with place branding but, in a broader context, it can be analysed as part of design culture. The emergence of design culture and the way it is structured is discussed before considering the language of place from a marketing perspective. This is followed by a series of examples that illustrate the way the design of a 'look' has become an increasingly important endeavour at the Olympic Games.

DESIGN CULTURE

According to Julier (2006), visual culture emerged in the 1990s through the combination of art history and cultural studies. The relationship between the viewer and the viewed was the key orientation for scholarly enquiries. This was in response to the belief that the visual had become a dominant characteristic of modernity and a commonplace feature of everyday life. It reflected the importance of visual technologies, the voracious demand for images in advertising (Julier, 2006) and the instantaneous gratification that is offered by the consumption of signs (Jirásek and Kohe, 2015). However, Julier (2006) suggests that the emphasis placed on 'a way of looking' at a produced object by an alienated viewer is not adequate to understand embodied engagement with design in contemporary society. With reference to Lash's (2002) idea of an architectonic, spatially based society with three-dimensional culture and Foster's (2002) writings about the re-making of space in the image of a commodity, Julier proposes that design is about 'the structuring of systems of encounter within the visual and material world' (2006: 67) in which people, rather than merely observing, step into and become immersed in objects. The engagement of youth culture in urban nightscapes of designer bars and clubs (Chatterton and Hollands, 2003) is cited as an example of 'immersion in a specific (designerly) ambiance' (Julier, 2006: 71). Information is presented in architectonic planes where convergent media offer experiential moments and it is necessary to recognise the role of spatial and temporal cognition in addition to visual cognition in order to understand design culture. Value is created by the reproduction of 'product nodes' where 'cultural information is filtered through a range of platforms and moments' (Julier, 2006: 74) with design mobilised by leisure practices that 'provide structures of engagement' (Julier, 2006: 74). Consistent with this framework, an eventscape equates to a design platform for an event where immersion offers experiential moments and encounters with a range of media.

Design culture is expressed in eventscapes. They are part of the flows of global culture and, while located in network society, they are also an instrument of it (Julier, 2006). They are subject to contextual influences such as the way features of a location produce particularised actions. This can be seen at events when local actors make distinctive adaptations in response to cultural and environmental characteristics. Systems of negotiation are central to the realization of design projects where teamwork is defined by creative empowerment and innovation (Julier, 2006). The model proposed by Julier concerns the interrelationships between designers and the production and consumption of objects, images and space. It requires an analysis of 'the dynamics and effects of material and immaterial relationships that are articulated by and through the multiple artifacts of design culture' (2006: 73). As a forum of communication, it is used to establish a symbolic value for a location where 'the systems of branding inhabit much of the space of design culture, turning information into an "all-around-us" architectonic form' (Julier, 2006: 75).

Trends in urban design are producing a city of surfaces (Degen, DeSilvey and Rose, 2008), which are exploited by outdoor advertising with the adoption of new technologies seeing a transition from two-dimensional (2D) to three- and four-dimensional (3D/4D) and to multidimensional forms of communication. This is producing a move from visual to embodied to performative marketing activities and is redefining the way people connect with the changing urban landscape (Koeck and Warnaby, 2014). The simplicity of 2D advertising makes it a very democratic form of communication and early printing technology made it possible to mass-produce messages that included colour images such as those that appeared on travel posters, as illustrated in Figures 3.2 and 3.3. They needed to be placed in locations where they would be seen by the target market. This remains true today and the relationship between promotional cycles and the rhythms of urban life was discussed in Chapter 3.

The place where an advertisement is located can be as important as the message in determining its effectiveness (Koeck and Warnaby, 2014). Outdoor advertisements also shape the affective geography of urban space (Cronin, 2010). When events seek to change affective experiences, they may be in competition with the commercial landscape. In addition, the normal rhythms of the city may be disturbed if train and bus timetables are changed to meet event needs. Criticism has been levelled at both events and outdoor advertising due to commercial interventions in public space (Iveson, 2012; McFall, 2004) with concerns expressed about an inability to avoid the impositions (Gannon and Lawson, 2010). Three-dimensional advertising is particularly intrusive as signs become space-defining architectural bodies (Koeck and Warnaby, 2014) when signs are wrapped around buildings. Laser scanning is used so the sign fits the exact dimensions of a façade. The building acts as a canvas and the message is physically linked to a specific location, contributing to the city's atmosphere and its brand (Koeck and Warnaby, 2014).

PLACE BRANDING

A recent article by Boise, Terlouw, Groote and Couweberg (2018) explains the differences between place promotion, place marketing and place branding and the discussion is used to identify the relationship between events and place from a marketing perspective. According to Boise *et al.* (2018), place promotion involves the provision of information about positive characteristics of a place. The characteristics may vary at different times and messages may reflect variations in the objectives of stakeholders and the needs of target markets. The desired results will be primarily cognitive in the form of enhanced knowledge about a place (Boise *et al.*, 2018). An event may serve as an instrument of promotion by capturing attention and communicating information about the host setting. Place marketing is a broader concept about market-led changes that add value to what the place has to offer. This may equate to place-making (Evans, 2015) and a strong mandate will be required to achieve change. So it is important to communicate with internal stakeholders, particularly local residents, as well as external markets in the formulation and implementation of policies. Combining the needs of both groups constitutes a challenge (Therkelsen, 2015). The development of an event is consistent with this type of change with success evaluated primarily from a conative perspective (Boise *et al.*, 2018) and consideration of the extent to which the event had a positive impact on the place.

According to Hankinson, the objective of place branding is 'to maximize economic value and social welfare on behalf of local residents and other stakeholders' (2015: 25). Who has a stake in the place is a key consideration as there will be a 'wide range of people, groups and organisations who have a vested interest in the place's success, and crucially, a point of view in terms of how this success will be achieved' (Stubbs and Warnaby, 2015). For Boise *et al.* (2018), the objective of place branding is simply to improve the image of a place. This has been called 're-imaging' (Ashworth, Kavaratzis and Warnaby, 2015) with iconic architecture and urban design (Evans, 2015) or signature structures, events and personality association regarded as the toolbox for re-imaging (Ashworth and Kavaratzis, 2015). The term 'signature' indicates uniqueness and suggests that 'the signature of a city is conveyed through the ensemble of related buildings, spaces and streetscape elements, including the signage, paving, street furniture and not least the labelling of the district' (Ashworth and Kavaratzis, 2015: 124). The brand should differentiate the place by identifying material and immaterial elements that are distinctive; a study in the Chatham Islands of New Zealand found that a sense of place was linked to four key themes:

> Time was explained as a localized concept that was reflected in the rhythm of life on the islands.

> Ancestry created a sense of belonging and prescribed roles and responsibilities.

> The landscape influenced relations between people, land and nature.

> Community captured the idea that interactions produce meaning.

Uniqueness associated with these themes should be communicated by the place brand (Campelo, Aitken, Thyne and Gnoth, 2013). It could be supported with stories generated from within the host community (Ashworth *et al.*, 2015) but, it is important to ensure that any patchwork of local stories is intelligible to external markets (Therkelsen, 2015). It seems odd to emphasise the importance of authenticity but at the 2010 FIFA World

Cup in South Africa, spectators were instructed how to behave in front of cameras in order to participate as active makers of the place brand. This branding also involved 'the purification of space through enclavization and exclusion' (Kolamo and Vuolteenaho, 2013: 513–514) and socio-spatial polarisation increased as urban transformations were restricted to privileged enclaves (Kolamo and Vuolteenaho, 2013). At the 2010 Olympic Games, using the language of 'marshalling' local residents and 'informal choreography', people who took to the streets and draped themselves in the Canadian flag 'were rebranded as purveyors of "patriotism" and "terrific spirit" that were doing their best to salvage the reputation of the Games for Vancouver and Canada' (Dyck and Gauvin, 2012: 202).

There are considerable implications if place branding is treated as an instrument of place marketing or if the reverse is the case. In a place marketing approach, branding may exist at different spatial scales to accommodate cultural quarters that operate as distinctive parts of a city (Evans, 2015) and an event may be developed as an intervention that affects the identity of the area where it is held. This may create a sub-regional brand within the overall city brand (Evans, 2015) and different brands may be developed for different target groups. For instance, an event with relevant place associations may be targeted to the teenage market whereas another event with different place associations may be targeted to an older market. These are examples of brand extension (Aaker and Keller, 1990) when the perception of one brand, the event, is transferred to another – the place. With this approach, there may be opportunities for different agencies to design place brands. However, an approach in which place branding is dominant would require all marketing activities, including event-related communications, to support a clearly defined brand. This is an example of a projective brand management strategy (Louro and Cunha, 2001), which involves projecting a consistent message to the consumer. This can be the basis for stakeholder cooperation when the place brand is treated as 'common ground' (Ashworth *et al.*, 2015) but it may mean that brand communications need to be managed by a single, central agency. This approach benefits from long-term consistency when support for the place brand is considered central to all urban strategies (Boise *et al.*, 2018). In contrast, in a relational brand paradigm (Louro and Cunha, 2001), the customer is a co-creator of brand meaning. This can happen when place experiences are posted on social media but also when consumers perform place-bound practices at events (Therkelsen, 2015). Relationships may be built and social networks established between 'consumer tribes' (Cova and Cova, 2002) who share a common enthusiasm for an event, reinforcing the brand of the place where the event is held.

Early academic interest in place branding was associated with urban policy and tourism with research about destination image reported extensively in the tourism literature (Hankinson, 2015). In studies of 'event tourism' which formalised the link between events and tourism (Getz, 1997), the relationship with image was acknowledged. It was defined as 'the systematic planning, development and marketing of festivals and special events as tourist attractions, catalysts and image builders' (Getz and Wicks, 1993: 2). Attention was directed to destination branding by Morgan, Pritchard and Pride (2002) where one of the chapters focused specifically on the role of events in destination branding (Brown, Chalip, Jago and Mules, 2002). Theories drawn from cognitive psychology were used to explain that, with knowledge represented in associative networks (Collins and Loftus, 1975), a transfer of brand image occurs when a consumer is able to assimilate a node from one association set to another. Brown *et al.* (2002) describe how place-based visuals about events can be built into a wide range of marketing communications. Examples were given from the 2000 Olympics where, according to the Managing Director of the Australian Tourist Commission, the Sydney Games changed forever the way the world saw Australia with the country's brand advanced by ten years (Morse, 2001). Organisations make a conscious decision to be associated with the Olympic brand due to the benefits that are expected to accrue but there can be costs. The Hudson's Bay Company store in Vancouver was the headquarters for the sale of official apparel and merchandise for the 2010 Olympics and this status was made clear by the design on the exterior façade of the building and by window displays. This visibility made the store a target for people protesting against the Games and the Bay's windows were smashed (Dyck and Gauvin, 2012).

OLYMPIC DESIGN

The Olympic Games with dramatic narratives, embedded genres of festivals and rituals and prominent symbols offer a polysemic structure that provides multiple opportunities for affective involvement (Chalip, 1992). Media coverage of the competitive events is enhanced by personal interest stories about athletes that find a patriotic resonance with the population of their home country. It is interesting to watch television coverage of the Games in different countries and note differences in the athletes who are profiled and variations in the style of presentation to their respective home audiences. Through personal narratives, Australians have become familiar with Dawn Fraser and Ian Thorpe in different sporting eras. In Britain, the rivalry between Steve Ovett and Sebastian Coe captured the attention of a large section of the public in the 1980s. There are equivalent examples in all countries. During the Games, the sporting narratives are communicated with the host city as a backdrop and not only are the settings selected for maximum visual appeal, much of what is seen has been designed specifically for the Games. The host city has become an important source of polysemy due to symbols embedded in the landscape many of which are the product of a conscious process of design. This symbolic construction can enhance visitor experiences, support brand identities and capture the attention of investors and tourists.

In *Designing the Olympics: Representation, Participation, Contestation*, the Olympics are said to involve both symbolic and systemic acts with Olympic design including 'architecture and urban development to graphic design, product design, fashion and the design of services' (Traganou, 2016: 6). Traganou uses the term 'Olympic city enforcement' to describe the application of planning and design in ways that 'alter the physical, social, financial and emotional landscape of the host location' (2016: 29). She suggests that by operating as socio-spatial engineering, the Olympics affect the physical landscape and the host environment while the texture, colour and forms associated with design have the capacity to create new sensations and feelings. This is similar to the imperative to create an atmosphere in the host city that is a blend of native self-understanding and tourism fantasies (Salazar, 2009) and Tzanelli's (2018) notion of imagineering. In the case of the Rio Olympics, it was glocal atmospheric formations that provided the blueprint for the city's mega-event design (Tzanelli, 2018).

In her book, Traganou (2016) devotes an entire chapter to the graphic design programme at the 1964 Tokyo Games, another to architecture and urban planning at the 2004 Athens Games and another to brand design at London 2012. She suggests that designers at the Tokyo Olympics were motivated by the ideals of internationalism and design idealism. The design of the pictograms and wayfinding symbols reflected a desire to create a universal visual language. This was achieved with each sport depicted as an abstract line drawing of a relevant body position. Under the direction of Katsumi Masura, prominent designers were invited to join a Colloquium and, in a break with a cult of individualism and design 'stars', collaborative teamwork was encouraged. In an attempt to establish a coherent identity for the Games, a set of principles were established governing the use the emblem, symbols and colours. For the first time at an Olympic Games, a design manual was developed. As an example of the democratic tendencies that were starting to emerge in Japan at this time, citizens were sent colour scales and asked to indicate what they considered to be the most suitable shade of red for the rising sun on the Olympic emblem (Traganou, 2016).

In an historical context, Traganou (2016) refers to the philosophical ideas of the founder of the modern Olympics who argued for unity between athlete, spectator, environment, decoration, landscape and ceremony. She notes de Coubertain's scenic requirements at the first modern Games in 1896 where public buildings and individual houses were adorned with bunting, multicoloured streamers and wreaths. She also suggests that the mix of urban festival and the quasi-religious elements of the event have made design inseparable from the Olympics from the start. In recent times, Traganou considers Olympic design to be part of design culture, acknowledging the role played by socio-political and cultural process. The Olympic brand and its products are regarded as commodities of a global marketplace where value is determined by geopolitical hierarchies. Consequently, products with local meanings may be less understood by and have limited appeal to outsiders (Traganou, 2016). With the Olympic world divided into nations, the use of national symbols can be observed and the Games become a terrain where identities are established and challenged and 'a battlefield of interpretations of this multifaceted design production' (Traganou, 2016: 10). Consistent with the conceptual model of eventscapes described in Chapter 3, Traganou examines the social and material world of Olympic design as an actor–network. The Olympics is regarded as a prime example of a social universe in which designers, construction companies and politicians are key actors. Sub-actors include standards established by products developed at previous Games and printing technologies that allow the use of new colours and materials. The role of forces such as weather conditions are acknowledged as is the flexibility of the actor network as members join and leave at different stages of the Olympiad (Traganou, 2016).

Drawing on MacAloon's (1984) ideas about the Olympics as a series of performative genres, Traganou explains the role of design at the games (venues, uniforms, communication systems etc.), in relation to the rituals (protocols associated with sanctioned symbols and performance scriptures etc.), the festival (decoration of the city, crowd management etc.) and spectacle (stage design, broadcast design etc.). Margolin's (1995) concept of product milieu is used to identify design at the levels of state, the market and individuals. Design at the Olympics is normally run by state institutions or their surrogates such as Olympic organising committees in conjunction with the IOC, as a supernational institution. The design work may be commissioned to private agencies or completed in-house by organising committees. Multinational corporations acting as Olympic sponsors are often active at the market level and the involvement of the public can take many forms when individuals or groups use the Olympics as a communication platform. Activities at this level can range from body decoration to organised celebrations or protests. There are frequently connections between the three levels such as when the public are encouraged to enter design competitions, run by organising committees in conjunction with sponsors. A spatial pattern associated with the enactment of Olympic design may take the form of concentric circles. Projects carried out by official actors at core locations such as sport venues would be at the centre where legally enforced controls are in place. In the next zone, authorised products may be displayed at transport hubs and at locations hosting event-related activities. In the outer circle, spaces that offer opportunities to display official and unofficial messages may be used. In addition to having a physical effect on the host city, Olympic design can create positive emotional reactions from producers and users (Traganou, 2016). An alternative analysis suggests that the arrangement of consumable signs, images and promised experiences (Urry and Larsen, 2011) is part of a game of magical make-believe that merely refashions a host city's 'various life-worlds as bits of a picture postcard' (Tzanelli, 2018: 25). However, Tzanelli (2018) rejects the view that mega-events are merely an exercise in appearances without meaningful and situated content, advocating a multi-sensory, aesthetic appreciation of the worlds that are modified by artwork and creative imagineering.

THE OLYMPIC LOOK

A temporary exhibition with the title *Olympic Cities: A Lasting Transformation* was held at the Olympic Museum in Lausanne in December 2017. Information, with an extensive display of objects, was provided about stadiums, urban regeneration, sustainability and a number of other themes. The stadiums were described as 'stars of the Games' as they play an important role in shaping the image of the Games. Designed by some of the world's leading architects, they were said to be the embodiment of innovative design and construction techniques (IOC, 2017). Plans of a patented design system that was used to construct Rome's Palazzetto dello Sport were displayed. The stadium, with its buttress-supported dome, was one a number of 'monumental sculptures' designed by engineer, architect, entrepreneur Pier Luigi Nervi for the 1960 Olympics. The iconic Munich stadium that featured on the official poster of the 1972 Olympics was described as an enduring symbol of the Games. There was a large model of Beijing's National Stadium that was the setting for the opening and closing ceremonies at the 2008 Games. It was explained that the Bird's Nest was designed by Swiss architects who were inspired by Chinese ceramics. Information accompanying a model of Beijing's Aquatic Centre drew attention to the building's distinctive design and the qualities of the material used in its construction. Clad in 4,000 energy efficient bubbles, the Water Cube is a colourful attraction at the entrance of the Olympic Park when lit at night.

A large part of the exhibition described the approaches taken to communicate the 'Look of the Games' with six host cities highlighted due to the contributions they have made to the development of the visual identity of the Olympic Games (Table 5.1).

The selection of these cities echoed a suggested list of the medal winners for graphic design at the Olympic Games, published in *Design Observer*:

Gold: Munich, 1972. For Otl Aicher's design system and the elegance of the pictograms.

Silver: Mexico City, 1968. For the ability of Lance Wyman's design to capture the spirit of the time with the concentric stripe pattern expanding in formats from words to stadia.

Bronze: Los Angeles, 1984. For the cohesive design scheme, based on the colours of southern California, developed by Deborah Sussman and Jon Jerde.

(Bierut, 2004)

The President of the Mexico Organising Committee commented that competitive events at the Games in 1968 would be of limited importance because records fade away but the image of a country does not (Rivas and Sarhandi, 2005, quoted in Barke, 2011). Innovative design played a major role in shaping this image, establishing a benchmark for graphic design. The logo was claimed to be a fusion of Mexican indigenous culture and psychedelic art with the number '68' generated from the geometry of the Olympic rings with MEXICO set in the middle of concentric swirls (Brewster, 2005, quoted in Barke, 2011). Interestingly, the graphic design component of the event was the only feature of the 1968 Games that was celebrated on its fortieth anniversary (Barke, 2011). The acclaimed design at the Munich Olympics focused on the host region (Bavaria) to distance the event from the nationalist imagery associated with the Berlin 1936 Olympics (Traganou, 2016). Recent evidence of the ongoing respect accorded to Otl Aicher was combined with commentary about how the design process has changed since the Munich Olympics. It was stated that the days are gone when a master designer like Aicher would be handed control of the visual identity of a major international sporting event as it is now necessary to satisfy multiple competing interests (Burgoyne, 2011). This complexity can be explained by the importance that is now placed on the Look at Olympic Games and the desire for each city to create a more distinctive visual identity than that of

Table 5.1 *Contribution to design by host cities*

Olympic Games	Heading	Contribution
Amsterdam 1928	The dawn of a new approach	The graphic designs by architect Jan Wils were matched with Art Deco style souvenirs.
Mexico 1968	The remarkable impact of a global design	Modern graphic identity and cultural traditions came together in the famous emblem.
Sapporo 1972	The convergence between tradition and modernity	The visual identity for the first Winter Games in Asia included Japanese symbols of a rising sun and a snowflake.
Munich 1972	A coherent and radiant image	Directed by Otl Aicher, founder of the Ulm Graduate School of Design, an integrated approach to the use of images in Olympic areas, the city and public transport was employed.
Los Angeles 1984	A high festival in colour	The lively use of a distinctive colour palette provided a coherence across the 75 separate sites of the Games.
Lillehammer 1994	An ode to nature and the environment	The design programme combined respect for nature with Norwegian cultural traditions.

Source: adapted from IOC (2017).

the previous host. It has become an accepted but complex and, increasingly, a resource-intensive part of staging the Olympic Games. The ability to make improvements is assisted by the Transfer of Knowledge programme which requires insights to be shared with the IOC and with representatives of future Games. A final Games Report is prepared by the organising committee and managers of the different departments make presentations at a conference that is held soon after the completion of the event. In addition to coffee-table books about Olympic posters and stadia design, scholarly analysis of Olympic design has featured in the book by Traganou (2016), in books about Olympic cities (e.g. Gold and Gold, 2011; Poynter and MacRury, 2009) and in a special issue of the *Journal of Design History* in 2012 (Traganou, 2016). A considerable amount of literature about the Look of the Games, produced by Olympic designers is now available in documents about visual communication strategies, style manuals and marketing reports. This material, combined with the outcomes of research conducted by the author in host cities, is used to provide examples of the way the Look has been applied at recent Olympic Games.

The Winter Olympic Games

Lillehammer 1994

The key features of the design programme for the 1994 Winter Olympic Games in Lillehammer were described in *The Look of the Games and the Visual Environment*, a document prepared by the organising committee two years before the Games (LOOC, 1992). While attempting to create a uniform visual image, emphasis was placed on conveying Norway's national character, a spirit of community and the close links between Norwegians and nature. The emblem included a graphic representation of the northern lights above a snow flurry. The natural environment, in the form of the crystalline structure found in rock, snow and ice was used as a device to integrate other design elements. Rock carvings provided the inspiration for the pictograms and the colour palette included traditional colours used in Norwegian folk art. Decorations applied to the venues and surrounding areas were called 'festival elements'. They sought to provide a scenic backdrop for television coverage, to enhance the festive atmosphere of the Games and to assist wayfinding. It was recommended that the elements such as signs and temporary structures should work in unison and 'must in no way dominate the rural landscape, townscape or the architecture of the arenas' (LOOC, 1992). The sense of celebration that was created in Lillehammer was considered to have been one of the most important benefits of hosting the Games (Spilling, 1996).

Salt Lake City 2002

One year before the 2002 Winter Olympics, monumental graphic images marked the first and most visually dramatic stage of the programme to create the look of the Salt Lake City Games. The images were produced on a scale that exceeded anything previously seen at an Olympics and transformed the city's skyline (Plate 7). Large buildings were wrapped with images of athletes participating in winter sports as representations of the theme of the Games; 'Light the Fire Within'. Contractual agreements were made by the Salt Lake Organising Committee (SLOC) so the images could be placed on particular buildings and to ensure that the surrounding environment was free from any conflicting messages or images that would disrupt the look (Brosnihan, 2006). The wraps were produced to meet the specifications of each building; they were printed in pieces and then sewn together. The largest banner was equivalent in size to 80 billboards. A local company, Fusion Imaging, installed over 500,000 square feet of mesh, perforated window film and vinyl banners to 14 buildings and produced hundreds of images that were displayed throughout the city (Fusion, 2002).

Vancouver 2010

The level of detail and critical analysis provided in the *Vancouver 2010 Visual Brand Presentation* (IOC, 2010) stand in marked contrast with the Lillehammer 'Look' document. The expectations for design and the nature of the design process had changed dramatically between 1994 and 2010. However, there were similarities in the vision associated with the Looks at Lillehammer and Vancouver as both sought to convey connections with nature and reflections of cultural traditions. There were more than 1,600 entries to a competition to select the Games emblem for Vancouver 2010 and a design based on the Inukshuk was selected by an international panel. It was a contemporary interpretation of the stone sculpture used by the Inuit as a directional marker. In addition to shaping the visual identity of the Games, the Olympic symbols influenced behaviour and encouraged engagement. The ability to construct a small version of the Inukshuk from stones or other objects gave rise to creative interpretations of the emblem on the streets of Vancouver and in the mountains. In places where the emblem stood as a large stone monument, it acted as a magnet for personalised photographs and where it appeared as an image, people posed beside other famous Canadian symbols (Figure 5.1). The Canadian Police, on foot or horseback, were never far from these markers and seemed happy to oblige.

Figure 5.1 *Vancouver 2010: posing with Canadian symbols.*

Source: Graham Brown

The Olympic rings were located at strategic locations such as in the Coal Harbor area of Vancouver, where the mountains provided a scenic backdrop. The rings appeared on the front of the victory podiums, which were made in the shape of Vancouver Island in wood from the forests of British Columbia. In the Opening ceremony and in fire and ice shows that were held each night at Whistler, skateboarders flew through the Olympic rings. In other locations, lines formed as people waited to pose for photographs at the rings with many proudly wearing red mittens which displayed a maple leaf on one side and Vancouver 2010 above the Olympic rings on the other. They became a popular way to express identification with Canada and the Olympics and by the close of the Games, 3.5 million pairs had been sold. In many ways, people stepped into the Look and made a statement, consistent with the objectives of Leo Obstbaum, Director of Design at VANOC who felt the Look should simply say, 'Hello. My name is Canada' (Gardiner, 2010).

VANOC's creative team, led by Alison Gardiner, brought a mix of expertise in branding, design and Games experience. After establishing the vision, the team worked on the design process over a six-year period. Insight into how the team operated is presented in a video that I highly recommend (see www.youtube.com/watch?v=7MsATxMHnO8). It shows an enthusiastic, youthful group responding to a once-in-a-lifetime opportunity to create a vision that captures ideas about Canada and its values at a significant point in the nation's history. Challenges and excitement were evident in the search for images from nature and from the everyday cityscape that could be abstracted to tell a distinctive story. It was also a very human story of group dynamics and tragedy with the death of Leo Obstbaum just months before the Games. He was the charismatic driving force who brought a creative perspective about what makes Canada special. Born in Argentina, this was a perspective seen through the eyes of a new Canadian. According to VANOC's manager of brand and creative services, the quintessentially Canadian element of the Vancouver 2010 identity had at its core the concept of a progressive, young, inclusive country that was at its best when taking inspiration from the country's diverse, ever-changing people and land and Ali Gardiner provides a personal reflection in **What Matters Most**.

WHAT MATTERS MOST

By Alison Gardiner, Former Manager Brand and Creative Services, Vancouver Organizing Committee for the Olympic Games

Before we started the process of creating the Vancouver 2010 branding and design programme, the organising committee developed a lofty vision: 'to inspire the world and touch the soul of the nation'. This set the tone for everything we did. We hired people that believed the Games could be a catalyst for pride, connection and 'celebrating the possible', as we described it in our brand essence.

Almost ten years after the Vancouver 2010 Winter Games, I believe the creativity, integration and visual and emotional impact of our graphic identity helped us realize this vision. The city and country stood taller as a result of our Games, and felt truly united and inspired for those 28 days. I think the experience remains an incredibly powerful memory of Canada's character and potential.

Our brand and creative team were the epitome of the Canadian story. We were mostly young, diverse, unknown and unproven on a project of this scale, but we were busting with heart and talent. I believe this kept us humble and curious enough to learn from those who had done it before us, while forging something totally different and in keeping with the young, adventurous Canadian spirit we were trying to capture.

We obsessed about every detail of every application. Beyond the large-scale expressions of our Look – on venues and in the city – we didn't waiver from our vision on touchpoints as small as souvenir packaging, staff meal vouchers and the hundreds of icons on maps that most of the world never saw. Like the details of a Wes Anderson film, we believed that it all added up and that every single Vancouver 2010 impression should connect to the overarching vision.

The thoughtfulness of our programme also went beyond the visual and extended to the functional element of various design applications. We didn't do things just because they had always been done that way. We sought to improve the design experience for the specific people and function it served. For example, our research on the packaging for athlete medals revealed that most medallists end up using socks and fabric bags to carry their medals instead of the bulky, fancy boxes of past Games. We designed a beautiful folding woollen pouch that considered the athletes' future trips to media interviews, schools and events.

With a project of this magnitude, where the eyes of the world were looking on us and there was such a massive opportunity as well as risk, I believe our young team succeeded because of the degree of trust and inspiration that our leadership gave us – particularly CEO John Furlong and Executive VP Dave

Cobb. This trust and support in the brand and design team to truly stretch from a creative standpoint while serving the Games mission was felt and helped us overcome many challenges, including limited budgets and time, the bureaucracy of brand approvals and sheer exhaustion.

In our final year, we faced the greatest challenge of all: finishing our work while battling the overwhelming grief that came with the sudden death of our brilliant Design Director, Leo Obstbaum. Somehow, we drew from the energy and passion he lived with, and we knew that achieving our goal of honouring and inspiring our country was also about honouring him.

The design team developed a visual framework using a 'Sea to Sky' colour palette in the form of a mountainous landscape of rolling green sandwiched between flowing ribbons in dark shades of blue in the foreground and misty blue and grey peaks in the background. The creation of the 'core fusion' graphic involved the addition of inlays, comprising illustrated textures drawn from Canada's natural, cultural and urban environments and overlays of images that depicted the close connection between Canadians and nature (Plate 8). The contours and many of the inlays were drawn from the natural environment but there was stronger representation of cultural images in the overlay symbols. The inlays included patterns of fir trees, maple leaves and ferns as well as references to urban patterns of brickwork and technology and First Nations representations of salmon. The overlays included whimsical images such as a sea plane with dragonfly wings, geese flying behind a kite and Chinese lanterns hanging from power lines. Each was selected for inclusion after an extensive process of identification and discussion within the design team and it was interesting note the way team members identified with particular images such as that of traffic signals attached to a tree that was thought to capture the essence of life in Vancouver. The core fusion with its thematic layers communicated a colourful, detailed storyline of Vancouver and the environment of British Columbia.

Plate 8 is from the *Broadcast Graphic Standards* manual. It was stated that:

Like the stage of a magnificent theatre, the visual images, pageantry and icons that surround the Olympic Games are part of their magic. – The image of Canada's Games – our land, our people and our vision

– is represented in the many elements of the Vancouver 2010 design program.

(VANOC, 2009: 1)

The manual provided guidelines for the use of the emblem, the Look of the Games, pictograms, sport overlays and mascots to assist rights-holding broadcasters to 'create a spectacular backdrop' to the Games. It explained that compliance with the approved standards was necessary to preserve the value of the graphics and marks for all authorised users (VANOC, 2009).

The visual identity was applied to everything from souvenir pins to building wraps and the design system needed the flexibility to respond to the needs of the many different stakeholders including sponsors and host city partners. Although the use of alternative inlays and overlays offered an infinite number of versions of the fusion, the design team decided to limit the number of options. The main evidence of variability was the addition of sport graphics in and around the respective venues. The artistic renditions of bodies in motion were effective wayfinding devices, appeared on tickets and provided memorable images of the different sports. The mountain resort of Whistler was allowed to develop a special version of the graphic and it was applied on local signage and at broadcast locations. It helped create a distinctive atmosphere at the live sites in the village.

Participation at free events where the Look was displayed was regarded as an influential factor in positive evaluations made by local residents about the Games. A survey that was conducted at regular intervals found that, as the Games progressed, people became more excited about the Olympics (Hillier and Wanner, 2015). However, the suitability of the heavily textured designs in venue applications was questioned in the *Vancouver 2010 Visual Brand Presentation* (IOC, 2010) where a refreshingly balanced review signalled notable successes, constraints and disappointing outcomes. The document covered 47 topics from athlete's bibs to Zamboni branding and commented on features that contributed to the success of the Look. This included the quality of the signage and the fence fabric at venues and the size and design of entry towers that served as impressive landmarks. However, it was noted that the city banners programme failed to make an impact as some of the key projects – to wrap buildings and brand bridges – had to be abandoned due to budget cuts. Any vacant space was readily exploited by sponsors and this was considered to be particularly noticeable at the airport due to the exclusive agreement signed with Samsung. It was suggested that an overtly commercial orientation compromised the desire to offer a welcoming experience (IOC, 2010).

The Summer Olympic Games

Barcelona 1992

The 1992 Olympics is widely regarded as having been one of the most successful in the history of the Games (Chalkley and Essex, 1999) due principally to the urban transformation linked to the Games. Major infrastructure projects included the construction of new roads and the complete redevelopment of the port and beachside areas and the exemplary nature of the changes has been referred to as the 'Barcelona model' (Monclús, 2011). Monclús (2011) explains that the regeneration of the seafront, under the slogan 'opening the city to the sea', was the fulfilment of plans that can be traced to the mid-1960s. He also believes that the most important effect of the Games on Barcelona was the way the city was put on the map. During the Games, television coverage provided dramatic images of the city and a leading sport journalist commented,

> I was there in the city where Fu Mingxia created the finest image of a sport ever seen, the 13-year old diving for gold at the Olympic complex at the top of Montjuic with the cityscape of Barcelona spread out beyond her.

> (Barnes, 2007)

Perceptions of the city changed and the scene was set for an extended period of economic growth, as Barcelona became one of the most successful tourist destinations in Europe. Promotion of the regional, Catalan identity was a key objective of the design strategy (Traganou, 2016) and Catalans continue to express pride about their 1992 Games. The event retains a visible presence in the streets of their city due to an eclectic mix of public art that was commissioned for the Olympics. They include the, Gaudi-inspired, sculpture of a woman's face by Roy Lichtenstein that stands 64-feet high near the port and, nearby, the huge cartoon-like lobster by Javier Mariscal (Figure 5.2), who also designed Cobi, the dog mascot of the Games.

Sydney 2000

John Moore, the Director of Marketing for the Sydney Organising Committee for the Olympic Games (SOCOG), suggested that you don't give the world's greatest party and not get dressed up for it (Gardiner 2010). The way Sydney was dressed helped create an infectious party atmosphere that encouraged interactions between strangers as stories were shared and recommendations volunteered about which places offered the best experiences. Headlines around the world recorded the emotional impact of the

Figure 5.2 *Barcelona 1992: street art.*

Source: Graham Brown

event with the *Independent* newspaper in Britain claiming that Sydney had dissolved into one gigantic street party (IOC, 2001). Among those experiencing the party were 40,000 people invited to the Games by Olympic sponsors and a survey of these guests confirmed the importance of the social dynamics and the role of the setting. In an open-ended question which asked respondents to nominate what they enjoyed most at the Games in Sydney, the most frequent response was a nominated event, such as the Opening Ceremony, but in second place was the friendliness of people and in the third was the beauty of the city (Brown, 2007). This encapsulates the city as an eventscape, reinforcing the view that it offers a distinctive social environment that is a product of the event and the environment where it is held. The significance and enduring nature of event experiences should not be underestimated. Over 18 years after the 2000 Olympics, I overheard a conversation in Adelaide when it was stated that an experience in Sydney during the Games had been one of the most enjoyable days of the speaker's life. This was made even more significant when I learned that the voice belonged to one of Australia's most famous AFL players who must have experienced a lot of special moments in his life including being elected to the sport's Hall of Fame in 2011.

He confirmed that the atmosphere and excitement of being in the Olympic city remained a cherished memory and also served as a reminder of what the world can be like when people are welcomed and friendship is shared.

According to Garcia, the Look of the Games in Sydney had 'a major impact on the feel of the city during the Olympic fortnight' (2011: 292) but she also suggested that the use of techniques in common with those used in other host cities represented 'a clear case of global standards dominating over place-specific trends' (2011: 293). Place-specificity presents opportunities to create distinctive outcomes as do unique qualities associated with timing. This was significant in 2000 as Australia had the chance to present a vision to the world at the dawn of a new millennium. SOCOG established Team Millennium Olympic Partners, the Millennium Marque was the exclusive site of sponsor hospitality at Sydney Olympic Park and the Echidna mascot, named Millie, was chosen to personify a sense of optimism at the time of the new millennium. The other mascots were called Syd and Ollie and together, they represented the optimism associated with the timing, the energy of the event and the beauty of the setting. These key ingredients helped deliver what Juan Antonio Samaranch, the President of the IOC, claimed to have been 'the best Games ever', in his speech at the Closing Ceremony.

The colours and movement associated with the look of the 2000 Olympic Games was based on elements of Sydney's beach culture (Plate 9) and the entrance to event venues were dominated by markers built in the form of lifeguard chairs. The colourful chairs displayed the fluid energy graphic that was at the heart of the visual identity at the Games. It was 'inspired by the vitality of the Australian environment and its people. Elegant, swirling shapes and concentric forms suggest the vibrant waters of Sydney Harbour at the heart of the host city' (SOCOG, 1998). The energetic movement implied by the graphic was embodied in performances at venues, on streets and the start of the Opening Ceremony was signalled by a lone horse rider galloping into the stadium before being joined by another 120 horsemen carrying fluttering flags. Colourful crowds moved through the streets, ushered by volunteers in uniforms that conspicuously displayed the fluid graphic. Many people gathered at the live sites such as Darling Harbour where banners marked the boundaries of these places that formed key elements of the Olympic eventscape. In addition to the planned environments, the city's beaches, parks and public spaces offered opportunities for informal gatherings and outdoor activities. Significantly, Sydney's landscape provided an ideal visual backdrop for the sporting events as athletes ran, cycled and swam past many of the city's most famous landmarks such as the Opera House that were decorated with the blue of the Look (Plate 10).

The excitement in parts the city may have been spontaneous but it was facilitated by many years of planning by SOCOG, the state government and many agencies, organisations and businesses. The provision of timely information by SOCOG was essential and helped establish a sense of engagement and ownership. SOCOG produced an Image Guidelines manual with sections about the Olympic symbol, the emblem, pictograms, mascots, language, the look of the Games and a number of other subjects. Each section included detailed explanations about how the images should be used. There were 26 pages devoted solely to the fluid graphic with examples of applications in single and double colours, vertical and horizontal configurations and in combination with other elements such as the emblem and the Olympic rings. Information sessions about how to use and adhere to the image guideline were given at SOCOG's offices and at presentations to the Tourism Olympic Forum (TOF). The role of the TOF was discussed in Chapter 2 but it is important to recognise that member organisations, that included transport operators, retail businesses and hospitality organisations, made a significant contribution to how the look of the Games was communicated. The Australian Tourist Commission (ATC), a member of the TOF, was fully aware of the opportunities presented by the Look to promote Australia and to enhance the nation's brand. A wide range of collaborative activities helped sponsors to benefit by identifying with Australian brand values and for Australia to extend its destination brand by featuring in promotions funded by sponsors. The ATC made available images for use in television advertisements that took the Look of the host country into homes around the world. A notable example was the 'Colors of Australia' advertisement that was produced by NBC and was broadcast in prime-time slots such as during coverage of the Super Bowl in the USA. The advertisement connected the colours of the Olympic rings with the colours of the Australian landscape and suggested that the colours could be visited 'now'.

Beijing 2008

During the bidding process, cities seek to make a favourable impression when receiving visits by members of the IOC and, in the case of Beijing, the situation was accentuated by a desire to change perceptions about the city's level of pollution. In addition to investments in infrastructure and new hotels, short-term initiatives included policies to reduce pollution by removing old cars from city streets and closing factories, painting old buildings and spraying the grass green (Cook and Miles, 2011). These improvements to the look of the city preceded a detailed brand programme that started with the Olympic Design Conference sponsored by the IOC in 2001 where international speakers shared knowledge gained at previous Games with Chinese design professionals. An international competition was announced to create the official emblem and, in 2003, 'Dancing Beijing' was selected by a panel of Chinese and international judges. It included elements of engraving, calligraphy, painting and poetry and combined the ancient and the modern (Cook and Miles, 2011). The emblem was launched at an impressive ceremony at the Temple of Heaven (IOC, 2008) that was characteristic of initiatives that sought continuity with the past while promoting the qualities of modern China. One of the official posters showed an image of the Temple of Heaven above the 'Water Cube' and another showed the Bird's Nest stadium next to the Forbidden City. The colour palette used modern gradients of traditional Chinese colours. The application of new technologies meant there were no longer limitations on the number of colours or the materials on which designs could be digitally printed.

The Beijing Games was notable for the number and size of construction projects and the cost of staging the event. The scale of the design programme was also unprecedented, involving 1,000 projects, many of which required subordinate projects (IOC, 2008). Activities to develop and apply the 'Kit of Parts' for the Look took place over a period of six years (Figure 5.3). A competition to select the theme for the Games attracted 300,000 entries.

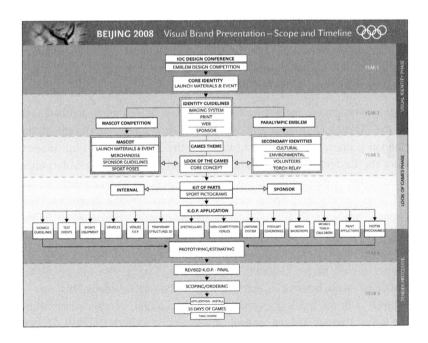

Figure 5.3 *Beijing 2008: visual brand – scope and timeline.*
Source: IOC, 2008.

'One World One Dream' was unveiled three years before the Games and gained extensive exposure. It was acknowledged in the Visual Brand Presentation document that brand saturation was evident in some parts of the city (IOC, 2008). This was partly because the Look was used to counter ambush marketing, to cover unwanted signs and to hide what were considered to be unattractive sights such as dilapidated housing. A more positive outcome concerned the attractive environment created by the Look at the airport and at hotels in city. Hotels used by members of the IOC were painted in gold.

London 2012

More surveys were conducted in London than in any previous Olympics and the findings revealed very positive attitudes towards the Games (Hillier and Wanner, 2015). Research by Ipsos MORI from 2003–2011 found that overall support for hosting the Olympics had remained steady at about 70 per cent prior to the Games but surveys conducted at regular intervals during the Games revealed interesting changes. The percentage who believed that the Olympics were having a very positive impact on the mood of British people increased from 29 per cent at the start to 53 per cent towards the end of the event. Data in another survey revealed that there was an increase from 20 per cent to 40 per cent in the percentage of people who were very happy that the Olympics were being held in the UK (Hillier and Wanner, 2015). A decrease in the number who were unhappy was explained by people becoming 'caught up in the celebratory atmosphere' (Hillier and Wanner, 2015: 679).

A geometric pattern emanating from the logo provided the visual language of the XXVII Olympiad and informed every aspect of design at the London Games. When launched in 2007, the logo received little support from the design community and was the subject of considerable public ridicule but, when applied as part of the Look, it was commended for delivering an effective brand identity, as promised by the designers, Wolf Ollins (Burgoyne, 2012b). Wolf Ollins deliberately broke many of the conventions established at previous Games by proposing that the brand identity should go beyond sport, beyond London and indicate that the Games should be for everyone (Shaughnessy, 2012). The use of clichés associated with landmarks and sporting icons was avoided. This was in contrast with the bid logo which showed a coloured ribbon, representing the River Thames, woven through the letters of LONDON 2012 (Traganou, 2016). However, the film that formed part of the final presentation made to the IOC did not include anything that was place-specific about London. Instead, the appeal related to Olympian ideals (Ward, 2011).

Although the shape of the Games logo was said to echo the host's qualities as a modern, edgy city (Designboom, 2012), the name London and the Olympic rings were relegated to subsidiary roles in what was an abstract representation of the year 2012. According to the Chairman of Wolf Ollins, rather than place branding, the objective was to make the date aspirational (Traganou, 2016). The initial objective to use the logo's architecture to promote participation and to encourage the creation of new versions proved to be unrealistic in an environment of brand manuals and laws to protect the interests of Olympic sponsors (Shaughnessy, 2012). But the design was still indicative of a paradigm shift with regard to the role of the logo: from representational to participatory accompanied by an increased emphasis on expressions of identity (Traganou, 2016).

The London 2012 Brand Expression Guidelines contained over 100 pages of detailed design specifications (LOCOG, 2010). Greg Nugent was appointed as Director of Brand, Marketing and Culture at LOCOG in 2009. He nominated the Games held in Mexico and Munich as the benchmarks for Olympic design but claimed that, in 2012, it was necessary to take advantage of opportunities presented by three-dimensional design and to develop a more consistent approach to the Look (Burgoyne, 2012a). FutureBrand was given the task of developing the Look and the approach it adopted is described in **Creating the Look of London 2102**. The task of delivering the Look included dressing hundreds of miles of streets, embedding the design at 21 sport venues and developing directional signage across the transport network.

CREATING THE LOOK OF LONDON 2012

By Nick Sykes, CEO FutureBrand

The company

McCann Worldgroup (MWG) was appointed in early 2009 as the official marketing services provider for the London 2012 Olympic and Paralympic Games. MWG was involved in all aspects of marketing services including ticketing, the Paralympics, Volunteers and the Cultural Olympiad. FutureBrand, one of six companies within MWG, was responsible for developing the Look of the Games as well as all the design assets required for the event. Under the creative direction of Matt Buckhurst, a team of 20 people worked on the project for three and a half years.

Context

FutureBrand had been involved in creating the Look at many major sport events previously, including the Sydney Olympic Games, Commonwealth Games, Cricket World Cups and European Football Championships. Sydney 2000 offered the most suitable Olympic reference point for London 2012. At Athens 2004, the organisers were focused on meeting deadlines for stadium construction and the scale of the Games in 2008 and difficulties in gaining relevant information made it difficult to draw lessons from the Beijing Olympics.

Sydney used look, design and brand to create real 'followership' but the world had manifestly changed since 2000 – in fact, with the growth in the role of social media, technology and the financial landscape, it was a very different place in 2012 compared with 2008. In 2012, political bodies, national and local governments, the IOC and Olympic sponsors had become more sophisticated and, in the media, the demand for transparency and financial accountability had become louder.

The London Organising Committee had a strong sense of direction with objectives expressed in the bid setting the parameters for the Games. There was a desire to encourage re-engagement with the Olympics, especially among younger audiences in the face of competition from other sports such as football and the technology explosion. To inspire a generation, the organising committee relied on its partners and we had to determine what was directly relevant to 'our piece of the pie'.

Approach

We drew on experience of analogous brands – and they were not restricted to sport. We examined Obama's political campaign in the USA and studied how he engaged with a generation of alienated Americans. We also knew that we needed to move away from two-dimensional brand design to create a series of total brand experiences. We treated the Games as a mix of a brand and a campaign, so we started with the development of a brand narrative from which we could then launch our campaign.

At the start, we locked key stakeholders in a room for four days! Two, two-day workshops were held to develop the brand narrative and then agree the direction of the campaign and to get everyone on board. In workshop 1, we engaged all the brand stakeholders including representatives of the Olympic and Paralympic Committees, local governments and sponsors. Together, we developed the brand narrative – to push past your personal best to help inspire a generation. In the following workshop, a series of marketing and communications campaigns were established and milestones were set – game-changing moments that demonstrated that targets were being met. The brand narrative was used to encourage engagement and to challenge levels of commitment. In one campaign, a list of demanding activities was followed by the question, 'Have you got what it takes to be a London 2012 Games Maker?'

Once the direction was set, we then focused on ideas about images and design. So we gathered a different set of stakeholders such as representatives of local councils, programme managers and stadium designers to identify factors that would influence how the Look would be developed. We needed to develop a single, unifying look that had the flexibility to differentiate sports and venues from one another. A lot of people had to be on board in order to develop a consistent Look from airport to venue in the host city and at places throughout the host country. We had to be sympathetic to concerns about the impact of design at venues such as Wimbledon and Lords and used the Look sparingly at iconic venues such as Horse Guards Parade. It was important to ensure that famous buildings were showcased rather than hidden so that the city helped brand the event.

The London Look became a derivative of the Games Look when city councils used the flexibility of the design system to communicate their involvement in the Games. Participation was critical and this was encouraged in many ways. Specially produced packs helped high streets around the country decorate celebration sites and become part of the Look. A competition was held to generate ideas about the Look of the education programme. It was won by a 16-year-old resident of one of the London boroughs who spent two weeks at FutureBrand finalising his design – this was design by the community for the community.

The Look helped present London and the UK to the world in a new way and it was a resounding success. Surveys conducted soon after the event found that 85 per cent of respondents liked the way the city had been decorated during the Games, 75 per cent agreed that London 2012 had made a positive difference to the UK, 61 per cent agreed that the Olympics had been a 'Games for Everyone' and 35 per cent of people inter-viewed overseas said the Olympics made the UK a more tempting place to study and do business.

The designers returned to the logo and the opportunities presented by its angular shape. It became the focal point from which shard-like shapes emerged that could reach out from London, across the country and to the world (Figure 5.4). The dynamic grid comprised 'bursts of energy radiat-ing from the heart of the 2012 logo' (McCann, 2012). A typeface that reflected the geometry of the grid pattern was developed specifically for the Games by Gareth Hague, the graphic designer for the London-based

Figure 5.4 *London 2012: the dynamic grid.*

Source: FutureBrand

company, Alias. It was applied as a powerful headline for use at large sizes (Designboom, 2012) and gave shape to the ever-present *Inspire a Generation* phrase and to messages on the large signs that marked the entrance to venues and on the giant beacons that were part of the wayfinding system. A desire to communicate and not decorate was one of the principles that guided the application of the Look and, in an echo of the approach adopted in Lillehammer, lightness of touch represented another principle in London. It meant that the Look should not act as a wallpaper or screen but should complement iconic backdrops (McCann, 2012).

Design was treated as a tool to influence behaviour and create emotional reactions, particularly in the way it was applied in and around the sport arenas. The idea of energy bursting from the stadium was seen as a way of drawing spectators towards the action within. The pattern of shards that were embedded in the concourse at the Olympic Park became denser as one approached the Olympic stadium. Giant pictograms were displayed on the outside of all of the venues as colourful markers that primed a sense of excitement. A distinctive identity for each venue was achieved by allocating specific colour combinations from the Look palette (Plate 11). Blue was used to denote water-based sports, purple was used at heritage venues such as Wimbledon and Lords and magenta and orange were used at indoor arenas that hosted fast contact sports. Deeper tones of the colours indicated dynamism. Decisions about the best locations to place logos and slogans were the product of detailed planning with Games broadcasters and venue managers (McCann, 2012).

For the first time, the logos of the Olympic and Paralympic Games at London were based on the same shape, reflecting a commitment to integrate the planning for both events. The countdown clock was one of a number of visible expressions of this integration. It was unveiled in the heart of London, at Trafalgar Square, 500 days before the start of the Games. Designed by FutureBrand and taking the angular shape of the logo, it was a tangible manifestation of the Look. On one side, it counted down to the Olympic Games and, on the other, it counted down to the Paralympic Games (Figure 5.5). In designing an identity for the Cultural Olympiad, Future-Brand sought to create a connection with the Games Look, although it was not able to include the Olympic rings. Branded as the 2012 Festival to encourage the idea of accessible culture, London 2012's magenta was the colour of shard-shaped ribbons that linked locations across the country that were part of the festival (Plate 12). The design created a three-dimensional presence on billboards and on free-standing signs and as a wrap on event venues. It announced a connection with the Festival while standing out against competing arts and cultural communications (McCann, 2012).

Figure 5.5 *London 2012: countdown clock.*

Source: Graham Brown

Partnerships with sponsors extended the reach of the Look and, in some cases, made it mobile. British Airways brought the Olympic flame to Heathrow airport on a plane bearing the gold and yellow colours of the Torch Relay and athletes, officials and members of the Olympic family travelled in vehicles branded in the Olympic livery. They were supplied by BMW as were bicycles decorated in the colours of the different venues. BMW even gained access to the field of play as remote control-led car models retrieved javelins, discuses and hammers thrown by athletes in the field events. Despite the temporary nature of the visual language that is created for the Games, there was a desire to leave a lasting legacy through design at London 2012 (McCann, 2012). By working with architects and planners, design features were embedded in concourse patterning, on bridges and on buildings that would remain long after the event. It was hoped that the integrated approach that was applied to create the 'One Look' across venues, the city and the country would serve as a benchmark for future organising committees (McCann, 2012).

Rio de Janeiro 2016

The first version of the *Look Manual* for the 2016 Olympics was produced six years before the Games (ROCOG, 2010). It contained the now familiar warnings about the need to ensure the integrity of official artwork and, under the registered title of BranDirection, explained how the brand should be expressed. Emphasis was placed on the human dimension of design, by suggesting that a brand needs to have a soul with material expression of secondary importance. In Rio, the brand sought to project the passion of the host city to the world (ROCOG, 2010). This was at the forefront of the thoughts of the team at Tátil, the Brazilian company selected to design the logo, in competition with 139 agencies. Tátil considered the Olympics to be the most complex visual identity project on the planet and 100 strategists, designers and copywriters collaborated in the creative process. The result was the first three-dimensional logo that had been designed for the Olympic Games. It was described as an object to be experienced – a message that was broadcast to 50 countries on the day of the launch (Tátil, 2016).

The logo sought to capture the warmth of Cariocas and their desire to share their way of life with others (Burgoyne, 2011). It depicted people joining together but it also represented the beauty of the city's landscape just as the city had been the star in an emotional video shown in the final presentation to the IOC by Rio's bid committee in 2009 (Ward, 2011). The bid document presented to the IOC had promised to make full use of the city's magnificent landscape (Silvestre and de Oliveira, 2012). The extensive use of superlatives in the documents in relation to the carnival, Copacabana and Ipanema beaches and Sugar Loaf mountain was considered to be 'simply acknowledgement that Rio contains more features that are readily recognizable to the outside world than any other Latin American city' (Gold, 2011: 399). The shape of the logo mapped the sensuous outline of Sugar Loaf Mountain. Sculptures of the logo were placed in public spaces and people who entered the shape were surrounded by colours that depicted Rio's lush environment (Plate 1). Yellow represented the sun and happiness, blue the ocean and a carefree way of life, and green the forests and optimism (ROCOG, 2010). The shape and the colours of the logo formed part of the visual language used by sponsors and sport federations. This is illustrated by the colourful transformation of the building on Avenida Atlantica that, for the period of the Games, became Volleyball House, the temporary home of the International Volleyball Federation (Plate 1). Large pictogrammes and the Olympic rings dominated the exterior of sport venues.

Speaking before the Games, the Director of *Celebrate*, the Games cultural programme, claimed that there would be artistic interventions and cultural performances in streets, squares, parks and beaches, humanising space while telling the story of the host city (Camurati, 2015). The Olympic Park at Barra de Tijuca was the setting for the largest artwork that was commissioned as part of *Celebrate*. The Aquatic Centre was encircled with a blue seascape mural by Rio artist Adriana Varajão that sought to create the sensation of a swimmer surrounded by waves. The artist was considered to be a bold choice for the Olympics as much of her work had been associated with racism, subjugation and Portugal's colonisation of Brazil (van Straaten, 2016). Indicative of competitive tensions between different Games, a news item compared the visual appeal of the mural with the architectural statements made by the Aquatic Centres in Beijing and London (Rio 2016, 2015).

SUMMARY

The Games are developed over a seven-year period and require a considerable investment of resources. In this context, the Look may be regarded as merely window dressing or a temporary mirage that seeks to mask local realities. It directs attention away from the undesirable to a preferred way of seeing, so it is part of the historical tradition of landscape representation as visual ideology. It offers a scenic backdrop to festivities, adding colour to the event experience and endless opportunities for immersive engagement in the contemporary design culture. It assists wayfinding and is a form of communication that seeks to express values about the event and the host city. The examples documented in this chapter show that the look of the Games has become increasingly important, resource intensive, complex and detailed in terms of specificity and controls. It is a very deliberate process that requires the support of the IOC and local political and business leaders. But, at its core, it is about creative people striving to develop a visual language that expresses what an historically significant moment means for a city and a nation.

A key question concerns the nature of the audience. Is the Look for local consumption by residents and visitors to the event or is it attempting to attract the attention of global markets? An evident desire to meet the needs of broadcast media would suggest the latter are very important and the use of social media may extend the reach of images but it is difficult to avoid the fact that physical presence is necessary to appreciate the Look in its many forms. This may suggest it cannot effectively communicate a place brand and this is supported by problems associated with the exceptional nature of the event. As an event, it has a clearly defined, temporary presence and is unsuitable to be part of a long-term strategy, requiring long-term integration with other initiatives. It also introduces a strange mix of non-traditional actors such as international corporations without local links and schoolchildren who win Olympic design competitions. However, much of the literature reviewed in this book has emphasised the fragmented, temporary nature of modern life which is subject to constant change and short-term planning horizons. So, the duration of the planning and implementation period of the Olympic Games provide a rare level of stability and the Olympic Look provides particular opportunities. It encourages a wide range of people to ask questions about the city where they live, what it stands for and what residents would like to say about themselves. The questions are asked with greater intensity at the Games and more resources are made available than at any other times to express the preferred answers. The answers can be checked with people from outside who are interested in the city at that moment in time. If managed well, the questions, the answers and the Look can bring the community together, enhance the sense of place and provide the foundation for ongoing narratives.

REFERENCES

Aaker, D. and Keller, K. L. (1990). Consumer Evaluation of Brand Extensions. *Journal of Marketing*, 54(January): 27–41.

Ashworth, G. J. and Kavaratzis, M. (2015). Rethinking the Roles of Culture in Place Branding. In: M. Kavaratzis, G. Warnaby and G. J. Ashworth, eds, *Rethinking Place Branding: Comprehensive Brand Development for Cities and Regions*. New York: Springer, 119–134.

Ashworth, G. J., Kavaratzis, M. and Warnaby, G. (2015). The Need to Rethink Place Branding. In: M. Kavaratzis, G. Warnaby and G. J. Ashworth, eds, *Rethinking Place Branding: Comprehensive Brand Development for Cities and Regions*. New York: Springer, 1–11.

Barke, M. (2011). Mexico City 1968. In: J. R. Gold and M. M. Gold, eds, *Olympic Cities*, 2nd edn. Abingdon: Routledge, 233–246.

Barnes, S. (2007). The Best Olympics. *The Times*, 21 February.

Bierut, M. (2004). The Graphic Design Olympics. *Design Observer*, 23 August. https://designobserver.com/feature/the-graphic-design-olympics/2517.

Boise, M., Terlouw, K., Groote, P. and Couweberg, O. (2018). Reframing Place Promotion, Place Marketing and Place Branding – Moving Beyond Conceptual Confusion. *Cities*, 80: 4–11.

Brewster, K. (2005). Patriotic Pastimes: The Role of Sport in Post-Revolutionary Mexico. *International Journal of the History of Sport*, 22: 139–157.

Brosnihan, T. (2006). The Olympic Cityscape Program: Light the Fire Within is the Theme of the Games This Year. *The Signs of the Times*. www.signsofthe times.com/content/the-olympic-cityscape-program.

Brown, G. (2007). Sponsor Hospitality at the Olympic Games: An Analysis of the Implications for Tourism. *International Journal of Tourism Management*, 9: 315–327.

Brown, G., Chalip, L., Jago, L. and Mules, T. (2002). Developing Brand Australia: Examining the Role of Events. In: N. Morgan, A. Pritchard and R. Pride, eds, *Destination Branding: Creating the Unique Destination Proposition*. Oxford: Elsevier Butterworth-Heinemann, 279–305.

Burgoyne, P. (2011). The Rio Olympics Logo: A Closer Look. *Creative Review*, 4 January. www.creativereview.co.uk/rio-2016-olympics-logo-a-closer-look/.

Burgoyne, P. (2012a). London 2012 Olympics: The Look of the Games. *Creative Review*, 12 July. www.creativereview.co.uk/london-2012-the-look-of-the-games/.

Burgoyne, P. (2012b). London 2012 Olympics: The Look. *Creative Review*, 31 July. www.creativereview.co.uk/the-look/.

Campelo, A., Aitken, R., Thyne, M. and Gnoth, J. (2013). Sense of Place: The Importance for Destination Branding. *Journal of Travel Research*, 53(2): 154–166.

Camurati, C. (2015). Artists to Fill Rio with Culture During the Olympic and Paralympic Games. *RIO 2016 News*, 7 July. www.rio2016.com/en/news/news/artists-to-fill-rio-with-culture-during-the-olympic-and-paralympic-games.

Chalip, L. (1992). The Construction and Use of Polysemic Structures: Olympic Lessons for Sport Marketing. *Journal of Sport Management*, 6: 87–98.

Chalkley, B. and Essex, S. (1999). Urban Development Through Hosting International Events: A History of the Olympic Games. *Planning Perspectives*, 14: 369–394.

Chatterton, P. and Hollands, R. (2003). *Urban Nightscapes, Youth Cultures, Pleasure Spaces and Corporate Power*. London: Routledge.

Collins, A. M. and Loftus, E. F. (1975). Theory of Semantic Processing. *Psychological Review*, 82: 407–428.

Cook, I. G. and Miles, S. (2011). Beijing 2008. In: J. R. Gold and M. M. Gold, eds, *Olympic Cities*, 2nd edn. Abingdon: Routledge, 340–358.

Cova, B. and Cova, V. (2002). Tribal Marketing: The Tribalization of Society and its Impact on the Conduct of Marketing. *European Journal of Marketing*, 36(5/6): 595–620.

Cronin, A. M. (2010). *Advertising, Commercial Spaces and the Urban*. Houndmills: Palgrave Macmillan.

Degen, M., DeSilvey, C. and Rose, G. (2008). Experiencing Visualities in Designed Urban Environments: Learning from Milton Keynes. *Environment and Planning A*, 40(8): 1901–1920.

Designboom (2012). London Olympics 2012: The Look of the Games. *Designboom Newsletter*. www.designboom.com/design/london-olympics-2012-the-look-of-the-games/.

Dyck, N. and Gauvin, R. (2012). Dressing Up to Join the Games: Vancouver 2010. *Visual Studies*, 27(2): 196–203.

Evans, G. (2015). Rethinking Place Branding and Place Making Through Creative and Cultural Quarters. In: M. Kavaratzis, G. Warnaby and G. J. Ashworth, eds, *Rethinking Place Branding: Comprehensive Brand Development for Cities and Regions*. New York: Springer, 135–158.

Foster, H. (2002). *Design and Crime (And Other Desirables)*. London: Verso.

Fusion (2002). *The 2002 Salt Lake City Olympic Games*. www.fusionimaging.com/2002-slc-olympics/.

Gannon, Z. and Lawson, N. (2010). *The Advertising Effect: How Do We Get The Balance of Advertising Right?* London: Compass.

Garcia, B. (2011). Sydney 2000. In: J. R. Gold and M. M. Gold, eds, *Olympic Cities*, 2nd edn. Abingdon: Routledge, 287–314.

Gardiner, A. (2010). Journey to 2010. *With Glowing Hearts: The Official Commemorative Book of the XXI Olympic Winter Games and the X Paralympic Winter Games*. Mississauga, ON: John Wiley.

Getz, D. (1997). *Event Management and Event Tourism*. New York: Cognizant Communications Corporation.

Getz, D. and Wicks, B. (1993). Editorial. *Festival Management and Event Tourism*, 2(2): 1–3.

Gold, J. R. (2011). Rio de Janeiro 2016. In: J. R. Gold and M. M. Gold, eds, *Olympic Cities*, 2nd edn. Abingdon: Routledge, 390–402.

Gold, J. R. and Gold, M. M., eds (2011). *Olympic Cities*, 2nd edn. Abingdon: Routledge.

Hankinson, G. (2015). Rethinking the Place Branding Construct. In: M. Kavaratzis, G. Warnaby and G. J. Ashworth, eds, *Rethinking Place Branding: Comprehensive Brand Development for Cities and Regions*. New York: Springer, 13–32.

Hillier, H. H. and Wanner, R. A. (2015). The Psycho-Social Impact of the Olympics as Urban Festival: A Leisure Perspective. *Leisure Studies*, 34(6): 672–688.

IOC (2001). *Sydney 2000: Marketing Report*. Lausanne: International Olympic Committee.

IOC (2008). *Beijing 2008: Visual Brand Presentation*. Lausanne: International Olympic Committee.

IOC (2010). *Vancouver 2010: Visual Brand Presentation*. Lausanne: International Olympic Committee.

IOC (2017). *Olympic Cities: A Lasting Transformation*. Temporary Exhibition at the Olympic Museum, Lausanne, Switzerland, December. International Olympic Committee.

Iveson, K. (2012). Branded Cities: Outdoor Advertising, Urban Governance, and the Outdoor Media Landscape. *Antipode*, 44(1): 151–174.

Jirásek, I. and Kohe, Z. (2015). Readjusting Our Sporting Sites/Sight: Sportifica-tion and the Theatricality of Social Life. *Sport, Ethics and Philosophy*, 9(3): 257–270.

Julier, G. (2006). From Visual Culture to Design Culture. *Design Issues*, 22(1): 64–76.

Koeck, R. and Warnaby, G. (2014). Outdoor Advertising in Urban Context: Spati-ality, Temporality and Individuality. *Journal of Marketing Management*, 30(13/14): 1402–1422.

Kolamo, S. and Vuolteenaho, J. (2013). The Interplay of Mediascapes and City-scapes in a Sport Mega Event: The Power Dynamics of Place Branding in the 2010 FIFA World Cup in South Africa. *International Communication Gazette*, 75(5–6): 502–520.

Lash, S. (2002). *Critique of Information*. London: Sage.

LOCOG (2010). *London 2012 Brand Expression Guidelines*. April, London Organising Committee for the Olympic Games.

LOOC (1992). The Look of the Games and the Visual Environment: Lillehammer '94. The Lillehammer Olympic Organising Committee, December.

Louro, M. J. and Cunha, P. V. (2001). Brand Management Paradigms. *Journal of Marketing Management*, 17: 849–875.

MacAloon, J. J. (1984). Olympic Games and the Theory of Spectacle in Modern Societies. In: J. J. MacAloon, ed., *Rite, Drama, Festival, Spectacle: Rehearsals Toward a Theory of Cultural Performance*. Philadelphia, PA: Institute for the Study of Human Issues.

McCann. (2012). *Our Personal Best? The Inspiration of a Nation*. London: McCann Worldgroup.

McFall, L. (2004). The Language of the Walls: Putting Promotional Saturation in Historical Context: Consumption. *Markets and Culture*, 7: 107–128.

Margolin, V. (1995). The Product Milieu and Social Action In: R. Buchanan and V. Margolin, eds, *Discovering Design: Explorations in Design Studies*. Chicago, IL: University of Chicago Press.

Monclús, F.-J. (2011). Barcelona 1992. In: J. R. Gold and M. M. Gold, eds, *Olympic Cities*, 2nd edn. Abingdon: Routledge, 268–286.

Morgan, N., Pritchard, A. and Pride, R., eds (2002). *Destination Branding: Creating the Unique Destination Proposition*. Oxford: Elsevier Butterworth-Heinemann.

Morse, J. (2001). The Olympic Games and Australian Tourism. Presentation made at the Sport Tourism Conference, Barcelona, Spain, 23 February.

Poynter, G. and MacRury, I., eds (2009). *Olympic Cities and the Remaking of London*. Farnham: Ashgate Press.

Rio 2016 (2015). The Sea and Angels in a Baroque Style – Introducing the Look of the 2016 Olympic Aquatic Stadium. *RIO 2016 News*, 16, December. www. rio2016.com/en/news/the-sea-and-angels-in-a-baroque-style-introducing-the-look-of-the-rio-olympic-aquatic-stadium.

Rivas, C. and Sarhandi, D. (2005). This is 1968 … This is Mexico. *Eye*, 56.

ROCOG. (2010). *2016 Rio Olympic Games Look Manual*. Version 1, December. Rio Organising Committee for the Olympic Games.

Salazar, N. B. (2009). Imaged or Imagined? Cultural Representations and the Tourismifaction of Peoples and Places. *Cashiers d'Études Africaines*, 49(1–2): 49–71.

Shaughnessy, A. (2012). London 2012: The Logo. *Creative Review*, 31 July. www.creativereview.co.uk/the-logo/.

Silvestre, G. and de Oliveira, N. G. (2012). The Revanchist Logic of Mega-Events: Community Displacement in Rio de Janeiro's West End. *Visual Studies*, 27(2): 204–210.

SOCOG (1998). Sydney 2000 Olympic Games Image Guidelines. Sydney Organising Committee for the Olympic Games.

Spilling, O. (1996). Mega Event as Strategy for Regional Development: The Case of the 1994 Lillehammer Winter Olympics. *Entrepreneurship and Regional Development*, 8: 321–343.

Stubbs, J. and Warnaby, G. (2015). Rethinking Place Branding from a Practice Perspective: Working with Stakeholders. In: M. Kavaratzis, G. Warnaby and G. J. Ashworth, eds, *Rethinking Place Branding: Comprehensive Brand Development for Cities and Regions*. New York: Springer, 101–118.

Tátil (2016). Rio 2016 Olympic Brand – The Dream Project. *Tátil.* http://tatil.com.br/en/projetos/rio-2016/.

Therkelsen, A. (2015). Rethinking Placebrand Communication: From Product-Oriented Monologue to Consumer-Engaging Dialogue. In: M. Kavaratzis, G. Warnaby and G. J. Ashworth, eds, *Rethinking Place Branding: Comprehensive Brand Development for Cities and Regions*. New York: Springer, 159–173.

Traganou, J. (2016). *Designing the Olympics: Representation, Participation, Contestation*. New York: Routledge.

Tzanelli, R. (2018). *Mega Events as Economies of the Imagination: Creating Atmospheres for Rio 2016 and Tokyo 2020*. London: Routledge.

Urry, J. and Larsen, J. (2011). *The Tourist Gaze*, 3rd edn. London: Sage.

VANOC (2009). *Broadcast Graphic Standards*. Vancouver 2010 Organising Committee, February.

Van Straaten, L. (2016). Waves of Dark History Break on an Olympic Pool. *New York Times*, 13 July. www.nytimes.com/2016/07/14/arts/design/waves-of-darker-history-break-on-an-artists-seas-in-rio.html.

Ward, S. V. (2011). Promoting the Olympic City. In: J. R. Gold and M. M. Gold, eds, *Olympic Cities*, 2nd edn. Abingdon: Routledge, 148–166.

6 Transformations by light

INTRODUCTION

This chapter discusses the awe and apprehension associated with dark and light, recognising the power of illumination to transform places. Many eventscapes are unrecognisable in the daytime. They blend into the fabric of the surrounding environment but at night they come alive, emerging from the darkness with lighting providing clarity, colour and much more. From the development of electricity to the contemporary use of lasers, 4D projection techniques and drones, technology and creativity have combined to redefine the visible world. Light is used to capture attention, to inform and entertain, to tell stories, to change the atmosphere and to create mystery and excitement. It is 'integral to the changing sensory characteristics of late modernity' (Gandy, 2017a: 354) and 'inseparable from the affective dynamics of capitalist urbanisation' (2017a: 368). The dynamics create atmospheres of distraction that are revitalising the public spaces of urban environments. In recent years, light festivals have been introduced in cities around the world. They vary in size and duration and have the ability to adapt to different environments. At the Event Awards in Australia in 2018, light festivals won the category for best tourism event (Vivid Sydney) and for the best small event (Lights of Christmas, Rockhampton). Other light festivals featured as finalists in the categories for best regional event and best community event. However, popularity does not come without criticism and it has been claimed that the projection of giant images on urban façades 'transform the city into a shocking night decoration' (Narboni, cited in Giordiano and Ong, 2017: 709). The artificial decorations add to light pollution which attracts and kills insects and birds, reduces the 'nocturnal commons' and impedes access to the natural wonders of the night sky (Gandy, 2017b). The chapter will describe the way eventscapes and the experiences they offer are transformed by light. It will start by considering the setting for night-time activities, as light invades darkness.

DAY AND NIGHT

And God said, Let there be light: and there was light.
And God saw the light, that it was good:
and God divided the light from the darkness.
And God called the light Day, and the darkness he called Night.

(Genesis 1:1–5, King James Bible)

The darkest building in the world was constructed at the 2018 Winter Olympic Games that was held in Pyeongchang, South Korea. The Hyundai Pavilion in the Olympic Plaza had been sprayed with a coating that absorbs 99 per cent of light. Pinpricks of light modelled the position of stars visible from the building's location. In the bright white interior, water droplets flowing along channels helped explain features of the car manufacturer's new hydrogen fuel cell vehicle. Here, the fundamental duality of the natural world: day and night, light and dark was on display. Also on display at the 2018 Olympics were 1,200 drones that made a dramatic appearance in the sky during the Opening Ceremony of the Games. The illuminations were programmed to take the shape of a snowboarder, a dove and the Olympic rings. Produced by the Intel Corporation, the 'shooting star' drones are designed specifically for use at light shows.

Although total darkness is absent from the natural world, we can only guess how humans, through the millennia, have felt when cloud cover rendered the nocturnal landscape largely invisible. It is likely that people drew on the full sensorium to a larger extent than we do today with, for instance, hearing more attuned to sounds in the night. It has been suggested that in the dark, landforms 'exist as presences: inferred, less substantial but more powerful for it' (MacFarlane, 2005: 75). So, how did people react to the visually spectacular, to the appearance of the moon beneath the surface of a lake, to a bolt of lightning or to the shimmering colours of an aurora? Contemporary light design remains fascinated by these phenomena and a light artwork, simulating the northern lights has featured at events in Switzerland, Japan and, in 2018, it was an important part of the Fringe's Parade of Light in Adelaide, Australia.

Throughout human history, darkness has been associated with fear, even for people living in powerful societies such as Imperial Rome (Brox, 2014) where, 'In normal times night fell over the city like the shadow of a great danger.... Everyone fled to his home, shut himself in, and barricaded the entrance' (Carcopino, 1940: 47). In Europe, during the Middle Ages, a curfew bell announced the end of day, gates were locked and chains were strung across roads to deny movement around the city after dark. In some cities, people were unable to leave their homes without approval from a magistrate (Brox, 2014). Attendance at religious festivals offered rare exceptions to escape from these restrictive regulations. The Dark Ages stand in contrast with the Age of Enlightenment, which brought radical ideas and scientific discoveries to Europe and provided the philosophical foundations for the American Declaration of Independence. Isaac Newton's optical theories serve as a metaphor for the start of this historical period characterised by new ways of seeing the world.

Contrasts between day and night 'form part of an ancient and extended set of symbols which are ubiquitous in theology, philosophy, literature and the arts' (Bach and Degenring, 2014: 46). Many festivals celebrate the victory of light over darkness, of good over evil, of knowledge over ignorance. This is the case with Diwali, the Hindu festival of lights that is held over five days every autumn. On day three, which coincides with the darkest night of the year in the northern hemisphere, temples, homes and offices are brightly illuminated. The festival can be traced to the middle of the first millennium and the tradition of lighting diyaes was recorded by Venetian merchants on visits to India in the fifteenth century. Today, it is popular around the world and the religious and historical significance of the festival was officially recognised in a resolution of the Congress of the United States in 2007. Since 2013, a celebration to mark Diwali has become an annual event at the US Capitol. In opening remarks in 2017, Democratic Congresswoman Tulsi Gabbard reminded the 400 people in attendance of what Diwali stands for and that it was important for truth to triumph over falsehood in Washington (Goindi, 2017).

The famous passage from the Bible, presented above, has had a major influence on art and literature and the English language is full of related references. 'I see' signifies understanding which contrasts with 'being kept in the dark' and a dark facial expression suggests the opposite of a bright smile. However, for Shakespeare, the night offers opportunities for both positive and negative personality traits to emerge and, in gothic literature, darkness is treated as being alluring as well as dangerous (Bach and Degenring, 2014). These issues continue to fascinate contemporary audiences and in an episode of the BBC series Civilisations with the title *Radiance*, the presenter, Simon Schama, suggested that the greatest art illuminates the universal search for salvation. The ability to explain artistic techniques, the use of colour, symbolic meanings and historical context associated with some of the world's most famous works of art demonstrated the power of television to inform, educate, entertain, shock, challenge and to inspire with visions of a shared humanity. A comparison of two paintings by the Spanish artist, Francisco Goya made a startling contrast between light and dark. The *San Isidro Meadow*, painted in 1788, shows people enjoying an annual festival and is full of colour. Thirty years later, Goya returns to the same setting but this time, according to Schama, 'the lights have been turned out' and the figures resemble 'a freak show'. The background is the colour of tar and the distorted shapes of faces reflect the pain and sorrow resulting from Napoleon's invasion of Spain during the Peninsular War (1808–1814). Schama's reference to the 'lights have been turned out' echoes the comment made by the British Foreign Secretary to a friend on the eve of the First World War that 'the lamps are going out all over Europe, we shall not see them lit again in our life-time'.

Radiance starts by illustrating the light that flooded into cathedrals where the stories on the jewel-like stained glass windows provide a glimpse of heaven. In the sixteenth century, the embrace of colour in Venetian art was in contrast with the classical style that was privileged in Florence. Bellini and Titian used harmonious combinations of colour with the most precious pigments reserved for the Madonna or powerful members of Venetian society. The *Celebration of Holi in a Garden Pavilion* (1729) shows a joyous celebration of sensual pleasure. The Hindu Festival of Holi continues today and is practised around the world to mark the victory of good over evil and the value of cherished relationships. Participants are showered in brightly coloured powders. According to Schama, another style of Indian art in the eighteenth century illustrated vibrant, colourful dreamscapes which told the stories of Hindu gods. At the same time in Japan, ten colours were used on wood blocks to print scenes of metropolitan life. By the 1830s, the leading exponent of this art, Katsushika Hokusai, was producing abstract interpretations of the spirituality embedded in the Japanese landscape. According to Buddhist beliefs, Mount Fuji is associated with immortality and it was depicted by Hokusai in 36 different prints with views from different perspectives and in different light. The Japanese prints were collected by and had a major influence on European Impressionist artists. They attempted to reinvent the way of seeing and, rather than showing light on objects, they wanted to paint light itself. Monet's equivalent of Mount Fuji was the cathedral in Rouen which he painted 30 times in different light, using colour to capture time. Schama suggests Van Gogh travelled to the south of France in search of 'Japanese light'. As the fulfilment of an obsessive desire to bring heaven to earth, he painted *Starry Night over the Rhône* in 1888 (Plate 13). Schama describes the painting's heavenly radiance with the trinity of gas lamps on the land, their reflections in the water and the explosion of stars in the sky. The glow of the gas lamps represented a visual connection between heaven and earth. This interpretation draws comparison with motivations attributed to some of the earliest forms of art and with the creation stories that are expressed in Australian Aboriginal art. Many of the dot paintings based on cultural traditions depict movements across the land and the sky.

In 2018, L'Atelier des Lumières (the studio of light), a digital art museum in Paris, brought Van Gogh's paintings to life in the form of an immersive art show that was attended by 1.2 million people. The paintings were projected onto the walls of a former foundry accompanied by a playlist of contemporary music (Stenson, 2019). The influence of Japanese art on Van Gogh was reflected in one part of the show. In *Dreamed Japan: Images of the Floating World*, people circled the floor as waves crashed around them to the sound of Claude Debussy's *The Sea* and the beat of the Japanese drums (Stenson, 2019). In another part, images of *Starry Night* covered the space from floor to ceiling, showing contrasts between light and dark and creating a sensation of standing in water, receiving reflections of the stars and lights of the town (Stenson, 2019). This exhibition demonstrates the enduring appeal of Van Gogh's art and its ability to create an immersive experience in a digital format. It is an example of Julier's (2005) design culture and the transformation of a foundry into an eventscape.

THEN THERE WAS LIGHT

Any temporal extension of daytime activities has been 'historically contingent and largely influenced by the means of individuals and societies to illuminate the night to a greater or lesser degree' (Bach and Degenring, 2014: 48). An ability to project light was usually associated with privilege. During the Middle Ages, the wealthy did not suffer the inquisitorial approach of the night watch because they could be seen from a distance. Their movements were made visible and their distinctive dress illuminated by the light from lanterns carried by servants. Later, when gaslight was introduced to cities, the gloominess of oil lamps marked the edges of poor neighbourhoods that were avoided by the well-to-do (Brox, 2014). Organised street lighting started when authorities required households to place a candle on street-facing windowsills and when movement through the nightscape was facilitated by lamps placed at regular intervals. People were attracted to the lights at taverns and coffeehouses which offered stimulants late into the night (Brox, 2014). The widespread introduction of oil lamps was very labour-intensive as they had to be lit and required attention to ensure that they continued to burn. An efficient system that operated in Amsterdam in the seventeenth century, meant that all the city's streetlamps could be attended by just 100 lamplighters. Municipal lighting grew as whale oil replaced locally produced rapeseed and linseed oils and, in 1846, more than 700 whaling vessels were leaving American ports to secure the necessary supply (Brox, 2014). Concerns were expressed at this time that 'if street lighting became common, festive and ceremonial lighting would lose some of its wonder' (Brox, 2014: 18).

Gaslight marked a big improvement in lighting with a more reliable flame and an interconnected delivery system from gasometers (Brox, 2014). After being used to light factories in Britain, lamps were introduced in a section of Pall Mall in 1907 to celebrate the King's birthday. By the 1820s, several hundred miles of underground gas mains supplied more than 40,000 gas lamps on the streets of London. Large, ugly storage tanks and gasworks were usually located in poor neighbourhoods and these tended to be the areas where gas leaks caused explosions. However, it would seem that the effect of industrial production was considered equal to that of the natural world. Brox refers to a quote in Clegg (1841) when it was claimed that gaslight offered,

> a brightness clear as summer's noon, but dazzling and soft as moonlight.... Those who have been used only to the brilliancy of oil and candle-light, can have no adequate idea of the effect of an illumination by gas. It so completely penetrates the whole atmosphere, and at the same time is so genial to the eyesight, that it appears as natural and pure as daylight, and it sheds also a warmth as purifying to the air as cheering to the spirits.
>
> (Clegg, 1841: 20–21)

For Robert Louis Stevenson (1893), the arrival of gaslight meant that 'sundown no longer emptied the promenade, and the day was lengthened out to every man's fancy' (quoted in Brox, 2014: 22).

From the middle of the nineteenth century, life was added to the word night as the gaslight era provided new leisure opportunities and created a nightlife for cities. The emerging middle class went window-shopping in the evenings when the glow from gas flames reflected against mirrors displayed merchandise with 'the art of dazzling illusion' (Gutzkow, quoted in Brox, 2014: 23). The first use of electric light was in department stores and the first arc streetlamps were introduced in London and Paris in 1878. Until then, change had been gradual as candles were replaced by lanterns that were then replaced by gaslight and throughout this time people moved between light and shadow in the streetscapes. But arc lights were much brighter and it became possible to shed light across entire cities. Not everyone was impressed and Robert Louis Stevenson protested that:

> a new sort of urban star now shines out nightly, horrible, unearthly, obnoxious to the human eye; a lamp for a nightmare! Such a light as this should shine only on murders and public crime, or along the corridors of lunatic asylums, a horror to heighten horror.
>
> (Stevenson, 1881: 295)

But few were daunted by such concerns as electric lighting 'emerged as a glamorous symbol of progress and cultural advancement' (Nye, 1997: 54) and municipalities large and small sought 'to test the boundaries of brilliance' (Brox, 2014: 25).

The potential of electricity was both tested and demonstrated at the Chicago World's Fair in 1893. The provision of electricity made it a test of the alternating current system that was at an early stage of development by the Westinghouse Company that won the contract to supply power to the event. Electricity was used to illuminate the buildings and fountains, and to power three large spotlights. Exhibits by the Westinghouse Company in a special Electricity Building showed the effects of electricity on devices developed by Nikola Tesla. A metal egg spinning on a disk demonstrated the effect of a magnetic field generated by an electric motor and a wireless lamp was lit in a high-voltage, high-frequency alternating current demonstration.

Light and technology continue to be showcased at events influencing the design of installations and the type of information they convey. The UK Pavilion at Expo 2010 in Shanghai, designed by Heatherwick Studio, sought to connect with the event's theme; *Better City, Better Life*, by exploring the relationship between nature and cities. This focused on London's green credentials and its pioneering role related to the provision of public parks and the study of botany. Kew Garden's Millennium Seedbank project was selected as the vehicle to communicate these ideas and the pavilion took the form of an architecturally iconic Seed Cathedral. At 20 metres in height, it was formed from 60,000 slender transparent fibre-optic rods (Figure 6.1). Each was 7.5 metres long and 3D computer modelling ensured the geometric accuracy of their placement. Each rod had seeds at its tip and drew daylight inwards to illuminate the interior of the pavilion. Changes in weather conditions caused fluctuations in the luminosity. Light sources inside each rod allowed the structure to glow at night. The fibre-optic array created an apparent halo around the structure while inside, visitors passed through a tranquil space surrounded by tens of thousands of points of light illuminating the seeds (Jordana, 2010).

Figure 6.1 *Expo 2010: UK Pavilion.*

Source: Daniele Mattioli

In a combination of art, fashion and technology, a 4D light show for a product launch by Ralph Lauren was described by a company executive as 'merchantainment' (Koeck and Warnaby, 2014). Laser scanning, computer modelling and animation culminated with the projection of moving images onto Ralph Lauren's flagship stores in London and New York. A recording that was accessible online extended the life of the promotion for both the brand and the places where the events were held. A similar product launch by Nokia included the biggest projection mapping ever staged in London and performances by a DJ and artists that appealed to young mobile phone users (Koeck and Warnaby, 2014). As urban spectacle, there is little to distinguish these events from key elements of the light festivals that are discussed later in this chapter.

RESPONSES TO LIGHT

Elizabethan plays were performed outdoors during the day and a candle was extinguished to signify darkness to the audience (Dessen, 1978). Today, when the curtain is raised in a darkened theatre, the world that is made visible on stage establishes the time and place for a dramatic performance. Revealing one part of the stage or shining a light on an object directs the attention of the audience and may dictate an emotional response. The use of light and shade is fundamental to the creation of dramatic effect and the movement of illumination through darkness can create 'a poetics of light' (Bille and Sørensen, 2007). Lighting provides meaning but meaning is also attached to the source of lighting. A single light bulb hanging from a ceiling in an apartment suggests poverty and possible danger while a dinner by candlelight expresses warmth and intimacy. A desire to conserve certain types of lighting has been described as 'place-bound technological nostalgia' (Gandy, 2017a: 366). This is illustrated by groups in Berlin who have campaigned to protect the largest remaining gas lighting network in Europe. Similarly, in Hong Kong, attempts have been made to save the famous multicoloured, handcrafted neon lights that date from the 1950s (Gandy, 2017a). With up to 90 per cent of the neon lights having disappeared in the last 20 years, the Hong Kong Neon Heritage Group was formed in 2017 to protect those that remain shining in the streets. Another response has been to create new indoor neon signs (Fernández, 2018). Bach and Degenring suggest that 'lighting situations are linked to social relationships, atmospheres, moods and characters' mental processes in a complex fashion, shaping them and in turn also being shaped by them' (2014: 61).

It is the task of designers to create appropriate 'light situations' that achieve desired outcomes at concerts, street festivals, product launches and other events. The scope of this work and the opportunities available for your entrepreneurs is outlined in **Developing Mapped Design**.

DEVELOPING MAPPED DESIGN

By David Musch

Mapped Design was established in 2018 to offer specialist services in visual design, and despite it being a relatively new entrant to the AV market, a number of formative development phases are evident.

Going back a number of years now to high school, I was responsible for the lighting at concerts and school plays and I became the theatre manager in Year 12. My weekends throughout this time were spent broadening my horizons in freelance lighting and sound production at parties. I had a thorough understanding of electronics and production technology for someone of my age and I established a solid network of contacts. The passion continued after leaving school when the parties I organised were starting to scale upwards in size. In addition, my personal branding and industry connections were rapidly growing. I didn't realise at the time, this would prove to be invaluable to me as my career progressed.

Post high school I was working full-time in an audio-visual role and looking for more creative, working opportunities – something more mentally stimulating that allowed me to combine my own freedom of expression while still seeking technologically complex solutions. I wanted to push beyond what I had achieved up until that point. I was also contracted casually as the 'sound and lighting guy' at the popular Adelaide nightclub, Sugar, where I was presented with opportunities to hone my skills with lighting and audio in a club capacity.

In 2017, I designed the space and lighting for 'Dark Matter', a temporary pop-up bar for Sugar in its neighbouring laneway as part of the Adelaide Fringe Festival. This further drove me to realise that this was where I wanted to focus my knowledge and energy. Taking a leap of freelance faith, I quit my full-time job and poured everything I had into the planning stages of what eventually would become Mapped. Within Mapped's first six months, I was contracted to design and build the staging and lighting installations at two separate techno music festivals that took place in the Adelaide Hills. They ended up being incredibly successful, were profitable and exceeded expectations for events of such niche music genre.

Then, 2018 was a big year. Once again in the realm of Adelaide's Fringe season, I was granted the opportunity of total creative freedom to develop an installation at Royal Croquet Club (since renamed as RCC Fringe), and so the idea of 'Neon Forest', the abstract, UV-lit, eccentric caravan park was conceived by myself and two colleagues. RCC Fringe has always been an incredibly successful, Adelaide-based event, and I have been fortunate enough to work with the founders for quite a while in the lead up to them asking me to take on such a huge project.

In the same year, for the Adelaide Fringe, I also designed and built the Infinity Box – an immersive, interactive experience of mirrors and light – a nod to Yayoi Kusama's work with Infinity Mirror Rooms. I found this project in particular to be truly reflective (pardon the pun) of the direction I want to go in with my work – using technology to deliver transformative experiences.

A referral from another local contact led to a meeting with the art director of a film production company, which led to a small lighting project on a feature film. The production designer and director of photography on the film were impressed by my work and suddenly this small project grew considerably in a short amount of time. I was suddenly managing a team of six, used about two kilometres of LED lighting and spent six weeks of pre-production and six weeks of production/shooting, working 18 hours each day. The gaffer from the film later introduced me to the creative agency Kojo who contracted me to design and programme lighting for various film shoots including for the Fremantle Dockers AFL team, and the Adelaide Strikers cricket team. A pipeline of work has been offered by Kojo.

My list of projects continues to grow, and with each one comes a new opportunity to use technology to deliver transformative experiences. Interaction should be more than touching a screen or playing with new tech. It should be meaningful and give the user something to take home with them, whether it be informative, a simple thought or simply joy. Throughout all my work, I am always striving to offer something that leaves the audience with a lasting memory.

One hundred years ago, lighting was used to achieve social engineering by Charles Bragdon, who organised Festivals of Song and Light from 1915–1918. Bragdon, an architect based in Rochester, New York, was driven by a theosophical world-view, based on Hindu and Buddhist cosmological principles in combination with modern Western science (Massey, 2006). For Bragdon, the festivals were a gathering of humanity and a way to unify people from different backgrounds. They represented the realization of his ideal of democracy as 'the rule of a people by its *demos*, or group soul' (Bragdon, 1926: 1). The ability to come together in a public place to share a collective experience is consistent with the notion of the commons and the politics of cooperation (Amin and Howell, 2016). Bragdon believed that the universal order of nature was manifest in mathematical patterns and the calculations used in his architectural designs were based on the ratios of the consonant intervals within the octave – principles of sound determined material volumes and geometric patterns.

Interestingly, geometry and music, with arithmetic and astronomy, were studied together as part of the quadrivium in medieval liberal arts scholarship (Cosgrove, 1985). Bragdon applied his beliefs in the construction of the Rochester railway terminal, where the resonance resulting from the performance of the diatonic scale by an opera singer brought the building to life and, in so doing, confirmed, for Bragdon, the satisfactory fulfilment of his design. At the festivals, 'using projective ornament and harmonic mathematics to synthesize architectural form with color and music on the model of Richard Wagner's "music drama", Bragdon created moments of cathartic unity among festival participants' (Massey, 2006: 579). Lighting played a key role in achieving these outcomes.

The first Song and Light Festival in New York was held in 1916 where 60,000 people gathered on the south shore of the lake in Central Park. It was organised by Bragdon with friends Harry Barnhart and Arthur Farwell. Farwell was a composer and was involved in music education and Barnhart was a concert performer and organiser of community choral groups (Massey, 2006). A 65-piece orchestra was seated on a wooden stage that projected over the water and 800 singers were assembled on the shore behind. Lamps were deployed in boats across the lake and overhead stretched cables bearing light fixtures with a colour palate based on correspondence between musical and chromatic harmonies. When the chorus began to sing 'the light fixtures were electrified. The chorus was illuminated by clear white light tempered for the eyes of the audience by colored lanterns and shields that glowed like stained glass windows' (Massey, 2006: 596). Bragdon modulated the flow of electricity for dramaturgical emphasis with low light levels coming from the multicoloured lanterns and bright white lights turned up at moments of intensity and to spotlight the chorus and the audience as they sang (Massey, 2006). According to Massey, Bragdon later wrote, 'Under the influence of the place, the lights, the music, favored by friendly darkness, the invisible audience found its voice and sang' (2006: 597). Bragdon described the design as a cathedral without walls and Massey suggests that, at his festivals, Bragdon 'created temporary environments defined by color, light, sound and ornament' (Massey, 2006: 597). During the Festival of Song and Light, Central Park was transformed into a precisely designed eventscape. After the First World War, Bragdon worked with colleagues to build a Luxorgam, a mechanism for simultaneously playing music and multicoloured projective ornament designs. He later made designs for colour-music film animations. He and his group of like-minded innovators called themselves 'The Prometheans' (Massey, 2006).

HEAT AND LIGHT

In Greek mythology, Prometheus steals fire from the Gods and gives it to man. Fire gave man heat and light: offering protection, an ability to cook food and ways to communicate. The light from a fire can be seen over long distances, so news can spread from one flaming hilltop to the next. Beacons were lit to warn of possible invasion as the Spanish Armada approached the English coast in 1588 and were lit again to celebrate victory. The lighting of bonfires throughout the UK has been used for other national celebrations, including Queen Victoria's Diamond Jubilee in 1897, the 400th anniversary of the defeat of the Spanish Armada in 1988 and Queen Elizabeth II's Golden Jubilee in 2002.

Fire can be spectacular and frightening and it has been associated with many types of events, from pagan rituals to modern celebrations. The diversity in the type of burning events is noteworthy as is their cultural significance. In the Hindu festival of Dussehra, effigies of Ravana, symbolising evil are burned in villages and towns throughout India, and particularly in cities in the north of the country. The festival was recognised by UNESCO as being of 'Intangible Cultural Heritage of Humanity' in 2008. In a very different context, a world record was set for the size of a bonfire on the campus of Texas A&M University in 1969. It had been built annually for 90 years to mark the university's burning desire to defeat the rival University of Texas in college football until it was stopped in 1999 following the death of 12 people who were killed when the bonfire collapsed during construction. In Britain, Bonfire Night commemorates the gunpowder plot of 1605 when an attempt was made to place explosives beneath the House of Lords in London. An official day of thanksgiving for the plot's failure became a cherished celebration for social gatherings and community events when an effigy of Guy Fawkes is burned on a bonfire to the accompaniment of fireworks. For generations, the 5th of November has provided an opportunity to buy fireworks from local shops, to spend days building a bonfire and to gather with family and friends on a cold night. When the last catherine wheel stops spinning, it is time to start thinking about Christmas.

Burning objects mark the dramatic conclusion at many events held in a wide range of environments. Up Helly Aa in Lerwick, Scotland is a 24-hour celebration of the Norse heritage of the Shetland Islands. It ends when torches are thrown into a Viking galley that has taken four months to build. A common characteristic among many burning events is the considerable investment by committed community members in the construction of symbolic objects that are then destroyed in a dramatic inferno. The flames provide an intense sensory experience when the objects are embraced by the natural world. As glowing embers start to fade, physics determines the form and duration of the event's final act. In 1986, a 'Man' was burned on a beach in San Francisco, giving rise to the 'Burning Man' event that is now held over nine days in late summer in the Nevada desert. About 70,000 people attend this annual celebration of self-expression, radical inclusion and community cooperation that is described in **Transformations at Burning Man**. Burning events present a fire hazard in much of Australia but bush doof festivals such as Pitch that is held in the Grampian Mountains of Victoria combine transformational qualities with an escapist engagement with nature. Participants are attracted by the mix of techno music genres that are offered and the atmospheric light displays that range from large LED screens displaying psychedelic images to doof sticks with colourful lights that sway in the hands of people in the crowd who made them. The individually designed doof sticks generate colourful illuminations at night and communicate humorous, counter-culture messages during the day.

TRANSFORMATIONS AT *BURNING MAN*

By Grant Hall

Transformational festivals tend to be found in remote natural locations. An emphasis is placed on expressive participation and co-creativity, environmental sensitivity and a social or gift-giving economy (Bottorff, 2015) and, in contrast with other types of festivals, they eschew corporate sponsorship and big-name performers (Ruane, 2017). Musical performances and psychedelic entertainment is complemented by yoga, chanting, meditation and ecstatic dance (Johner, 2015). According to Bottorff, 'it is common to hear participants at transformational festivals say they seek positive and life-altering experiences that will lead them to greater happiness, competence, and connectedness' (2015: 58). Famous examples include Rainbow Serpent in Australia, BOOM in Portugal and *Burning Man* in the USA, which is considered to be the 'prototypical transformational festival' (Rogg, 2017: 15).

Burning Man

First staged in 1986, in San Francisco, *Burning Man* is a week-long annual outdoor festival which takes place in the desert of

Nevada, USA. It has been described as bohemian, counter-cultural, party-like and drug infused, attracting anarchists, drifters and mystics in its community alongside the artists, engineers and academics and is especially popular with people who work in innovation intensive roles (Radziwill and Benton, 2013: 8). It has been reported that attendance at *Burning Man* inspired innovations in tech-based companies (Dawson, 2017), fashion design (Brennan, 2017), music and visual art (Mendoza, 2015) and the production of other festivals (Hillier, 2016). Google's founders, Larry Page and Sergey Brin, 'chose Eric Schmidt as their CEO because he was the only candidate for the job who had been a burner' (Taylor, 2007).

With annual attendances in the order of 70,000, a temporary city is established called 'Black Rock City', which is dedicated to 'community art, self-expression and self-reliance' (Radziwill and Benton, 2013: 8). As it is situated in a harsh environment, festival pilgrims 'must be prepared to endure physical hardship and moments of trial', amid 'the extremes of heat and cold, unforgiving winds, unavoidable dust, and the persistent risk of dehydration' (Gilmore, 2010: 124). Participants have reported that the challenges of existing in the harsh conditions can contribute to the 'breaking down of self', and as such, has played a role in the transformational personal experiences that people report in relation to their *Burning Man* experience. The festival is symbolised by the ritual burning of a large male effigy, which represents 'a metaphor for the process of purification of the individual from market constraints' (Cova and Dalli, 2017: 8). It is best known for its abundant art, including large-scale installations that protrude from the monotone earth, like surreal trees in an unruly forest (Limbach, 2014). Buying and selling is not permitted and 'people bestow handmade trinkets, artwork, or experiences upon others without expectation of immediate reciprocation' (Chen, 2012: 571). Burners are involved in artistic and other creative activities such as 'elaborate costuming, designing and decorating a campsite, constructing and driving an art car, performing dance or music, engaging in performance art and other collective activities at theme camps' (Chen, 2012: 581). 'No spectators' is a Festival slogan (Chen, 2012: 571).

Burning Man is widely labelled as a transformational festival within the popular media and academic publications, but the organisers prefer to refer to it as a 'culture', which incorporates a broad range of non-traditional activities. They draw attention to initiatives by *Burning Man* communities that exist around the world. Burners Without Borders is an international NGO, which undertakes activities such as beach clean-ups, disaster relief efforts, providing assistance in refugee camps and the planting of community gardens.

The elemental forces of fire and water have been combined to spectacular effect at events held at two of Europe's major rivers – the Thames and the Rhine. The River Thames became an eventscape in September 2016, when a 'Take me to the River' programme promoted over 150 events. They included opportunities to *get active*: by walking, swimming, kayaking; *to get onboard* classic boats and tall ships; and *to get involved* in photography competitions and clean-up activities. *Floating Dreams*, a three-storey-high, illuminated lantern in the centre of the river, was constructed from drawings by people who had fled from North to South Korea. But it was *London's Burning* that captured international attention. It was produced by Artichoke, the company responsible for bringing the Sultan's Elephant to the streets of London (see Chapter 4). A series of art events, performances and talks to commemorate the 350th anniversary of the Great Fire of London included an interactive fire garden in the grounds of the Tate Modern Art Gallery and large-scale video projections on the National Theatre and St Paul's Cathedral. It came to a spectacular close when a 120-metre-long wooden sculpture, floating on the river, was set alight (Figure 6.2). The sculpture depicted the skyline of London as it was at the time of the Fire in 1666. *London's Burning* was ambitious in creative scope, planning and delivery. An area in the heart of London including part of the River Thames became a stage with spectators having free access to the riverbank to watch the event. Training was offered to young unemployed people and hundreds of schoolchildren designed decorative panels for the sculpture. The organisers had to work closely with police, fire, ambulance and transport services but also with groups such as tug boat operators, the Port of London Authority and the London river-based Fire Brigade. Over 50,000 spectators attended the event and there was an online audience in excess of one million live viewers. In evaluating the Public Relations impact of the event, O'Donnell (2016) reported that it received press coverage in 25 countries including India, China, Russia and

Figure 6.2 *London's Burning: sculpture on the Thames.*

Source: Matthew Andrews

the USA and from every national newspaper in the UK with *London's Burning* picture stories running on four consecutive days in *The Times* with two 'Picture of the Day' features appearing in the *Telegraph*. Three months after the event, the figure for online views stood at 6.5 million.

The cultural landscape plays a critical role at the *Rhine in Flames* when, on five occasions between May and September each year, Europe's biggest parade of illuminated ships makes the trip from Spay to Koblenz in Germany. Both sides of the river are lit with torches, as are many of the villages and, at the end of the event, large fireworks light the skies above the Ehrenbreitstein Fortress and the Deutsches Eck in Koblenz (Rhineland-Palatinate Tourist Board, 2018). Fireworks were used in festivals as early as the ninth century in China where it was believed they bring good fortune. From the seventeenth century, they became popular in Europe where coloured fireworks were invented in the nineteenth century. Today, they feature at the opening and closing ceremonies of the Olympic Games and television coverage of New Year's Eve showcases a competition to see which major city can stage the longest and most spectacular firework display. The choice of location for television crews is dictated by an ability to capture the pyrotechnic displays set against stunning backdrops at, in chronological order of presentation to a global audience, Sydney Harbour, Red Square, the Eiffel Tower or Times Square.

Events have always taken advantage of the ability to carry a flame. Ancient landscapes were witness to processions of people carrying burning torches and, today, candles are carried into cathedrals, as they have been for thousands of years, to set the scene for religious ceremonies. Despite the development of new technologies, there remain continuities with practices based in belief systems that have survived for thousands of years. However, applications constantly evolve in response to social trends and environmental affordances. At the start of the ski season, mountains are transformed by the appearance of a moving line of twinkling lights on distant slopes. The scene gradually changes as skiers holding torches approach the resort before the sound of the skis and the heat from the flames are experienced as the skiers sweep past the waiting spectators. Similar performances form part of Fire and Ice events that are staged as evening entertainment in many ski resorts. At the Speed of Light event at the Edinburgh Festival, choreographed staging of walkers and runners with lighting technology harnessed to their bodies produced a 'kinetic cultural spectacle' (Edensor and Lorimer, 2015: 1).

The longest, most famous and symbolically important torch procession is the relay of the Olympic Flame as it is carried from Olympia in Greece to the host city to mark the start of the Games. Although it has connections with practices associated with ancient Greece, the first time the relay was held was at the 1936 Berlin Olympic Games. Since then, the torch has demonstrated a unique power to capture the attention of people of all ages and backgrounds and to bring communities together. While wrapped in the national flag, people try to get as close as possible to the torch. Open displays of emotion betray a belief that a special moment in the country's history is being shared. The route equates to an extensive eventscape connecting dispersed communities and linking them to national values and those espoused by the IOC and corporations which sponsor the relay. The route is planned to ensure that the torch passes sites of national importance with media coverage capturing images of places as tourist destinations.

ILLUMINATIONS

Illuminated manuscripts were decorated with gold, silver and colourful miniature pictures. The early examples that survive today were religious documents such as translations of the gospels produced by monks. The vivid embellishments were designed to capture attention, add interest in the documents and enhance their ability to convey information. Similar outcomes are sought when colourful light is projected onto outdoor structures. The illumination of heritage buildings such as castles enhances their visual appeal and is used to proclaim their cultural importance. This practice is applied so consistently to iconic structures that it is possible to make a statement by turning the lights off. This occurred in 2016 when the Eiffel Tower was placed in darkness as a sign of solidarity with the people of Aleppo during the war in Syria. The French have long recognised opportunities to communicate and entertain on a grand scale and were the pioneers of various forms of creative outdoor performances. In 1952, the Chateau de Chambord was the setting for the first Son et Lumière and, by the end of the twentieth century, there were 50 productions of this type in France, mainly in the Loire Valley. The effect of projecting lighting onto historical buildings synchronised with music and narration has attracted tourists to some of the world's most famous sites including the Forum in Rome, the Parthenon in Athens, the Pyramids of Giza in Egypt and the Temples at Teotihuacán in Mexico. French electronic music composer Jean-Michel Jarre included Son et Lumière productions at outdoor concerts which attracted more than 1 million spectators. A Son et Lumière was held at Canterbury Cathedral in 2005 as part of the European Cathedrales en Lumière project and the Eden Project in Cornwall, England produced a Son et Lumière as a Christmas attraction in 2016. Lasers created a canopy of light, painting the biomes with festive colours, set to a soundscape of music and stories (Dixon, 2016). It was listed as one of the top Christmas light festivals in the UK in 2016. The list included the Capability Brown sculptured parkland at Blenheim Palace, where there was a one-mile multisensory path, a scented fire garden and fibre-optic lawns. At Longleat Safari Park, there were lanterns in the shape of some of the park's animals and the displays used 12 miles of silk, 30,000 bulbs and 2½ miles of LED lighting (Dixon, 2016).

Winter illuminations have become popular throughout Japan and Kobe's Luminarie was produced by Italian designers as a memorial to the victims of the 1995 earthquake. It is held for ten days in December but some of the festivals last much longer. The Kingdom of Light at Nagasaki runs from late October to early May at a theme park where music accompanies a canal cruise that passes illuminated waterfalls and flowers. Music is synchronised to a light show at the Ashikaga Flower Fantasy in Tochigi where four million LED lights cover a park and hanging lights are made in the shape of flowers (Japan Guide, 2018). Temperatures below freezing provide an opportunity to create ice sculptures. On a small scale, some hotels located next to lakes build structures on the ice as a temporary attraction for guests. On a larger scale, cities in Japan, Norway and Canada take advantage of long, cold winters to stage ice sculpture competitions. The most famous example is the Harbin International Ice and Snow Sculpture Competition in China, which attracts more than ten million visitors each year (China Highlights, 2019). The festival, which began as an organised show in 1963, can be traced back to the Qing dynasty when fishermen placed candles inside blocks of ice cut from the Songhua River to create lanterns (Recker, 2019). Today, the number and size of the sculptures in Harbin make the eventscape resemble a colourful, frozen city. Photos that accompany news items about the event (cf. Goldberg, 2019; Recker, 2019) support promotional claims that it is the beauty of the lighting that sets it apart from other festivals. The role of lanterns in Chinese culture and continuities between former and present-day practices are discussed in **Light Festivals in China**.

LIGHT FESTIVALS IN CHINA

By Hailian Gao

Lanterns were developed when fire was discovered and were used for reading and working. The protection provided by the shade stopped the wind blowing out the flame (Song, 2015). The light gave protection due to the belief that fire had the power to drive away all evils in the dark. The display of lanterns became a festival in the Han Dynasty more than 2,000 years ago. During the reign of Emperor Ming of the Eastern Han Dynasty, Buddhism began to spread from India throughout China. Emperor Ming had heard that Buddhist monks would pray to Buddhist relics on the fifteenth day of first lunar month, so he ordered that lanterns should be lit to pay respect to the Buddha. People were allowed to go out to see the lanterns under the full moon (Song, 2015). The lanterns in Buddhism symbolise light and wisdom, which will bring supreme happiness. With the advocacy of the emperor, lantern festivals became a folk custom (Huang and Zhu, 2013).

Lantern festivals are also rooted in the China's indigenous religion: Taoism, which celebrates the Shangyuan festival. In Taoism, people worship the three most powerful gods: Tianguan (the god of the sky), Diguan (the god of the earth) and Shuiguan (the god of the water). The fifteenth day of the first lunar month is the birthday of Tianguan. 'Shangyuan' means the first full-moon night in a year. Legend has it that Tianguan was fond of entertainment, so people would light colourful lanterns on his birthday to amuse him (Qiao, 2009).

Lantern festivals developed into a grand events in Tang Dynasty (Song, 2015). Lanterns were put up everywhere in the imperial palace, streets, even in common people's houses. People made lanterns to celebrate their peaceful life whilst the magnificent public displays symbolised and celebrated a prosperous, strong and powerful country. High lantern wheels, lantern towers and lantern trees were built in the imperial palace and many popular ancient poets described the grand occasions. The strong tradition from Tang Dynasty carried on to the Song Dynasty. Later on, lantern riddles, dances and operas were developed as part of the festival customs in the Ming and Qing dynasties (Song, 2015). Attendees continue their celebrations by eating sticky rice balls and performing Lion and Dragon dances. Lantern festivals are also about love. In ancient times, single men and women were provided a precious opportunity to meet face to face at a time when they were not allowed to move freely in public except during festivals (Zhang, 2008). During the Lantern Festival, the government cancelled the curfew and allowed people to go out at night and to places that were not normally permitted. People were permitted to break space and time regulations (Zhang, 2012). Nowadays, people have transformed the thirst for light to longing for a better life. Therefore, at the beginning of a new year, people light a lantern to light up the long, depressing winter and open up the hope for a good year.

The lanterns in the ancient China were a work of art. With a history of nearly 2,000 years, the workmanship of Chinese lanterns is a perfect combination of Chinese painting, paper-cutting, paper arts, embroidery, sewing, as well as the lighting function. The materials to make Chinese lantern include bamboo, wood, rattan, straw, animal horns, metal, silk, damask, etc. (Liang, 2007). In addition to the traditional oval-shaped lanterns, there are square, rectangular and spherical lanterns. Lanterns can be as small as a baseball or as large as a person (Song, 2015). Traditionally, they are red and round-shaped, decorated with red and gold tassels. The round shape symbolises wholeness and togetherness in China, reminiscent of the full moon. In Chinese culture, the colour red is believed to symbolise warmth, happiness and good fortune. Lanterns have become a symbol of national pride in China and are used to decorate homes and public places for most major festivals (Song, 2015). By lighting a lantern, people pray for a good year, a prosperous family, good health, longevity, wealth, promotion and all kinds of good luck for the coming year. Different patterns are drawn on the lantern cover to symbolise various wishes. For instance, peony symbolises wealth and pomegranate symbolises many children in the family (Yang, 2011).

Nowadays, with the development of science and technology, the art of lanterns has been refurbished, and new types of lanterns are emerging every year. New technologies and processes such as electronics, construction, machinery, remote control, acoustics and optical fibres are used in the design and production of lanterns. The combination of shape, colour, light, sound and movement creates a magical atmosphere that attracts millions of people. The modern festival is a platform for new ideas, new creations and new social exhibitions to emerge; a stage for humanities and sciences to display; a platform for cultural communication; a classroom for aesthetic education; a channel for international cultural exchanges; and also a bridge to connect the common people. In June 2008, Lantern Festival was designated a national Intangible Cultural Heritage by the Chinese government.

With the continuous advancement of modernisation, Chinese and foreign cultural exchanges are deepening, and the festive elements of traditional Chinese festivals are enjoyed by people around the world. The festival has become a bridge for foreign cultural exchanges and cooperation (Xi, 2017). It also allows people to learn to appreciate one another's traditions and culture (Bong, 2014). One of the most popular festivals that has become a tourism attraction worldwide is the Qinhuai Lantern Festival.

Dating back to the early Six Dynasties (about 1,800 years ago), the Qinhuai Lantern Festival, also known as 'Jinling Lantern Festival' and 'Confucius Temple Lantern Festival', is a popular folk cultural activity that is held in the Nanjing area. It is mainly held from the Spring Festival to the Lantern Festival. During this period, various lanterns are displayed along the

Qinhuai River, mostly concentrated in the Confucius Temple District. It incorporates light show, lantern festival and lantern market and is the first large-scale integrated lantern festival in China. An old Nanjing saying states that, 'Without enjoying lanterns in the Confucius Temple, you haven't spent the Nian (the Lunar New Year); without having a lantern from the Confucius Temple, you haven't had a good Nian.' In recognition of its popularity and importance, Qinhuai Lantern Festival was named as one of the Intangible Cultural Heritage of China by the government in 2006. In 2017, more than 15 million people participated in the festival. The colourful lanterns attract local people and visitors from other provinces and international tourists. The sale of lanterns reached ten million yuan. Catering, accommodation, shopping as well as lantern making all benefited from the festival (Zhang and Zhang, 2018). The lanterns not only bloom in Nanjing, but light up all over the world. Lantern craftsmen have travelled to more than 40 countries in Europe, America, Africa and Asia to promote the art of Nanjing Lantern (Wei, 2018). They have become the best carrier to endorse Nanjing and tell the Chinese story to the world.

At Christmas, houses and gardens in many countries are decorated with lights, seemingly, in an attempt to make a display that is more impressive than others in the street. A sense of competition is enhanced by reports in local newspapers about where to find the best decorated neighbourhoods. But, a study in England found that householders 'regarded their displays as productive of seasonal festivity, conviviality, good neighbourliness and community spirit' (Edensor and Millington, 2013: 149). In Europe and North America, the long hours of darkness and the low demand at many tourist attractions combine to encourage the use of Christmas lighting as a form of product augmentation. In London, the festive, gift-giving, shopping season formally starts when the Christmas lights that line Regent Street are switched on. The tradition which began in 1954 was organised by local retailers and businesses. During the 1950s and 1960s, the installations spread to other streets and the lights became a key part of London's festive calendar. However, they have not escaped criticism and the involvement of corporate sponsors led to complaints that they had become too commercial and vulgar. In 1998, the visibility of a soft drink sponsor with its prominent banners proclaiming 'Tis the season to be Tango'd' was met with public scorn (Linden and Linden, 2017).

Illuminations have featured as an attraction at traditional seaside resorts in Britain for over 100 years, famously at Blackpool. First shown in 1879 when they were described as 'artificial sunshine', eight carbon arc lamps illuminated Blackpool's promenade. The model for the modern-day displays first appeared in May 1912 to mark the visit of Princess Louise who opened a new section of the Promenade which was decorated with 10,000 light bulbs. At the request of the local Chamber of trade, the display was repeated in September of the same year and, from then, it was held annually, as an extension of the summer season. After a break during the First World War, the displays returned in 1925 and in 1932, and the illuminations were extended to the current length. After another break during the Second World War, the lights returned in 1949 and, in the post-war period, displays have contained more than 5,000 square meters of illuminated tableaux with the Blackpool Tramway running along the length of the illuminations. 'The world-famous illuminations', as they are described in destination promotion material, have helped Blackpool retain the status as Britain's most popular resort throughout much of the post-war period. It attracted 18 million visitors in 2016 (Gavell, 2017). More people visit the illuminations than the Edinburgh Festival (Cook, 2006) but it has been the subject of unfavourable reviews from many sources.

Writing in 1995, Bill Bryson made forthright observations about the Blackpool illuminations. He noted the risks associated with long-held expectations describing the level of disappointment he experienced. He explained:

> there was just a rumbling procession of old trams decorated as rocket ships or Christmas crackers, and several miles of paltry decorations on lampposts. – tacky and inadequate on rather a grand scale – What was no less amazing – were the crowds of people who had come to witness the spectacle.
>
> (Bryson, 1996: 269)

He also noted with incredulity that half of all visitors to Blackpool had been there at least ten times. Irrespective of the humorous style adopted by Bryson, it is likely that Edensor and Millington (2013) would consider his comments to be consistent with the preferences of the creative class. In their sociological analysis, they criticise a lack of unawareness of the situated expertise which is responsible for much of the production of the illuminations and comments that are dismissive of the cultural values of the visitors. Contradictory attitudes towards the illuminations are seen as evidence of an aesthetic gulf associated with serial production, which imposes cosmopolitan design and metropolitan 'good taste' on one side and vernacular practices on the other. The former is said to produce a generic place design whereas the latter allows for the creation and retention of a distinctive sense of place. The differences are highlighted in Blackpool due to its status as 'the world's first working-class holiday resort' that 'functions as a cultural repository, exemplifying the protean, dynamic qualities of popular culture' (Edensor and Millington, 2013: 147). The authors point to the fact that most of the illuminations have always been produced in the resort ensuring a continuity in aesthetic traditions and innovative practices. An illuminations depot was described as 'a socially embedded craft workshop' (Edensor and Millington, 2013: 157). The study by Edensor and Millington sought the views of people who visited the illuminations and the pleasure created by the lights, weather, smells and noises along the promenade were reported consistently. The shared familiarity of the scene and the opportunity for nostalgic reconnections were appreciated by many of the visitors and a view that the illuminations stood in distinction from the outside world was revealing. A lady in her sixties observed 'there's such a lot of awful things going on in the world, come to Blackpool and see the lights and lighten yourself up' (Edensor and Milington, 2013: 155). Since 2007, A Festival of Light has been held in conjunction with the illuminations in an attempt to attract a new, higher-spending, visitor market. Artists were recruited and new installations 'rather than standing apart as differently sophisticated and of higher quality, have tended to become absorbed into the overall eclectic mélange' (Edensor and Millington, 2013: 153).

FESTIVALS OF LIGHT

Light plays a central role in events which seek to energise the nocturnal lives of cities, helping people rediscover and reclaim urban space (Alves, 2007). Light festivals are testing the boundaries of brilliance as technology and creativity combine to create visually spectacular eventscapes. International networks are forged as people come together to share technical expertise, to identify new meanings about the relationship between people and place and to raise awareness of environmental issues and the sustainable use of power. In the last 20 years, large festivals that feature artistic light installations and light projections have become a global phenomenon. There are now approximately 100 large light festivals in the world, most of which have been developed in the last five years (Giordano and Ong, 2017). This has been driven partly by inter-urban competition, the creative city paradigm (Landry, 2000) and the search for innovative practices that can be applied quickly to achieve development objectives (Giordano and Ong, 2017). The global dissemination of light festivals has been consistent with what McCann (2011) has described as a 'policies mobilities' perspective with characteristics that reflect 'local globalness' (McCann, 2011: 109 and 120). Assisted by international consultants and networks of lighting professionals, the festival ideas have been appropriated by local actors who have adapted them to reflect local circumstances. Figure 6.3 traces the process and indicates that successful local festivals may become examples on the international circuit of similar events.

A number of authors (Alves, 2007; Edensor, 2014; Giordano and Ong, 2017) consider Lyon's Fête des Lumières to be the prototype for light festivals and to have influenced the way similar festivals have been established in other cities. The Fête des Lumières was held for the first time in 1999 for three nights in December around the Christian Feast of Immaculate Conception, drawing on the tradition of putting candles on window ledges to propitiate the Virgin Mary (Giordano and Ong, 2017). In 2003, almost one million people were present on a single night to witness the lighting displays and temporary installations designed by international artists (Alves, 2007). The festival 'transforms the city into a phantasmagorical landscape and creates affective and evocative atmospheres' (Giordano and Ong, 2017: 705). In 2002, the city of Lyons established the Lighting Urban Community International (LUCI) to offer technical and policy

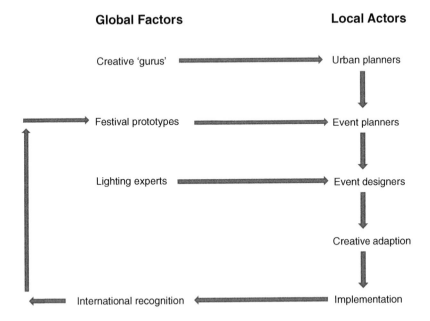

Figure 6.3 *Light festivals: development process.*

Source: Graham Brown

development support to other cities. It organises conferences that attract lighting companies and public authorities from around the world and, since 2012, the Lyon Light Festival Forum has been held annually as part of the Fête des Lumières. Consequently, the Fête has become 'an international showcase to demonstrate the potential for illumination to transform space and is a global magnet for those planning light festivals' (Edensor, 2014: 88). The Festival's technical team acts like a consultancy firm, assisting in the development and organisation of other light festivals (Giordano and Ong, 2017).

In 2016, Quito, the capital of Ecuador, staged the Fiesta de la Luz over five nights to coincide with the Habitat III United Nations Conference on Housing and Sustainable Urban Development. In a joint initiative with the city of Lyon, it included a collaborations between French and Ecuadorian artists and a local adaptation of Lyon's Fête des Lumières. The theme of light was pertinent as Quito was one of the first cities to declare independence from Spanish rule, providing the spark that lit the flames of a revolution throughout much of South America. Consequently, the city is known as 'Luz de America' – the light of America (Klassen, 2018). Quito was also the first city to be placed on the World Heritage list by UNESCO and, during the light festival, images of pre-Columbian, baroque and contemporary art were projected onto heritage buildings. According to one report,

> the meticulously-preserved architecture of Ecuador's capital is being 'renovated' by 3-D video projections. Buildings came alive as special indigenous figures emerged from the baroque walls of churches and angels ascended to the bell towers, soon making way for dancing floral patterns and intricate designs that wrapped themselves around the Renaissance-era columns and archways of the historical center.
>
> (TeleSUR, 2016)

It had been necessary to take precise measurements, mapping the buildings, so the projections would adapt to the exact shape of the façades. The level of air pollution in the city imposed additional challenges for the projections sent from a distance of 50 metres onto surfaces measuring 50×30 metres and 45×30 metres. The images were powered by Christie 3DLP 20,000 lumen projectors supplied by Christie Digital Systems, USA, a Japanese-owned, global visual and audio technologies company (Christie, 2017). In another example, Luzboa was held in Lisbon for the first time in 2004 and was a two-week festival of light art animations, conferences and workshops. It promoted the animation of public spaces and encouraged local engagement as children's drawings turned into light sculptures and passengers travelling on illuminated transport vehicles acted as both actors and observers. Lighting on warehouses encouraged people to walk through and reconnect with the city's historic waterfront area, an approach that was consistent with views that walking is the best way to explore and exploit what cities offer (De Certeau, 1984; Sinclair, 1997; Solnit, 2001). Significantly, Luzboa was an attempt to place Lisbon on a cultural route of cities with light festivals, pioneered by Lyon, Paris (Nuit Blanche), Geneva (Christmas Tree Festival) and Turin (Luci d'Artista) (Alves, 2007).

There is considerable variability in the form and duration of the ever-expanding range of light festivals due to differences in objectives and their physical and cultural contexts. They include spectacular, multi-installation events that disrupt normal rhythms across urban environments and single productions in small spaces. Light is associated with shifting geometries of perception (Gandy, 2017a) and illuminated environments are defamiliarised as beams of light provide architectural structure and buildings under projections become fluid. Projections with narratives that provide historical information can enhance a sense of place and encourage nostalgic recollections (Edensor, 2014). The unfamiliar appearance of lights moving overhead or standing as a column in the distance capture attention and create a questioning sense of excitement. On approach, the atmosphere changes and affective and sensual forces shape experience. The ludic dimension of light festivals seduce people into a convivial disposition towards others and immersive, 'thick' atmospheres 'are saturated with intense modes of sensual, emotional and affective involvement' (Edensor, 2014: 94). The environment offers participants spaces of latent possibilities (Stewart, 2011) but some light festivals have been developed as part of 'territorial marketing' (Alves, 2007 1252), when tourism development and international positioning are important objectives. These objectives played an important role in the development of Vivid Sydney.

Vivid Sydney

Vivid Sydney illustrates how technology is used to change the appearance of a city by creating a visually stunning eventscape. The image on the book cover was taken in 2017 and supplied by Destination NSW with a caption that stated that the Harbour Lights installations turned the waters of Sydney Harbour into a Vivid Sydney precinct. The projection of light during Vivid Sydney integrates different parts of the urban environment while individual installations transform intimate settings. It is a 23-day winter festival, held in the capital of New South Wales (NSW) and has three elements: Vivid Light, Vivid Music and Vivid Ideas. It was first staged in 2009 and is owned and managed by Destination NSW. It attracted 2.32 million people in 2017, making it the largest festival in Australia and demonstrating the appeal of the event format. It has been classed as a Hallmark Event by the New South Wales (NSW) government. The harbour provides an ideal setting to display artwork and to project moving images onto iconic structures such as the UNESCO World Heritage-listed sails of the Sydney Opera House. The scale and dispersed nature of the events requires a long period of planning and collaboration between multiple government agencies. The imagery and associations of the event seek to reinforce Sydney's brand identity as a colourful and creative global city.

In 2017, the light artistry of more than 185 artists from 22 countries in 109 installations was enjoyed along a 4 km 'light walk' through the CBD, Royal Botanic Garden and the Sydney Harbour Foreshore. Each year, the use of technology, such as augmented reality and motion sensing, has challenged perceptions and encouraged interaction and engagement. People have been able to use a touch screen to direct colour illuminations onto buildings and to create music by walking on stairs which appear as a giant piano keyboard. The tone of a talking car depended on how it was touched and lights on a tree turned and answered back to people when spoken to (Farelly, 2018). In 2018, the shells of the Opera House were illuminated by artist Jonathan Zawada (Plate 14). The kinetic digital sculptures of botanical images morphed into geometric designs (Morris, 2018). The title, Metamathemagical, captures the combination of art and technology that underpins this type of production. Aqueous, one of the main features in the Botanic Gardens had been brought from the *Burning Man* festival, demonstrating the growing relationships between the producers of light festivals. Aqueous was described as 'an interactive landscape of meandering pathways of light. Reflection and shifting colour and light react to audience participants as they run and walk along the pathway' (Vivid Sydney, 2018). Echoing a theme espoused by many festival directors, the Creative Director of Vivid attributed the event's success to its accessibility. 'What we've done is take art off the wall and onto the streets where people can touch it' (Jones, quoted in Morris, 2018). The event is described in **Vivid Sydney – Festival Development** by the CEO of the company that developed the festival.

VIVID SYDNEY – FESTIVAL DEVELOPMENT

By Anthony Bastic, CEO and Creative Director,
AGB Events, Sydney

The company

Founded in 2016, AGB Events specialises in the creation of public celebrations, iconic events and innovative experiences and has produced events across Australia, Asia, United Kingdom and the United States. AGB Events delivered the creative and production elements for Vivid Sydney from its inception and for its first ten years, The founder and Creative Director of AGB who was instrumental in the establishment of the festival, has held positions of Director of Vivid Light and Curator of Light for Vivid Sydney.

Developing Vivid Sydney

Coming from a background in creating and producing large-scale events, I had recently returned to Sydney and was thinking about the next chapter of my career.

I was introduced to a light artist by a colleague who works in PR for major events. We agreed that we were entering an interesting time in the field of lighting as Australia was the first government to 'ban the bulb', that is, phase out incandescent lighting and replace it with modern lighting technology. This action, we believed, could be the premise for the introduction of a light festival!

I began by conducting research into light-related events, and after visiting Switched On London – a small lighting event in 2007 – thought that a similar style of event might work in Sydney. We then visited other events around the world, met with several light artists and began to develop a concept. The initial idea was to create a 'light walk' around Sydney Harbour, through the Botanic Gardens and ending in Hyde Park.

The next step was to convince government that this was a great idea and would attract tourists. Our timing was perfect as Events New South Wales had recently been established and the organisation wanted to create a winter festival and our concept fitted the bill, almost! The NSW state government did not want a narrow focus on light so, since 2009, Vivid Sydney was broadened and has been a highly successful festival of Light, Music and Ideas. Each element is important because they attract a different audience and people like choices. We designed a festival that celebrates creativity and ingenuity and each year Vivid is different to the year before. It is curated from scratch every year, with expressions of interest sought from artists from all around the world. There is no doubt that continually offering something new and reinventing light as an art form are some of the reasons for Vivid's continued success.

The success of Vivid

Vivid has become a global phenomenon and many people ask why it has become so popular? Through working with many international established artists and outstanding local artists, the event immediately captured the attention of the world. This international visibility is important as it means that artists, designers, architects and students can experiment and show-case their talent on a world stage. Vivid provides a platform for careers as it has a currency among international employers in the creative industries. Our success is related to the setting, the relationship between creativity and technology and the nature of the event experience.

Sydney has a reputation as a city that lends itself to celebration. This was demonstrated by the size of celebrations in 2000 when Sydney hosted the 2000 Olympic and Paralympic Games, and Sydney put on a show like never before. This positive thirst for celebrating together in public spaces continues to this day. People like to see their city re-imagined and Vivid offers a creative experience that can be shared on a grand scale. This is significant because many people can feel a sense of isolation living in a city and become alienated – relying on mobile devices to communicate. In contrast, people come together at Vivid. They can celebrate with their friends and tell everybody what they see and experience. They use social media to say 'Look where I am. Look what has been created for me in my city'. By sharing the moment, people construct an experience for themselves and for others. These experiences occur in a special place. Sydney gives us such a lot to play with. The footprint of Vivid has expanded over the years to include old Sydney (the Rocks, Colonial Sydney) and modern Sydney with its imposing skyscrapers. The Light Walk is a journey of artistic creativity through the Botanic Gardens with striking contrasts between glowing light installations and the nocturnal urban parkland. It offers a new interpretation of surrounding buildings, where illuminations emerge brilliantly from the darkened façades. Then we have the harbour, and one of the most celebrated buildings in the world. In winter, reflecting light on the harbour can be so effective. At the Sydney Opera House, Jørn Utzen created a sculpture and Vivid allows artists to re-imagine this breathtaking building as a stage. Applying the latest technology to project artists' images onto the sails, we create vibrant digital compositions in continuous motion. You just can't create and present artists' work like this in many other cities.

For the past ten years, I have had the great fortune to work with artists, emerging and established, to re-imagine Sydney at night; it has been one of the most rewarding opportunities of my career.

The Vivid Ideas component of Vivid Sydney explores innovation across the creative industries and, in 2017, 36,000 professionals participated representing animation, architecture, design, electronic games, fashion, film and screen arts, lighting, music, performing and visual arts. As part of the Ideas Talk Series, a 15-storey high outdoor mural was commissioned to celebrate the power to change through public art (Destination NSW, 2017). In 2018, a number of the Vivid Ideas talks were combined with musical performances. At Vivid Music, performances by Australian and international acts were held in a wide range of small venues across the city as well as at iconic venues including the Sydney Opera House. Vivid Sydney is an example of successful product development, as an event and as a tourist attraction and details of the latter are explained in **Vivid Sydney – Tourism Development**.

VIVID SYDNEY – TOURISM DEVELOPMENT

*By Sandra Chipchase, Chief Executive Officer,
Destination NSW and Executive Producer,
Vivid Sydney*

The organisation

Destination NSW is the lead government agency with responsibility for achieving economic and social benefits for the people of New South Wales through the development of tourism and securing major events. It seeks to position Sydney and NSW as premier, global tourism and major events destinations. Vivid Sydney is owned, managed and produced by Destination NSW.

The event

In 2009, Vivid Sydney was established as a winter event to showcase smart light technology and drive additional visitation to the city in what was traditionally a low tourism season. In its first year, the festival attracted just over 200,000 people. In 2017, Vivid Sydney attracted 2.33 million visitors to the city to enjoy the annual celebration of light, music and ideas. The Festival is held over 23 days and nights and has reinforced Sydney's position as the creative services hub of the Asia-Pacific region. It has won global recognition and multiple awards including at the national Event Awards for both the 'Best Tourism Event' and the 'Best Cultural, Arts or Music Event in Australia'. Strategies developed by Destination NSW have been the key to driving this phenomenal growth and success.

When Destination NSW was formed in 2011, the new State Government questioned whether Vivid should continue. The challenge was to change it from a local Sydney event to an international event. This was achieved by making it international in scope, raising its profile with international creatives and by increasing engagement with overseas travel trade and tourism markets. International competitions are held to design and deliver light sculptures and 3D mapping for the event and invitations are sent to thought-leaders and leading international and local creatives and innovators and musicians to share their talent. International tourism campaigns and travel packages for the event have been developed with travel wholesalers to drive visitation. In 2017, the travel packages generated 65,000 international visitors and 70,000 interstate visitors. In addition to the impact in the city, the 'Sydney Plus' Vivid packages created 94,000 room nights in regional NSW and delivered an increased spend of $AUS16.5 million.

Vivid is an international event that is delivered in a very Australian way. It is daring, fun, cheeky, bold, sexy – in fact, very Sydney. It draws on the city's spectacular setting and its friendly people. Sydney Harbour serves as a huge art canvas and differentiates Vivid from all other light festivals around the world. The boats and cruise chips carry onboard technology used to make lights on ships change in colour as they move around the harbour. People on the Bridge Climb wear illuminated vests and 3D mapped projections bring the sails of the Opera House to life. Visitors are welcomed by over 400 Volunteers comprising international students, retirees and others wanting to welcome festival guests. The event generates tremendous goodwill and, as an inclusive event, has special provisions and assistance for visitors with a disability or needing additional assistance. It has sustainability partners to reduce its environmental impact as the light walk is 100 per cent green power accredited. Sydneysiders have a great sense of ownership and pride in Vivid Sydney. Children are inspired by what they see and can identify new career opportunities such as being lighting designers, animators or creators of light sculptures and animatronics. The festival also impacts the visitors' psyche: when people are happy, they spoil themselves. For example, the sales by ice cream vendors at Circular Quay are greater during the three weeks of Vivid in winter, than through the summer. Emotional connections to light, music and ideas make Vivid an event for everyone. It is not an exclusive or ticketed only event. The light walk is free!

The support provided by the New South Wales State Government has been fantastic. The event's success has required a whole of government approach and cross-city collaboration. A wide range of agencies responsible for roads, transport and emergency services and precinct management are all embedded in the event with their staff being on call 23 days and nights. Many organisations seek to leverage the event and Business Events Sydney and the city's Convention Bureau, bring some of their top clients to the city for meetings, conventions and incentive reward trips during Vivid.

Vivid Sydney relies on the inter-connected work of a lot of people and organisations but Destination NSW acts as the machine that drives the event throughout much of the year. This involves working with travel industry partners, providing retail promotion support, city dressing with posters and banners and a massive media communications programme. We are able to attract high-quality staff because everyone wants to work on Vivid. At Destination NSW, we believe in the power of events to drive economic growth, jobs, innovation, change perceptions and deliver unbridled joy. Alongside some of our famous sport and arts events, Vivid Sydney has helped to shape the city's creative brand and further establish Sydney's reputation for staging world-class events.

Vivid Sydney may be exceptional in terms of size, setting and technological sophistication but transformation by light has become the norm at events held in cities. It remains relatively rare in areas away from the permanent glare of urban lights where the impact of lighting can be dramatic due to the visual expectations attached to these environments. This is confirmed in the description of the *Enchanted Forest* festival in Scotland, where 'the usual sensual and symbolic apprehension of the forest is made strange by an array of lighting techniques, displays and choreographed sounds' (Edensor, 2014: 88). The illumination of individual trees with colour projected onto trunks and flickering leaves can be used to magical effect in urban parks that stage events as well as in remote forests. On an expansive scale, the Parrtjima festival of light transformed parts of the natural environment in central Australia in 2016. The event was considered to be an 'outstanding success' (NT Gov., 2017) and was held again in 2017. For ten nights, indigenous art was illuminated onto 2.5 kilometres of the 300-million-year-old MacDonnell Ranges, near Alice Springs. According to the festival website, 'the vision is to host a meeting place where the newest light and projection technologies create an experience of wonder and respect for the world's oldest living culture' (Parrtjima, 2017). However, the media reported the concerns of scientists about the possible impact of lasers on wildlife (NITV, 2016) and the views of an aboriginal elder who stated, 'That's not a man-made canvas. That is our whole being tied up in that site. That has a life, blood in it from what's around, and it is the lifeblood of my connection to country' (Guardian, 2017).

Few people live in outback Australia and in many cities the creation of 'a man-made canvas' is an objective of urban design. The infinity pool on the roof of the Marina Bay Sands hotel offers a view across Singapore and, at night, the scene below is transformed by a spectacular sound and light show in the Gardens by the Bay (Plate 15). The hyperreality of the Gardens is suggested by a mechanical forest of 18 'supertree' towers that are vertical gardens in the day and brightly coloured illuminations at night. It may be hard to distinguish between the ecosystem of light that is on display every night in Gardens by the Bay and the transformations in Sydney during Vivid.

SUMMARY

Residents of most modern cities live in an age of illumination where the quality of light influences the quality of life. The question was raised about the ability of light festivals to add value to urban life. From an historical perspective, this is not a new concern as it was suggested that the arrival of street lighting might make ceremonial lighting lose some of its wonder. At the present time, such fears would seem to be misplaced as light festivals are being developed around the world and are attracting large, enthusiastic crowds. As with most types of events, the opportunities for social inter-action are one the main benefits they offer. In the case of Vivid Sydney, Anthony Bastic made insightful observations about beliefs that the event had been created for the benefit of individual residents who wanted to share the experience with others. This was seen to be an antidote to rela-tionships that depend on social media. There was frequent reference to the atmosphere created by creatively combining light and sound. This was evident at a wide range of scales and in both indoor and outdoor settings.

The chapter identified the mystical relationship between light and dark and the way simple light technologies have transformed environments for thousands of years. Artists and photographers have attempted to capture light and have been sensitive to the variability of light conditions at different times of the day, at different latitudes and in different levels of air pollution. Costs associated with light and sound pollution are starting to be recognised, giving rise to the creation of dark sky parks and silence projects which promote natural soundscapes. The largest Dark Sky Park in Europe is at Kielder Forest in Northumberland, England, where an observatory stages events that use the night sky as a source of inspiration.

For Van Gogh, light was of cosmological significance and there are provocative similarities between *Starry Night* (Plate 13) and the image of Sydney Harbour taken during Vivid Sydney (Plate 14) where light is reflected in the water and lasers replace stars to make a visual connection between heaven and earth. It is intriguing to note the frequent use and the importance placed on representations of the natural world in illuminations and at light festivals. A long list of examples would include the use of both real trees and artificial forests as the setting for light projection, pulses of light at a concert with the title 'neon forest', the botanical images on the sails of the Sydney Opera House and installations that simulate the Northern Lights.

The chapter included many examples of globalisation, the application of ideas form international experts and the serial production of festivals that have been developed in other parts of the world. But there were also many examples of the importance of local adaptation, the incorporation of vernacular products and the scope for local creativity. Light festivals have become an important part of local economies and symbolise many of the values associated with creative cities. It was interesting to note that enhancing employment in the creative industries was stated by the CEO of Destination NSW as an objective of Vivid Sydney. This may be stimulated by curatorial decisions or may be organic as creative, young artists and engineers find outlets to apply skills at concerts, product launches and light festivals.

REFERENCES

Alves, T. (2007). Art Light and Landscape: New Agendas for Urban Development. *European Planning Studies*, 15(9): 1247–1260.

Amin, A. and Howell, P. (2016). Thinking the Commons. In: A. Amin and P. Howell, eds, *Rethinking the Commons: Rethinking the Futures of the Commons*. London: Routledge, 1–17.

Bach, S. and Degenring, F. (2014). From Shakespearean Nights to Light Pollution: Artificial Light in Anglophone Literature. In: J. Meier, U. Hasenöhrl, K. Krause and M. Pottharst, eds, *Urban Lighting, Light Pollution and Society*. London: Routledge, 46–65.

Bille, M. and Sørensen, T. (2007). An Anthropology of Luminosity: The Agency of Light. *Journal of Material Culture*, 12(3): 263–284.

Bong, K. (2014). Karim: Cultural Festivals Great Platform to Strengthen Unity. *The Borneo Post*, 7 September. www.theborneopost.com/2014/09/07/karim-cultural-festivals-great-platform-to-strengthen-unity/.

Bottorff, D. (2015). Emerging Influence of Transmodernism and Transpersonal Psychology Reflected in Rising Popularity of Transformational Festivals. *Journal of Spirituality in Mental Health*, 17(1): 50–74.

Bragdon, C. (1926). *Architecture and Democracy*, 2nd edn. New York: A. A. Knopf.

Brennan, S. (2017). Model Couple Who Set Up Fashion Site to Rival ASOS in their Bedroom are Set to Make MILLIONS, *Mail Online*, 3 May. www.daily mail.co.uk/femail/article-4466960/Couple-set-fashion-site-course-make-milions. html#ixzz4rCeB8LOp.

Brox, J. (2014). Out of the Dark: A Brief History of Artificial Light in Outdoor Spaces. In: J. Meier, U. Hasenöhrl, K. Krause and M. Pottharst, eds, *Urban Lighting, Light Pollution and Society*. London: Routledge, 13–29.

Bryson, B. (1996). *Notes From a Small Island*. London: Black Swan.

Carcapino, J. (1940). *Daily Life in Ancient Rome: The People and the City at the Height of the Empire*. New Haven, CT: Yale University Press.

Chen, K. (2012). Artistic Prosumption: Cocreative Destruction at Burning Man. *American Behavioral Scientist*, 56(4): 570–595.

China Highlights (2019). *Harbin International Ice and Snow Festival 2019.* www. chinahighlights.com/festivals/harbin-ice-and-snow-festival.htm.

Christie (2017). Lyon's Festival of Lights Arrives in Quito with Christie Mapping Projection. *Christie Press Release*, 31 January. www.christiedigital.com/en-us/ about-christie/news-room/press-releases/lyons-festival-of-lights-arrives-in-quito.

Clegg, S. (1841). *Practical Treatise on the Manufacture and Distribution of Coal-Gas*. London: John Weale.

Cook, W. (2006). The Blackpool Illuminations Attract More Visitors Than the Edinburgh Festival, but are Ignored by Snooty Arts Critics. *The New Statesman*, August.

Cosgrove, D. (1985). Prospect, Perspective and the Evolution of the Landscape Idea. *Transactions of the Institute of British Geographers*, 10: 45–62.

Cova, B. and Dalli, D. (2017). From Communal Resistance to Tribal Value Creation. *First International Conference on Consumption and Consumer Resistance.* www.researchgate.net/publication/228611587_From_Communal_ Resistance_to_Tribal_Value_Creation.

Dawson, M. (2017). Book Says Zappos CEO Didn't Just Want a Company – He Wanted a Cult. *New York Post*, 20 February. http://nypost.com/2017/02/20/ zappos-ceo-didnt-just-want-a-company-he-wanted-a-cult/.

De Certeau, M. (1984). *The Practice of Everyday Life*, trans. S. Rendell. Berkeley, CA: University of California Press.

Dessen, A. C. (1978). Night and Darkness on the Elizabethan Stage: Yesterday's Conventions and Today's Distortions. In: G. W. Williams, ed., *Renaissance Papers 1978*. Columbia, SC: Camden House, 22–30.

Destination NSW (2017). Submission to the Australian Event Awards, 2017.

Dixon, S. (2016). Ten of the Best Christmas Light Festivals in the UK. *Guardian*, 6 December. www.theguardian.com/travel/2016/dec/06/10-best-christmas-light-festivals-uk.

Edensor, T. (2014). The Rich Potentialities of Light Festivals. In: J. Meier, U. Hasenöhrl, K. Krause and M. Pottharst, eds, *Urban Lighting, Light Pollution and Society*. London: Routledge, 85–98.

Edensor, T. and Lorimer, H. (2015). 'Landscapism' at the Speed of Light: Darkness and Illumination in Motion. *Geografiska Annaler: Series B, Human Geography*, 97(1): 1–16.

Edensor, T. and Millington, S. (2013). Blackpool Illuminations: Revealing Local Cultural Production, Situated Creativity and Working-Class Values. *International Journal of Cultural Policy*, 19(2): 145–161.

Farelly, E. (2018). 'Kind of Tacky': Sydney's Vivid has Lost its Mojo. *Sydney Morning Herald*, 8 June. www.smh.com.au/national/nsw/kind-of-tacky-sydney-s-vivid-has-lost-its-mojo-20180607-p4zk6r.html.

Fernández, E. (2018). Hong Kong's Fight to Save its Neon Shimmer – A Photo Essay. *Guardian*, 25 July. www.theguardian.com/travel/2018/jul/25/hong-kong-neon-lighting-threat-chinese-regulations?CMP=share_btn_link.

Gandy, M. (2017a). Urban Atmospheres. *Cultural Geographies*, 24(3): 353–374.

Gandy, M. (2017b). Negative Luminescence. *Annals of the American Association of Geographers*, 107(5): 1090–1107.

Gavell, T. (2017). Blackpool Visitor Number Rise Driven by Big Events. *The Gazette*, 12 October. www.blackpoolgazette.co.uk/whats-on/blackpool-visitor-number-rise-driven-by-big-events-1-8800966.

Gilmore, L. (2010). *Theater in a Crowded Fire Ritual and Spirituality at Burning Man*. Berkeley, CA: University of California Press.

Giordano, E. and Ong, C.-E. (2017). Light Festivals, Policy Mobilities and Urban Tourism. *Tourism Geographies*, 19(5): 699–716.

Goindi, G. (2017). Fourth Sparkling Diwali Celebration in US Congress Draws Over 400 Guests. *The American Bazaar*, 9 November. www.americanbazaar online.com/2017/11/09/fourth-sparkling-diwali-celebration-us-congress-draws-400-guests/.

Goldberg, M. (2019). World's Largest Annual Ice Festival Transforms North-Eastern China. *Archinect News*. 9 January. https://archinect.com/news/article/150113733/world-s-largest-annual-ice-festival-transforms-north-eastern-china.

Guardian (2017). Our Sites are Not to be Used for Money-Making: The Row Over Alice Springs Light Festival. *Guardian*, 20 September. www.theguardian.com/artanddesign/2017/sep/30/our-sites-are-not-to-be-used-for-money-making-the-row-over-the-alice-springs-light-festival.

Hillier, D. (2016). How Burning Man Culture Changed Festivals Around the World. *Vice*, 10 March. www.vice.com/en_us/article/gqy95y/how-burning-man-culture-made-its-way-around-the-world.

Huang, L. and Zhu, Y. (2013). On the Festival Lights of Folk Culture. *Journal of Chinese Culture*, 10: 107–110.

Japan Guide (2018). Winter Illuminations. *Japan Guide*. www.japan-guide.com/e/e2304.html.

Johner, A. (2015). Transformational Festivals: A New Religious Movement? In: E. Simao, A. da Silva and S. de Magalhaes, eds, *Exploring Psychedelic Trance and Electronic Dance Music in Modern Culture*. Hershey, PA: IGI Global, 58–86.

Jordana, S. (2010). UK Pavilion for Shanghai Expo2010. *Heatherwick Studio.* www.archdaily.com/58591/uk-pavilion-for-shanghai-world-expo-2010-heatherwick-studio.

Julier, G. (2005). Urban Designscapes and the Production of Aesthetic Consent. *Urban Studies*, 42(5–6): 869–887.

Klassen, C. (2018). What is Quito's Fiesta de la Luz (Festival of Light) 2018 Event? *Metropolitan Touring.* www.metropolitan-touring.com/quito-fiesta-de-la-luz/.

Koeck, R. and Warnaby, G. (2014). Outdoor Advertising in Urban Context: Spatiality, Temporality and Individuality. *Journal of Marketing Management*, 30(13/14): 1402–1422.

Landry, C. (2000). *The Creative City: A Toolkit for Urban Innovators*. London: Earthscan Publications.

Liang, C. (2007). Lantern Art Development and Festival Culture Creation. *Journal of Leshan Teachers College*, 22(3): 122–126.

Limbach, E. (2014). The Wonderful, Weird Economy of Burning Man. *The Atlantic*, 18 August. www.theatlantic.com/business/archive/2014/08/the-wonderful-weird-economics-of-burning-man/376108/.

Linden, H. and Linden, S. (2017). A Brief History of London's Christmas Lights. *City Metric*, 5 December. www.citymetric.com/business/brief-history-london-s-christmas-lights-3485.

McCann, E. (2011). Urban Policy Mobilities and Global Circuits of Knowledge: Towards a Research Agenda. *Annals of the Association of American Geographers*, 101(1): 107–130.

MacFarlane, R. (2005). The Via Negativa. In: A. Farquhar, ed., *The Storr: Unfolding Landscape*. Edinburgh: Luath Press, 73–78.

Massey, J. (2006). Organic Architecture and Direct Democracy: Claude Bragdon's Festivals of Song and Light. *Journal of the Society of Architectural Historians*, 65(4): 578–613.

Mendoza, H. (2015). The 2SQUARED Mini: 3D Printing Illuminated Art Inspired by Burning Man. *3DPrint*, 22 May. https://3dprint.com/66629/2squared-mini-illuminated-art/.

Morris, L. (2018). Sydney's Most Popular Festival Celebrates 10 Years in the Spotlights. *Sydney Morning Herald*, 20 March. www.smh.com.au/entertainment/art-and-design/sydney-s-most-popular-festival-celebrates-10-years-in-the-spotlights-20180320-p4z5a5.html.

NITV (2016). Parrtijma Festival Lights Up the MacDonnell Ranges amid controversy. *SBS TV*, 28 September. www.sbs.com.au/nitv/article/2016/09/28/parrtjima-festival-lights-macdonnells-ranges-amidst-controversy.

NT Gov. (2017). Parrtjima – A Festival to Illuminate the Territory in 2017. *Northern Territory Government.* https://nt.gov.au/news/2017/march/parrtjima-a-festival-in-light-to-illuminate-the-territory-in-2017.

Nye, D. E. (1997). *Electrifying America: Social Meanings of a New Technology, 1880–1940.* Cambridge, MA: The MIT Press.

O'Donnell, R. (2016). PR Case Study: London's Burning. *CISION Gorkana*. www. gorkana.com/2016/12/pr-case-study-londons-burning/.

Parrtjima (2017). Mission and Values. *Parrtjima*. https://parrtjimaaustralia.com.au/culture/.

Qiao, D. (2009). *Pictured Chinese Festival*. Beijing: China Social Science Press, 36–46.

Radziwill, N. and Benton, M. (2013). Burning Man: Quality and Innovation in the Spirit of Deming. *The Journal for Quality and Participation*, 36(1): 7–11.

Recker, J. (2019). Step Inside Winter's Most Spectacular Wonderland at the Harbin Ice and Snow Festival in Northeast China. *Smithsonian.com*, 10 January. www. smithsonianmag.com/travel/harbin-ice-snow-festival-2019-180971227/.

Rhineland-Palatinate Tourist Board (2018). Rhine in Flames. Rheinland-Pfalz Tourismus GmbH. www.romantic-germany.info/things-to-do/leisure-tips/rhine-in-flames/.

Rogg, M. (2017). Convergence Citizen: Innovative Designs of Mediated Citizenship: A Case Study of the Swedish Convergence Festival Gather. Masters thesis. Södertörn University, Stockholm.

Ruane, D. (2017). 'Wearing Down of the Self': Embodiment, Writing and Disruptions of Identity in Transformational Festival Fieldwork. *Methodological Innovations*, 10(1): 1–11.

Sinclair, I. (1997). *Lights Out for the Territory*. London: Granata Books.

Solnit, R. (2001). *Wanderlust: A History of Walking*. London: Verso.

Song, L. (2015). Lantern Festival. *Paths International*. http://ebookcentral.proquest.com/lib/unisa/detail.action?docID=1977479.

Stenson, B. (2019). Immersive Van Gogh Show Opens in Paris. *Guardian*, 5 March. www.theguardian.com/travel/gallery/2019/mar/04/immersive-vincent-van-gogh-show-opens-paris-digital-art.

Stevenson, R. L. (1881). A Plea for Gas Lamps. In: R. L. Stevenson. *Virginbus Puerisque and Other Papers*. London: C. Kegan Paul & Co., 286–288.

Stewart, K. (2011). Atmospheric Attunements. *Environment and Planning D: Society and Space*, 29: 445–453.

Taylor, C. (2007). Burning Man Grows Up. *CNN Money International*, 1 July. http://money.cnn.com/magazines/business2/business2_archive/2007/07/01/1001 17064/.

TeleSUR (2016). Festival of Lights: Quito's Historical Center Bathed in Color. *TeleSUR News*, 18 October. www.telesurtv.net/english/news/Festival-of-Lights-Quitos-Historical-Center-Bathed-in-Color-20161018-0011.html.

Vivid Sydney (2018). *Vivid Sydney*. www.vividsydney.com/event/light/aqueous.

Wei, R. (2018). Qinhuai Lantern Festival: Ambilight 1700 years. *Xinhua News*. 2 March. http://xh.xhby.net/mp3/pc/c/201803/02/c450056.html.

Xi, H. (2017). The Ceremonial Sense of the Lantern Festival Carries the Rhythm of Chinese Culture. *Xinhua Daily Press*. 10 February. http://news.xhby.net/system/2017/02/09/030545923.shtml?winzoom=1.

Yang, L. (2011). Development of Lantern Art. *National Arts*, 8: 139.

Zhang, B. (2012). Praying and Carnival: The Cultural Connotation of the Lantern Festival. *China Culture Daily*, 6 February, 7.

Zhang, H. (2008). *Traditional Chinese Festivals and Culture*. Taiyang, China: Shuhai Publishing House.

Zhang, Y. and Zhang, X. (2018). Nanjing Qinhuai Lantern Festival Released Big Data: 32 Years, Participants Exceeded 120 million. *People's Daily*, 12 February. www.yangtse.com/app/jiangsu/nanjing/2018-02-12/518305.html.

7 Conclusion

REFLECTIONS

An academic colleague explained to me that he sought to confuse students in his class. He believed that this would encourage them to seek answers to questions and create a desire for knowledge. This book may have caused some confusion as the subject provides ample opportunity for what Gandy calls 'complex entanglements between space and subjectivity' (2017a: 368). Examples of entanglements at eventscapes include:

- Place dependence resulting in place transformation.
- Space dictating the need for surveillance but surveillance determining the use of space.
- Expressive participation and creativity emerging from environments with hidden structures of control.
- Settings that engender respect for the commons and the preservation of public spaces while others result in private encroachment and commodification.
- Mega-event organisations engaged in partnerships with businesses in host cities while imposing restrictive regulations and denying access to their brands.

To add to the complexity, eventscapes provide examples of the blurred boundaries between architecture, infrastructure and information (Gandy, 2017b). They include architecture that is replete with symbolic meaning, infrastructure that reflects the values of decision makers where costs and benefits are not evenly distributed across the community and information that communicates a visual identity for the event and the host city. There was frequent reference to the tension between a desire for locally inspired production in the face of powerful external forces and the unhinging of territorial moorings caused by globalisation (Amin, 2006). This theme has been expressed in the literature of a wide range of disciplines but the discussion of some events has demonstrated that it is possible to achieve a successful blend of these contradictory forces. For example, the Olympic look is a compromise that reflects a desire to project local values in ways that have global resonance and many light festivals benefit from international expertise while providing opportunities for local creativity to emerge. Future research should examine the cumulative effect of these processes for the preservation of local distinctiveness and the creation of a sense of place.

Eventscapes was used as an analytical framework to examine the spatial expression of event activities, adopting a similar approach to that employed by Bale (1994) in his studies of the landscapes of sport. The spatial patterns of events were compared with Wynn's (2015) ideal types model that he applied to music festivals. It was well suited to an examination of events that are restricted to a single, self-contained site and, to a certain extent, to events that use venues across a city but it was less relevant to fluid events that create connections across widely dispersed environments. Similarly, a separate interpretation was needed for parades that transform space in urban environments when spectators actively participate in the production of experiences and determine the boundaries of the eventscape. The discussions benefited from insight provided by what Getz (2012) has called the foundation disciples of event studies (Cultural Anthropology, Management, Environmental Studies, Geography, Philosophy, Political Science/Law, Psychology and Sociology). In addition, Art History, Leisure Studies, Sport Management, Urban Studies and Design were important parts of the book's ontological map with concepts tested against a wide range of events held in many different countries. Factors that have created a global network of light festivals were identified and music festivals in Europe and Australia can be compared in terms of sustainability practices. Trends that were identified include the increasing importance of interactivity in situations that ranged from the use of maps to immersive experiences with light installations. The case studies provided an 'insiders' perspective revealing perceived opportunities, constraints and political realities in event management. They also demonstrate the variability in the type of businesses involved in event design and the scope for entrepreneurial start-ups. The examples range from the young group who formed ID&T in Holland and the development of Mapped Design by David Musch in Adelaide to the large teams that devote their energies to the creation of a visual identity at the Olympic Games and the diverse services provided by major media corporations such as the McCann Worldgroup.

An analysis of eventscapes helps establish spatial anchors that place an event in a particular environmental context making it possible to better understand the places that host events. This includes their history, cultural traditions and socio-political characteristics. These characteristics influence events and are impacted by them. The profile of places that host certain events is boosted each year by news reports accompanied by spectacular images that report the latest iteration of famous events such as the Rio Carnival and the Harbin Ice Sculpture Festival. Richard's (2015) description of iterative and pulsar events makes a valuable contribution to the literature but, as he acknowledges, there are examples of events which do not correspond to the categories. This is the case at large light festivals such as Vivid Sydney where the diversity of the programme and the mix of factors that influence the design mean that it can be classed as both an iterative and a pulsar event. Light festivals are not normally classed as mega-events and would not meet the criteria advanced by Muller (2015). However, Vivid Sydney can make a strong claim to be in this category based on its spatial footprint, the number of government agencies, business organisations and staff involved in staging the event and the large number of participants and visitors who attend.

The flexibility of events means they can move and adapt to new settings but they still rely on place-based resources and this can provide a competitive advantage for places that wish to attract events. Event management must also take account of mobilities and the flows of information that enter eventscapes. The relevant processes were discussed in the context of an actor–network framework (Van der Duim, 2007) but the spatial characteristics of such networks needs more detailed analysis. It is difficult to locate the source of information flows and, for this reason, they have been called 'non-spaces' (Tzanelli, 2018) but it would be possible to identify the spatial pattern of local networks that contribute the 'interactional intelligence' (Thrift, 2005) of events. This could include places of production such as the craft workshops that produce many of the installations for the Blackpool Illuminations (Edensor and Millington, 2013), the favelas where the performances are designed and the costumes are produced for the Rio Carnival and the schools where the decorative panels for the London's Burning sculpture were designed. A map of the networks of production sites would reveal an extended spatial pattern of an eventscape, depicting connections between communities. With reference to alternative epistemologies, the language used to communicate the spatial patterns could be derivative of geographical information systems to reveal statistical relationships or of artistic creativity to present visually appealing descriptions. The latter is illustrated in Plate 16, which is titled *Pirkurna Wiltarninthi tapa Purruna-ans* (Strengthening communities through culture). It was painted by Allan Sumner, a Ngarrindjeri-Kaurna-Yankunytjatjara artist, to describe the widely dispersed communities who access the South Australia Integrated Health Clinic. The colours indicate the diversity of the cultural background of the users and the spiritual connections between them. The large circle depicts the Clinic, as a place of togetherness and story-sharing. The eight small circles represent the restorative, healing, services offered by the Clinic. The journey lines show people returning to their homes, taking strength, healing and knowledge to their communities. Further to the references to art in the book, this painting offers an appealing prospect to communicate information about relationships across eventscapes. It could make visible and provide a narrative of the hidden structures of eventscapes.

The reference to scapes in a wide range of disciplines required a diverse literature review and the concept of servicescapes (Bitner, 1992) was shown to be particularly influential. Examples of its application demonstrated how environmental variables are manipulated to achieve management objectives in a wide range of settings. This type of flexibility is needed at eventscapes due to their variability in size, structure and setting. This makes it inappropriate to impose a precise definition of eventscapes. The model that was developed sought to illustrate key characteristics and formative processes. Although a wide range of eventscapes were described, there was a bias towards mega-events and a lot of examples were taken from the Olympic Games. This should not be surprising as the longevity of the event makes it possible to identify trends and factors that have been influential at different times and the large number of host cities reveals the significance of geographical and cultural characteristics in the way the event is organised. There is a wealth of academic literature about the Games and a growing library of manuals and specialist reports including those which describe how the look of the Games has been designed. Mega-events invest considerable resources, which means they can be innovative and test new ideas. Small events cannot call on the same level of resources but they can learn from what has been implemented at mega-events while the need for creativity remains. A key task is being able to adapt to local circumstances and a distinctive event look can be created by using the artistic skills of local schoolchildren rather than an international design agency. The annual competition to design the poster for the Adelaide Fringe attracts entrants of all ages and backgrounds and the winning design is displayed throughout the city.

Graphic design and illuminations were discussed in detail in Chapters 5 and 6 with examples provided of the images displayed in different types of eventscapes. The visual representations in eventscapes are no less ideological than those in landscape paintings or on maps. This highlights the need for research to identify the nature of the gaze among different audiences and the meanings attached to various forms of engagement with environmental settings. The multiple opportunities for immersive experiences at eventscapes positions events as part of contemporary design culture (Julier, 2005). Separate chapters were devoted to transformation by design and by light but this may be an artificial distinction as, in many eventscapes, graphic art, light and music are used in combination. Together, they create atmospheres of varying intensity and rather than being concerned with whether light adds value to urban experiences, it may be more appropriate to consider how the introduction of a combinations of effects changes the atmospheres of places. Atmospheres can be characterised as a multi-layered space of latent possibilities or a force field in which people find themselves (Stewart, 2011) and there is a growing literature about urban atmospheres (Gandy, 2017a), their impact in public spaces (Amin, 2008) and the relationship between light and atmosphere (Edensor, 2015). Light is a powerful determinant of atmospheres but they are multi-sensorial, intangible and may generate a variety of responses with sensitivity influenced by personal predispositions. They vary in spatial reach, can overlap and are porous as sounds and smells move through or around physical barriers. The role of soundscapes at events has been discussed in the book and it would be interesting to apply the techniques used to develop maps of urban smellscapes (Henshaw, 2014; Quercia, Schifanella, Aiello and McLean, 2015) at eventscapes.

Although spatial characteristics and visual features are prioritised within the eventscapes perspective adopted in this book, it is important to take account of the 'aesthetic of atmospheres' – the 'tuned space' that is responsible for the way we feel about ourselves in an environment (Böhme, 2016). It is also important to remember that spatial patterns and images at an eventscape tell a story about place that can be read and interpreted. This is more difficult in the case of atmospheres. With reference to McCormack's (2014) suggestion that circumstances, via partial enclosure, offer a way of giving consistency to atmospheres, Edensor notes the atmospheric potentiality of events 'in constituting occasions freighted with an affective and sensual difference that contrasts with normative mundane experience, evincing poignancy sharpened by their fleeting qualities' (2015: 332). This commentary on the nature of events demonstrates the reflexive relationship between events and urban rhythms and events and urban atmospheres. The former was the first theme that was discussed in Chapter 2, setting the scene for the multidisciplinary analysis of eventscapes that was subsequently developed. It is revealing that the intangible phenomena of rhythms and atmospheres act as bookends. This is of relevance to the question of whether we need planned events (Getz, 2012) as it suggests that we should not just look for an answer in the findings of economic impact studies. But neither can the answer be found in surveys of attitudes towards a single event because the object of analysis needs to be the complex entanglements of events with lifestyles and sensory perceptions. Events are a powerful force that shape the rhythms and atmospheres of contemporary life, to which citizens respond. These rhythms and atmospheres find expression at eventscapes.

RESEARCH DIRECTIONS

The book will conclude by briefly reviewing research that can shed further light on eventscapes and their impacts. There is scope for an entire book to be devoted to this subject so this section can do little more than indicate directions. An edited book about methodological approaches to event studies provides a useful starting point (Pernecky, 2016) as does an earlier book about methods related to tourism and visual culture (Burns, Lester and Bibbings, 2010). Visual analysis has attracted the interest of sociologists (Blaikie, 2001; Sweetman, 2009; and Wheaton, 2003) and, not surprisingly, the journal of *Visual Studies* is a rich source of insight about visual methodologies and many of the articles describe the use of photographs in research design (Bendiner-Viani, 2016; Drew and Guillemin, 2014; Harper, 2002; Guillemin and Drew, 2010). Landscape perception is of interest to environmental psychologists and a study by Nasar and Terzano (2010) required respondents to rate photographs of natural scenes, skylines after dark and skylines during the day on a scale developed to measure the perceived pleasantness of the scenes. A special issue of *Visual Studies* included a number of articles about visual interpretation of the Olympic Games (Coles, Knowles and Newbury, 2012; Dyck and Gauvin, 2012; Marrero-Guillamón, 2012). The analysis of images in the cityscape during the Olympic Games has been reported from a marketing perspective (Nadeau, O'Reilly and Heslop, 2015) and as a dialectic representation of official and counter branding (Maiello and Pasquinelli, 2015). The former used an observation-based approach and the latter used an internet-based content analysis. The iconography at events has been studied (Xie and Groves, 2003) and the analysis of tourism sites as semiotic signs (Knudsen and Rickly-Boyd, 2012) would be equally valuable at eventscapes.

Some of the themes identified in the book require further research. They include the analysis of event networks (Richards, 2015; Van der Duim,

2007), the psychic income generated by events (Kim and Walker, 2012) and emotional reactions to eventscapes (Maguire and Geiger, 2015). The study by Maguire and Geiger (2015) used mobile phone diaries to capture emotions at the time and in the environment where they were felt. New technologies are providing increased opportunities for this type of interventionist research but there remains value in the post-experience interpretations of meanings. The use of personal meaning mapping was used to understand personal constructs of festival experiences (Van Winkle and Falk, 2015) and Kelly's (1955) theory of personal constructs has been used as the foundation for repertory grid analysis in tourism studies (Botterill and Crompton, 1987; Pearce, 1982). There are considerable opportunities to combine photo-elicitation of scenes at eventscapes with repertory grid analysis to understand the attribution of personal meanings.

Meaning can be produced by reflective researchers (Cohen, 2013) and autoethnography has been used in event research (Huang, 2010) and as a tool to assist cross-cultural interpretation of event settings (Brown and Huang, 2015). A contrasting, quantitative approach has been used to measure attachment to event venues and a study by Brown, Smith and Assaker (2016) at the London 2012 Olympic Games asked respondents to rate items for place dependence, place symbolism, place affect and place identity. The study found that venue attachment had a strong effect on intentions to revisit the host city. Observation of behaviour in eventscapes can reveal valuable findings and a study by Frew and McGillivray (2008) used Foucauldian theory to interpret the way 'Fan Parks' manufactured dramaturgical experiences at the FIFA World Cup. Finally, I will refer to a study by Tim Edensor and his colleague Hayden Lorimer (2015) in recognition that Edensor's work has been of great value in preparing several sections of this book. The study of the 'Speed of Light' at the Edinburgh Festival presents an intriguing picture of event research. It describes the distinctive effect created by illuminated performers moving through space but it also uses evocative language to explain the immersive, multi-sensorial experience of the researcher. In the pursuit of knowledge, there are endless opportunities to shed light on the nature of eventscapes.

REFERENCES

Amin, A. (2006). The Good City. *Urban Studies*, 43(5/6): 1009–1023.

Amin, A. (2008). Collective Culture and Urban Public Space. *City*, 12(1): 5–24.

Bale, J. (1994). *Landscapes of Modern Sport*. London: Leicester University Press.

Bendiner-Viani, G. (2016). Bringing Their Worlds Back: Using Photographs to spur Conversations on Everyday Place. *Visual Studies*, 31(1): 1–21.

Bitner, M. J. (1992). Servicescapes: The Impact of Physical Surroundings on Customers and Employees. *Journal of Marketing*, 55(April): 57–71.

Blaikie, A. (2001). Photographs in the Cultural Account: Contested Narratives and Collective Memory in the Scottish Islands. *The Sociological Review*, 49(3): 345–367.

Böhme, G. (2016). *The Aesthetics of Atmospheres*, edited by J.-P. Thibaud. London: Routledge.

Botterill, T. D. and Crompton, J. L. (1987). Personal Constructs of Holiday Snapshots. *Annals of Tourism Research*, 14: 152–156.

Brown, G., Smith, A. and Assaker, G. (2016). Revisiting the Host City: An Empirical Examination of Sport Involvement, Place Attachment, Event Satisfaction and Spectator Intentions at the London Olympics. *Tourism Management*, 55: 160–172.

Brown, G. and Huang, S. (2015). Interpreting Tourism at Olympic Sites: A Cross-Cultural Analysis of the Beijing Olympic Green. *International Journal of Tourism Research*, 17(4): 364–374.

Burns, P. M., Lester, J.-A. and Bibbings, L., eds (2010). *Tourism and Visual Culture, Volume 2: Methods and Cases.* Wallingford: CABI.

Cohen, A. A. (2013). Reflections and Reflexivity in Leisure and Tourism Studies. *Leisure Studies*, 32(3): 333–337.

Coles, P., Knowles, C. and Newbury, D. (2012). Seeing the Olympics: Images, Spaces, Legacies. *Visual Studies*, 27(2): 117–118.

Drew, S. and Guillemin, M. (2014). From Photographs to Findings: Visual Meaning-Making and Interpretive Engagement in the Analysis of Participant-Generated Images. *Visual Studies*, 29(10): 54–67.

Dyck, N. and Gauvin, R. (2012). Dressing Up to Join the Games: Vancouver 2010. *Visual Studies*, 27(2): 196–203.

Edensor, T. (2015). Light Design and Atmosphere. *Visual Communication*, 14(3): 331–350.

Edensor, T. and Lorimer, H. (2015). 'Landscapism' at the *Speed of Light*: Darkness and Illumination in Motion. *Geografiska Annaler: Series B Human Geography*, 97(1): 1–16.

Edensor, T. and Millington, S. (2013). Blackpool Illuminations: Revealing Local Cultural Production, Situated Creativity and Working-Class Values. *International Journal of Cultural Policy*, 19(2): 145–161.

Frew, M. and McGillivray, D. (2008). Exploring Hyper-Experiences: Performing the Fan at Germany 2006. *Journal of Sport & Tourism*, 13(3): 181–198.

Gandy, M. (2017a). Urban Atmospheres. *Cultural Geographies*, 24(3): 353–374.

Gandy, M. (2017b). Negative Luminescence. *Annals of the American Association of Geographers*, 107(5): 1090–1107.

Getz, D. (2012). Event Studies: Discourses and Future Directions. *Event Management*, 16: 171–187.

Guillemin, M. and Drew, S. (2010). Questions of Process in Participant-Generated Visual Methodologies. *Visual Studies*, 25(2): 175–188.

Harper, D. (2002). Talking About Pictures: A Case for Photo Elicitation. *Visual Studies*, 17(1): 13–26.

Henshaw, V. (2014). *Urban Smellscapes: Understanding and Designing City Smell Environments*. New York: Routledge.

Huang, S. (2010). Post-Olympic Tourist Experience: An Autoethnographic Perspective. *Journal of China Tourism Research*, 6(2): 104–122.

Julier, G. (2005). Urban Designscapes and the Production of Aesthetic Consent. *Urban Studies*, 42(5–6): 869–887.

Kelly, G. A. (1955). *The Psychology of Personal Constructs*, Vols 1 and 2. New York: Norton.

Kim, W. and Walker, M. (2012). Measuring the Social Impacts Associated with Super Bowl XLIII: Preliminary Development of a Psychic Income Scale. *Sport Management Review*, 15: 91–108.

Knudsen, D. C. and Rickly-Boyd, J. M. (2012). Tourism Sites as Semiotic Signs: A Critique. *Annals of Tourism Research*, 39: 1242–1263.

McCormack, D. (2014). Atmospheric Things and Circumstantial Excursions. *Cultural Geographies*, 21(4): 605–625.

Maguire, L. and Geiger, S. (2015). Emotional Timescapes: The Temporal Perspective and Consumption Emotions in Services. *Journal of Services Marketing*, 29(3): 211–223.

Maiello, A. and Pasquinelli, C. (2015). Destruction or Construction? A (Counter) Branding Analysis of Sport Mega-Events in Rio de Janeiro. *Cities*, 48: 116–124.

Marrero-Guillamón, I. (2012). Photography Against the Olympic Spectacle. *Visual Studies*, 27(2): 133–139.

Muller, M. (2015). What Makes an Event a Mega-Event? Definitions and Sizes. *Leisure Studies*, 34(6): 627–642.

Nadeau, J., O'Reilly, N. and Heslop, L. A. (2015). Cityscape Promotions and the Use of Place Images at the Olympic Games. *Marketing Intelligence & Planning*, 33(2): 147–163.

Nasar, J. L. and Terzano, K. (2010). The Desirability of Views of City Skylines and After Dark. *Journal of Environmental Psychology*, 30: 215–225.

Pearce, P. L. (1982). Perceived Changes in Holiday Destinations. *Annals of Tourism Research*, 9(2): 145–164.

Pernecky, T., ed. (2016). *Approaches and Methods in Event Studies*. Abingdon: Routledge.

Quercia, D., Schifanella, R., Aiello, L. M. and McLean, K. (2015). Smelly Maps: The Digital Life of Urban Smellscapes. *Association for the Advancement of Artificial Intelligence*. https://researchswinger.org/publications/icwsm15_smell.pdf.

Richards, G. (2015). Events in the Network Society: The Role of Pulsar and Iterative Events. *Event Management*, 19: 553–566.

Stewart, K. (2011). Atmospheric Attunements. *Environment and Planning Planning D: Society and Space*, 29: 445–453.

Sweetman, P. (2009). Revealing Habitus, Illuminating Practice: Bourdieu, Photography and Visual Methods. *The Sociological Review*, 57(3): 491–511.

Thrift, N. (2005). But Malice Aforethought: Cities and the Natural History of Hatred. *Transactions of the Institute of British Geographers NS*, 30: 133–150.

Tzanelli, R. (2018). *Mega Events as Economies of the Imagination: Creating Atmospheres for Rio 2016 and Tokyo 2020*. London: Routledge.

Van der Duim, R. (2007). Tourismscapes: An Actor–Network Perspective. *Annals of Tourism Research*, 34(4): 961–976.

Van Winkle, C. M. and Falk, J. H. (2015). Personal Meaning Mapping at Festivals: A Useful Tool for Challenging Context. *Event Management*, 19: 143–150.

Wheaton, B. (2003). Lifestyle Sport Magazines and the Discourses of Sporting Masculinity. *The Sociological Review*, 51(1): 193–221.

Wynn, J. (2015*). Music City. American Festivals and Placemaking in Austin, Nashville, and Newport*. Chicago, IL: University of Chicago Press.

Xie, P. F. and Groves, D. (2003). Identifying Cultural Iconography: A Case Study of Canadian-American Festival. *Event Management*, 8: 91–97.

Index

Page numbers in **bold** denote tables, those in *italics* denote figures.

aboriginal communities **30**
active engagement in events 11, 37
activities, daily programmes of 38
actor–network relations 60
actor–network theory 60
Adelaide Festivals 13, 109, 122
Adelaide Fringe 119–122
advertising/advertisement 49, 74, 146–147, 166; images in 145; three-dimensional 147
aesthetic of atmospheres 228
aesthetic preferences 57
Agnew, J. 71
Amin, A. 7, 82
Appadurai, K. 49
architecture 12, 15, 48, 62–63, 78, 112, 148, 151, 208, 213, 224
arc lights 187–188
arousal leading, levels of 72
artificial light 51
artificial sunshine 205
artistic cartography at London 134–135, *135*
arts, impacts on **30**
ATC *see* Australian Tourist Commission (ATC)
atmospheres 80, 95, 122, 125, 126, 151, 162–163, 228, 229; festival 14; importance of 50; of place 5; of seduction 74

atmospherics 81
Australian Tourist Commission (ATC) 27, 34, 131–132, 166; Visiting Journalist Programme 34
'Australia Prefers Visa' campaign 34
authenticity 148–149
avoiders 32

Bale, J. 68, 70, 71, 225
Barcelona 1992 163, *164*
Barker, C. 9
basal experience 36
beach volleyball games 95, *95*, *96*
behaviour: fundamental role of 82; patterns of 8
Beijing's Aquatic Centre 153–154
Berlin Olympic Games 166–168, *167*, 199
Berridge, G. 21–22
Bitner, M.J. 4, 72
blandscapes, nocturnal 51–52
blitzkrieg planning 17
Boise, M. 147
Bragdon, C. 193
brand 33; identity 168; management strategy 149; manuals, environment of 169; meaning 149
brandscape 78
Brannen, C. 74
Bridlington poster 65
Brighenti, A.M. 71

Brown, G. 150
'Burning Man' event 195–197
business partnerships 27–28
business revenue 27–28
Byron Bay Bluesfest 99; eventscape of 100

Canadian symbols 157, *158*
capitalisation of city landscapes 12
capsular civilisation 13
carnivals 123–124
cartographic silence 133
cartography 133; totalising vision of 138
Castells, M. 11
casuals 32
category membership 38–39
Celebration Sites programme 20, *20*
ceremonial lighting 217
changers 28
Chinese culture 113
Chinese philosophy 113
chorography 133
Christie Digital Systems 208
Christmas light festivals 200
city: festive appearance of 1; landscapes,
    capitalisation of 12; perceptions of 163;
    rankings of 7
cityscapes 95; consumption of 81–82;
    manifestation of 48; post-modern 78
Clegg, S. 187
Coachella Valley Festival 103
coastal environments 54–55
cognitive psychology 150
collective effervescence 9
Collins, R. 9
Colomb, C. 82
commercialisation 82
commercial landscape 147
Commonwealth Games (2018) 19
communication systems 12
communities 2–3, **30**, 37–38; activities,
    outdoor spaces for 126; groups 124;
    space 21
complexity, level of 72
confetti pattern 119
consumer behaviour 52
consumer tribes 149
consumption 11–12
contemporary geography 53
contemporary light design 182

Cooper, R. 81
corporate hospitality 15
corporate sponsors: involvement of 204
Cosgrove, D. 51
counter-mapping 136
Cox, P. 61–63
creative class 12
creativity 66; culture and 12
Crown Lands Act 103
Cullen, G. 60
cultural information 146
cultural landscape 198
cultural traditions, nature and reflections of
    157
culture 145–147; Chinese 113; and
    creativity 12; design 146; global 146;
    impacts on **30**; local 63; music 101–102;
    representatives of 12; visual 145; youth
    146
cycle races 128–129

darkness 182–183
design 52; and construction techniques
    153; contribution to **155**; culture 146;
    idealism 151
designscapes 49, 79; production of 83
design, transformations by 145; culture
    145–147; Olympic design 150–153;
    Olympic look 153–176; place branding
    147–150
destination, visual representation of 64, *64,*
    65
disruptive cartography at London *137*
distinctive identity 173
Dreamscapes (Drebin) 49
Durkheim, E. 9
Dussehra 194
Dyck, N. 9

Economist Intelligence Unit 7
eco-system, reference to 15
Edensor, T. 7–8, 48, 230
Edinburgh Festivals 13, 52, 205
education landscape 50
Eiffel Tower 200
electricity: potential of 188; provision of
    188
electric lighting 187, 188
emotions 35, 74; in eventscapes *75*

entanglements 224
entertainment 11–12; daily programmes of 38
environmental sustainability 19
environments 54, 125
ethnographic map 138
ethnoscapes 49
Event Awards in Australia 182
eventilisation 14, 82
Event Marketing at St Moritz 96–98
event-related donations 127
events: behaviour 39; design 21–27, 113; development of 148; evaluation and planning 33; eventful cities 11–14; experiences 35–40; flexibility of 226; impacts 27–35; intangible benefits of 27–28; legacies 35; leveraging 33; mapping 138; mega-events 14–17; nature of 228; participation **10–11**; planning 17–21; processes of planning 9–10; quality of 7; quasi-religious elements of 152; spaces 63; sponsors 33; symphonies of 74; and tourism 150; types of 217; urban rhythms 7–11; visitors 28
eventscape map 138
eventscapes 80–83, 93, 224, 225; analysis of 81, 226; boundaries of 122; of Byron Bay Bluesfest 100; characteristics of 82; conceptual model of 49, 82–83, *83*; context of 16, 68; emotion in *75*; evolving 104–108; formation and impact 127; forms of 3, 49; mapping 123, 132–138; multidisciplinary analysis of 228–229; observation of behaviour in 230; operation of 66; pattern of 127; resource base 93–99; spatial patterns: multiple settings 119–122; precincts 104–118; routes 123–131; single sites 99–103; temporary 81; translocal 49; types of 93, 128; views of **69–70**
exhibition centres 63
experience economy, defined 12
experiences, events 35–40; guest of Olympic sponsor 40; level of 36; resident of host city 39
Expo '88, 104–106
Expo 2010 *189*
extentioners 28

external landscapes 53, 54

fantasy city 38
fantasy-scapes 51–52
festivalisation 14
festivals 192, 193; elements of 156; historical significance of 184; of light 206–217; marketing of 150; music 94, 99–101, 103, 225; and music culture 101–102; religious 184
festivalscapes 80–81
Fiasco Design 138
FIFA World Cup 9, 17
financial capitalism 16
fire 194
firms, business practices of 12
foodscapes 52
for-profit industries **32**
Foucault, M. 14, 57, 68
4D light show 189
Four Magical Days in May 126–127
freelance lighting 190
free-standing signs 173
Fusion Imaging 157
'fuzzy' places 71

Gandy, M. 224
Gardiner, A. 159
gas lighting 187–188, 190
Gauvin, R. 9
geographical landscapes 52, 53–56
geographical scholarship 53
geographical scope 131–132
geopolitical indignities 136
Getz, D. 2, 21, 22, 36
giant pictograms 173
Glacier Express 58
Glastonbury Festival in England 103
global culture 146
global economic recession 37
globalisation 61, 62–63, 225; ambassadors for 63; mobility and 59
The Globalised Landscape 61–63
Goffman, E. 21–22
Gold Coast City Council 17–18
golfscape 71
Google Maps 134–135
Goya, Francisco 185
graphic design 154; benchmark for 154

grid pattern, geometry of 172
Gunn, C. 60, 61

Hagerstrand, T. 60
Hankinson, G. 148
Harvey, D. 66
Heidegger, M. 16
heritage buildings 208
home stayers 28
humanistic geography 50
Hyde Park in London 103

ice sculptures 200
iconographic map 138
'identikit' destinations 64
identity 55–56; distinctive 173; national
    62; place 112; regional 62; visual
    154–155, 157, 162, 174, 224, 225
ideoscapes 49
illuminations 199–206; Blackpool 205;
    conjunction with 206; contradictory
    attitudes towards 205; of heritage
    buildings 199–200; winter 200
imagescapes 75; tourist attractions as
    74–75
imagineering 16, 74, 75
informal choreography 149
infrastructure 19, 35, 97–98, 166, 224
Ingold, T. 138
innovative design 154
institutions **30**
interactional intelligence 226
internationalism 53–54, 151; antithesis of
    61
International Olympic Committee (IOC)
    15, 37
IOC *see* International Olympic Committee
    (IOC)

Jacob, D. 82
Japanese art 186
Japanese light 185
Julier, G. 78, 145, 146, 186

Kaplan, S. 72
Klauser, F. 13

lamps 193
landmarks 115, 168; familiarity of 134

landscape 48, 49, 55–56, 134–135, 165;
    analysis, framework of 65; commercial
    147; conference and 52; by geographers
    52; geographical 52; incorporation of
    114; of leisure 60–67; as natural
    resource 61; painting 50, 51; perception
    229; representations of 50, 51; social
    construction of 66; of sport 225; study
    of 56; visual preferences of 72
landscapism 52
laser 200; scanning 147
Lash, S. 146
L'Atelier des Lumières (the studio of light)
    186
Lauren, Ralph 189
leisure, geographies of 65
leisure researchers 59
lifestyle architecture, components of 15
light art animations 208–209
light festivals 206–217; development
    process 206, *207*; elements of 189;
    global network of 225; ludic dimension
    of 209
Light Festivals in China 201–204
lights/lighting 192; of bonfires 194;
    houses and gardens 204; show 200;
    situations 190; source of 189–190; and
    technology 188; types of 190; on
    warehouses 209
light, transformations by 182–183; day and
    night 183–186; festivals of 206–217;
    heat and 194–199; illuminations
    199–206; responses to 189–193; at
    taverns and coffeehouses 186
Lillehammer 1994 156
live music 21
Live Sites 19, 39
local cultures 63
LOCOG website 134–135
logo: sculptures of 175; shape of 175
London Olympics 49, 95, 168–172, *172*,
    174
London's Burning 197, *198*
Lorimer, Hayden 230
Luz de America 208
Lyon Light Festival Forum 208

Mapped Design 190–192

maps 137, 138; of Brazil 138; design of 134; importance and relevance of 133–134; information and imagery on 132–133; proportional symbols on 136; published by media organisations 135; trends in 133; of UK 138
marine environments 54–55
marketing scholars 71
Marrero-Guillamón 16
McCann Worldgroup (MWG) 169–172
media 20, 37; coverage 37, 150; events in 132; landscape 50
mediascapes 48–49
medieval cities, life in 8
mega-events 14–17, 36–37, 75, 93 see events
Melbourne 7; sporting events 7
memorable experiences 36
Midsummer Night's Dream, A (Shakespeare) 51
Millennium Marquee, designing 22–26
mnemonic map 138
mobile phones 59
mobility 8, 13; and displacement 67; and globalisation 59
modernity, dominant characteristics of 145
monumental sculptures 153
Moore, J. 163–164
moorings 16
mountains 95
Muller, M. 226
Munich Olympic Park 114–118, *115*
music: culture 101–102; festivals 94, 99–101, 103, 225; landscapes 55–56; and narration 200
musicscapes 49
MWG see McCann Worldgroup (MWG)
Mysteryland Case Study 100–103

narration, music and 200
national identity 62
national symbols 152
natural light, conditions of 51
nature: space 74; universal order of 192
negotiation: processes of 60; systems of 146
neoliberal urban policies 11
neon lights 190
network-centric model 14

networks 35; society 11; value 14
Niemeyer, O. 124–125
nocturnal blandscapes 51–52
nocturnal commons 182
Nohl, W. 57
nostalgiascapes 49
not-for-profit organisations **31**
novelty, level of 72

OCA see Olympic Coordination Authority (OCA)
ODA see Olympic Delivery Authority (ODA)
oil lamps 186–187
Ollins, W. 168
Olympic accreditation 38–39
Olympic Coordination Authority (OCA) 18–19
Olympic Delivery Authority (ODA) 16
Olympic design 151
Olympic Design Conference 166
Olympic Flame 199
Olympic Games 32; visual identity at 225
Olympic Green, Beijing *113*, 114
Olympic Museum in Lausanne 76, *77*
Olympic Roads and Transport Authority (ORTA) 18
Olympics: hospitality at 15; sponsors 152; sponsor-scape 81; sponsorship, benefits of 22–23
Olympic Task Force 17–18
Olympic Torch Relay 129–130
ontological genesis 132
ORTA see Olympic Roads and Transport Authority (ORTA)

paintings 186; hierarchies of 51
Palio horse race in Siena 99
pedestrian management 19
pedestrian stroll 20, *20*
Pérez-Gómez, A. 133
performance facility 21
performative map 138
personal communication 136
personal space 57
physical co-presence 9
physical space 74
pictorial intentionality 16

pictorial realism 50
place-based visuals 150
place brand/branding 147, 149; academic interest in 150; objective of 148
place identity, architectural signifiers of 112
place-making 147–148; politics of 16
place marketing 147–149
places 8; animation of 13–14; attachment, applications of 59; distinctive sense of 206; fuzzy 71; memories of 61–62; promotion 147; sense of 70, 148; uniqueness of 61–62
place-specificity 165
planning: of events 17–21; process 21; transport 18
Plato 7, 133
playscapes 67
policy 35
political landscape 50
polysemy 151
post-industrial cities 11
post-modern cityscapes 78
potentialities, identification of 13
power relations 78–79
precincts 104–118; attractive feature of 109; in Melbourne 108; Riverbank *109*
presence events 14
PriceWaterhouseCoopers 27, 28
print advertising 97–98
privatisation 82
process design 22
psychographic map 138
psychological bonds, development of 59
psychological separation 26
public buildings 152
public events, social eco-system of 15
public faces of geography 53
public place 99
public spaces 13, 22; art productions in 126; privatisation of 13; of urban environments 182
pulsar events 9
pyrotechnic displays 198

radiance 185
real estate 12
reference 67
reflective researchers 230

regional identity 62
regionalism 61
re-imaging 148
religious festivals 184
renaissance art 50
REPAC *see* Riverbank Entertainment Precinct Advisory Committee (REPAC)
resistance 66
re-use legacy 19
rhythmanalysis 7–8, 52
Rio Carnival 9
Rio de Janeiro 2016 175–176
Riverbank Entertainment Precinct Advisory Committee (REPAC) 109–111
rock carvings 156
'Route and Pub Finder' map 135
Royal de Luxe 125, 126
royal events 123
runaways 28
rural landscape 156

Salisbury Festival 126
Salt Lake Organising Committee (SLOC) 157
Samaranch, Juan Antonio 165
Sambadrome 124–125
sandscapes 52
Santos Tour Down Under (TDU) 128
Sassen, S. 16
SATC *see* South Australian Tourism Commission (SATC)
scapes, study of 79; eventscapes 80–83; landscapes 49–67; reference to 227; servicescapes 71–80; sportscapes 67–71; types of 52; visions of world 48–49
Schama, S. 184, 185–186
schools 37–38
sculpture 197
SeaBus 36
seascapes 52, 54–55; description of 52; visualising 54
seasonal festivity 204
sector-centric model 14
securitisation 82
sensuous geographies 68–69
serial events 14
service contexts, environmental variables in **73**

servicescapes 49, 71–81; of casinos 76; concept of 76, 80, 227; expansive approach towards 79; experiences in 74; external setting 77; ideas about 82–83; research 79; similarities with landscapes 72; types of staging 74
shopping 12
SkyDome in Toronto 70
SkyTrain 36
SLOC *see* Salt Lake Organising Committee (SLOC)
Snow & Glow event 21
social inclusion/exclusion 66
social interaction 78
socialisation processes 56
social networks 149
social relations 59
social-servicescape 78
social space 57
social ties, development of 9
social values 56
SOCOG *see* Sydney Organising Committee for the Olympic Games (SOCOG)
SOL *see* South of Litchfield (SOL)
Song and Light Festival in New York 193
sonic spaces 55–56
soundscapes 52, 55–56; role of 228
South Australian Tourism Commission (SATC) 128
South Bank 107–108
South of Litchfield (SOL) 78
spaces: blocs of 71; management of 13; mapping of 16; planning 22
spatial segmentation, analysis of 71
special events, marketing of 150
splintering 13
sponsors/sponsorship 19, 22–26, 98; conjunction with 153; hospitality suite 40; partnerships with 174; representatives of 40
sporting events 165; in Melbourne 7
sporting facilities 18
sporting icons 168
sportscapes 49, 67–71; ambiguity of 68; description of 67
Sports Geography (Bale) 68
sports stadium, integrity of 68
Stevenson, Robert Louis 187–188

'sticky' places 60
St Moritz Polo World Cup 98
storyscapes 49
street lighting 186
street performers 21
sub environments 24
Sultan's Elephant *125*
Summer Olympic Games: Barcelona 1992 163, *164*; Beijing 2008 166–168, *167*; London 2012 168–172, *172*, *174*; Rio de Janeiro 2016 175–176; Sydney 2000 163–166
surveillance, machine of 16
Swiss landscape, framing 57–59
Sydney Olympics 9, 18, 163–166
Sydney Organising Committee for the Olympic Games (SOCOG) 1, 23–26, 34, 163, 165; planning by 166; workshops 39
Sydney Airport Authority 19
Sydney 2000 Torch Relay 130–132
symbolic novelty 12
symbolism 50, 113

Taipei Lantern Festival 80
'Take me to the River' programme 197
target markets 147
Tattersall, J. 81
tax revenue 27–28
TBL *see* Triple Bottom Line (TBL)
TDU *see* Santos Tour Down Under (TDU)
technology, light and 188
television coverage 163
territorialisation 71
theatres 122, 189–190
ticketing procedures 39
time-geography 7–8
timescapes 52
time switchers 32
TOF *see* Tourism Olympic Forum (TOF)
topophilia 70
torches 198–199
tourism 131–132; development 61; events and 150; geographies of 65; impact map for 28, *29*; landscapes 56; literature, contexts in 64; planning 60–61; spaces 60, 67; study of 60
Tourism Olympic Forum (TOF) 33–34, 166

'touristed seascape' 64
townscape 156
Townscape (Cullen) 60
Traganou, J. 151–152, 156
training 197
transformation of eventscapes 145
transforming experiences 36
transport/transportation 20; infrastructure 14; planning 18; schedules 8; strategy 18
travel patterns 39
Triple Bottom Line (TBL) 28
Tuan, Y.-F. 59, 70, 71
Tzanelli, R. 15, 16, 151, 153

UCI *see* Union Cycliste Internationale (UCI)
Union Cycliste Internationale (UCI) 127–128
uniqueness 148
urban areas, bright lights of 51
urban atmospheres 228
urban designscapes 78
urban design, trends in 146–147
Urban Development Institute of Australia 19
Urban Domain Planning Team 18
urban ecology 17
urban environments 82; visual characteristics of 48
urban experience, development of 17
urbanization of events 13
urban landscape 74, 114, 147
urban nightscapes, youth culture in 146
urban outdoor spaces 50
urban places, timescape of 74
urban planning 12, 48
urban public spaces 8
urban spaces: affective geography of 147; representations of 48–49
urban spectatorship 133

urban strategies 149
Utrecht Conference Centre in 1993 100

vacationscape 60–61
value 146; systems 78–79
Vancouver Olympic Games 2010 130, 157; branding and design programme 159–160; design applications 160; opening ceremony 158
Vancouver Olympics 36
VANOC 159, 162
Venice Carnival 123–124
venue applications 162
vernacular architecture 62
vernacular expression 62
Vienna 7
visitors **31**
visual communication strategies 156
visual culture 145
visual framework 161
visual identity 154–155, 157, 162, 174, 224
visual image 156
visual landscape 3
visual language 168; temporary nature of 174
visual technologies, importance of 145
visual transformations 3
Vivid Sydney 209–217
volleyball stadium 94–95

Wagner, R. 193
Weber, M. 99
White Turf racing 98
winescape 79–80
winter illuminations 200
Winter Olympic Games 20; Lillehammer 1994 156; Salt Lake City 2002 157; Vancouver 2010 157–162
Wynn, J. 3, 99, 104, 119, 123, 225

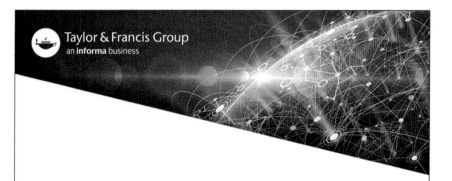